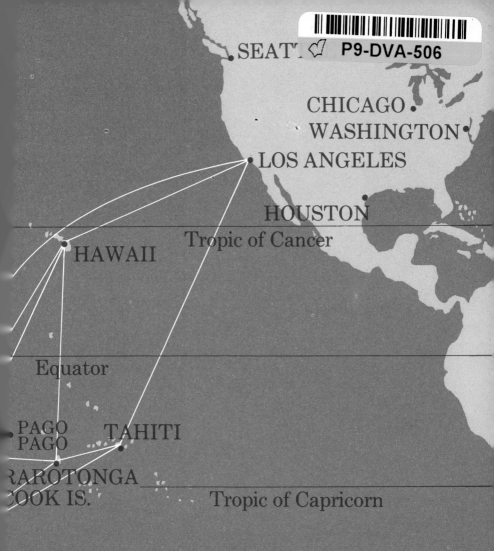

SEATT P9-DVA-506

CHICAGO
WASHINGTON
LOS ANGELES

HOUSTON

Tropic of Cancer

HAWAII

Equator

PAGO
PAGO   TAHITI

RAROTONGA
COOK IS.   Tropic of Capricorn

AND

NGTON
CHURCH

Air New Zealand International Route Network

ACIFIC OCEAN

How To
Get Lost
And Found
In New Zealand

How to Get Lost and Found in New Zealand is a travel experience rather than a guide book. In its pages the adventure of two American travellers in New Zealand unfolds as a constantly-moving, constantly-informing, constantly-entertaining voyage of discovery.

Where-to-go and what-to-see are paramount, but underlying all the practicalities are the warmth of New Zealanders met and the wonder of New Zealand in its infinite variety. These are reflected by the sympathetic eyes, ears and interpretation of a widely-travelled author, who loves New Zealand deeply and aims to introduce the "Land of the Long White Cloud" to his fellow-Americans and to travellers around the world.

New Zealand lies in the South Pacific, an outpost of Polynesia that retains a large Maori population, integrated and sharing all social advantages with the descendants of, in the main, British settlers.

It is judged by many to be the most beautiful country in the world. It is certainly one of the most blessed – under-populated by Northern Hemisphere standards, agricultural rather than industrial, relatively free of pollution of all kinds, equable of climate, and packed with travel experiences and a kaleidoscope of dazzling scenery and natural wonders.

John W. McDermott, aided by the observations and comments of the Lady Navigator, makes New Zealand come alive as few travel books have done.

First Published 1976

A. H. & A. W. REED LTD
65-67 Taranaki Street, Wellington

Second edition 1978
WAIKIKI PUBLISHING COMPANY
1441 Kapiolani Boulevard, Honolulu.

ISBN 0 589 00000 0

Typeset by Printset Processes (1973) Ltd, Christchurch
Printed by Dai Nippon Printing Company (Hong Kong) Limited

How To
Get Lost
And Found
In New Zealand

by John W. McDermott

Waikiki Publishing Co.,
Honolulu, Hawaii

To Rita and Berney Bookman,
Our loyal nannies for six months. . .
And to the Lady Navigator,
my tough but tasty editor.

Contents

List of Maps

(Maps by Genesis Designs)

Introduction

The Pacific Basin is a fascinating area.

The variety of cultures, the famous landmarks and cities, the appeal of different recreational facilities make the vast spread of ocean and land a huge box of travel chocolates from which a traveller can pick and choose.

Who can blame the first-time voyager – or the many-time, thoroughly experienced traveller – from putting together a trip to include Honolulu, Papeete, Auckland, Sydney, Singapore, Hong Kong and Tokyo? Unfortunately, this kiss-and-run schedule permits the traveller to experience only the most superficial attractions of a country – particularly a country like New Zealand.

New Zealand, tucked down in the corner of the Pacific Ocean, is off the beaten track of world traffic: which in the end is a blessing.

New Zealand is unspoiled. In a crowded world, over-trampled, weary in spots and testy, New Zealand is still fresh. And that is its first charm.

Not a tiny country, with over 100,000 square miles, New Zealand has only three million people and, as a result, the countryside is virgin, uncrowded.

The country is divided into two narrowly parted islands, the North Island and the South Island.

Americans have a difficult time remembering that New Zealand being below the equator makes the American summer New Zealand's winter, and vice versa. And that the north is warm and the south is cool. Thus in looking at the scenery in New Zealand you go from the balmy days at the north end of the North Island to the Scandinavian fjords in the south of the South Island.

And what would you like in between? Name it.

Alpine peaks and sweeping glaciers or verdant plains and rich pastures. Lovely beaches or forest-covered mountain trails. Isolated lakes and sweet-water rivers or volcanic mud-pots and thermal geysers.

There are enough scenic vistas to stun the most ardent outdoorist. It is a country for the camera.

And what would you like to do in between? Name it.

There is every sport under the sun.

All of this is contained in a land stretching less than 1,000 miles tip to tip and so narrow that you are never more than 80 miles from the sea.

Yet there is so much to see and do. The longer a visitor stays, the more rewarding the vacation will be.

We had visited and written about New Zealand previously which only served to accentuate our hunger to stay longer and do more until we finally launched on a sabbatical of a Year of Saturdays and spent the first six months in New Zealand going from Cape Reinga in the extreme north to Stewart Island in the extreme south. We saw everything and did everything we could . . . which left an ambition to return again and see still more and do more.

Besides the scenery and the activities, there are the New Zealanders. Here we must distinguish between the Pakeha (a New Zealander of European descent) and the Maori of Polynesian origin. Both are New Zealanders . . . and proud of it and of each other. In very rough figures the Pakeha outnumber the Maori by about nine to one, though this proportion varies from district to district. There is no racial discrimination. Intermarriage has been a social commonplace ever since the first Pakeha settlers arrived, and still is. The words "native" or "colored" are never applied to the Maori: he is a New Zealander.

The Pakeha is for the most part British by descent and related in spirit to Australian and American farmers and colonists-frontiersmen. But basically he is an individual with a fierce pride in being a *Kiwi.*

A word of caution: if a New Zealander adopts you, you are endangered of being fed like a fattened calf and beveraged like a town drunk. Your midriff is threatened by new horizons and your liver may never be the same color again.

If there is an application of "kill you with hospitality" it belongs to the New Zealander.

The Lady Navigator and I enjoy golf and tennis and swimming and hiking and trout fishing and horseback riding and the reader is apt to find our personal tastes reflected in our experiences. On the other hand we are not keen on deep-sea fishing (nausea) or mountain climbing (coward) or hunting (fainting at the sight of blood). However these sports are duly documented. We are also fond of good food and good wine and shopping for antiques.

In spectator sports we enjoy horse racing and rugby. New Zealand is famous for its horses and its rugby.

In fact New Zealand is famous for all of its sports . . . and sportsmen and women. But you don't have to be an athlete to enjoy New Zealand. With all of that spectacular scenery there is a tremendous vacation waiting for you on the open road. If you do enjoy sports, you are travelling in the world's Eden of sports.

So pack a bag and come along on a leisurely tour of what the first Polynesians, seeing the snow-tipped mountains called "the land of the long white cloud".

What a country!

The prices quoted in New Zealand dollars were valid in 1978. They should be used as a yardstick of the costs of goods and services. (We have found as a rule of thumb that each year increases the general cost of travel about 10%).

A few personal friends knew of our plans to write a book. We paid full fare for all travel expenses going, as it were, as an average overseas couple without influence or professional favours.

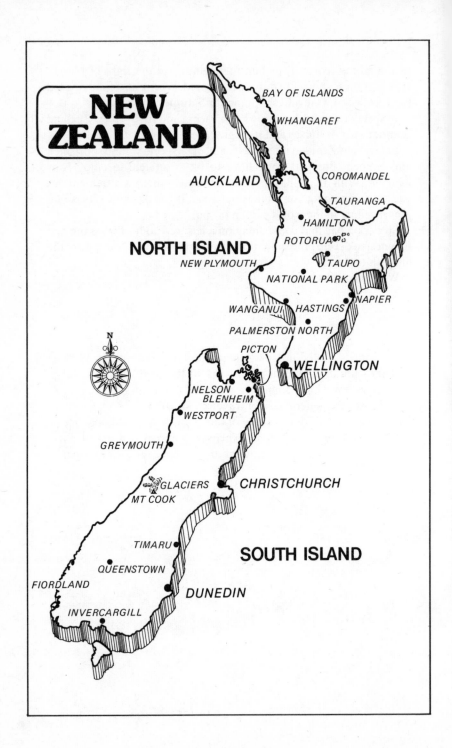

NEW ZEALAND

BAY OF ISLANDS
WHANGAREI
AUCKLAND
COROMANDEL
TAURANGA
HAMILTON
NORTH ISLAND
ROTORUA
NEW PLYMOUTH
TAUPO
NATIONAL PARK
NAPIER
WANGANUI HASTINGS
PALMERSTON NORTH
PICTON
WELLINGTON
NELSON
BLENHEIM
WESTPORT
GREYMOUTH
GLACIERS
MT COOK
CHRISTCHURCH
TIMARU
SOUTH ISLAND
QUEENSTOWN
FIORDLAND
DUNEDIN
INVERCARGILL

N

1. How To Get "Found" Before You Get Lost

Or ... What We Wished We Knew Before We Came To New Zealand

Travel Formalities And Other Niceties
If you come to New Zealand from Australia, all you need is a clean shirt.

If you come from the United States and are staying less than thirty days, you need only your passport. Innoculations are not required unless you come from an endemic fever area.

If you are staying more than thirty days you need a visa and proof of onward passage and proof of funds. Visas can be obtained from travel commissioners' offices in Los Angeles, San Francisco and New York.

If you stay beyond three months, you first must register as an alien – take two passport photos – and with a letter saying you have registered from the Alien Registration Office in Wellington, you go to the Department of Labor (Social Welfare Division!) and turn over your letter together with onward passage as to date and flight number or ship reservation and, again, proof of funds.

If you want to stay longer than six months as a visitor or if you wish to migrate to New Zealand, you must contact the Department of Labor, Private Bag, Te Aro, Wellington.

The general international standards of Customs found around the world are also found in New Zealand. One carton of cigarettes. One bottle of spirits plus one bottle of wine, etc. You can't bring in sidearms (Good!) You can bring in a car for twelve months but you must take it out again.

There is no restriction on the amount of money you may want to bring in but there are formalities about removing money from the country. No large problem.

Being an agricultural society, the New Zealand Customs is sensitive to any dirt, plant life, fruit, etc. and even if you have hiking boots or golf shoes, make sure they are clean because you'll probably have to have them inspected.

1

The electrical current is rated at 230 volts, 50 cycle, alternating current and is not suitable for American direct current of 110 volts although most hotels and motels provided 110-volt a.c. sockets for electric razors.

If you are travelling with a lady who won't leave the house without her electric haircurlers, the bane of any male traveller, you will need a converter/transformer which will also accept the New Zealand three flat-pin plug, an oddity you won't find in any travelling kit. The transformer can be found in America but the three-pin plug will have to be picked up in New Zealand.

Medical facilities are of a high order. You can avail yourself of free medical facilities at public hospitals, however there are faster, private facilities available and the fees are nominal compared to United States levels.

A visitor is covered for personal injury by accident under New Zealand law. If you get hurt, irrespective of fault, you will receive free medical and hospital treatment or payment for expenses.

Tipping is an exception and not the rule. We found it difficult to break ourselves of the habit of scattering change over porters, bartenders, waitresses and taxi drivers, but once rid of the guilt complex, it was like entering a lovely new world! Better hotels and restaurants, however, are tainted.

The police force is a national organization. Interestingly the police do not carry sidearms and only in an extreme emergency is an armed squad called in. (There were two uses of the armed squad when we were in New Zealand resulting in two deaths, the first in several years. The country went into shock.) New Zealand is not a violent land.

Duffi, a vacationing daughter from school in Italy, sensed almost immediately a characteristic of New Zealand we had missed. "You know," she said, "it is a country without tensions."

Weather And What To Wear
New Zealand climate is relatively mild without extreme variations in heat or cold even though in the northern end of the country there are citrus groves and in the colder southern end of the country the winter months can bring frost and snow.

Fluctuations, however, in weather can be sudden.

New Zealand is a country where you can bring your bikini and your ski jacket and never be certain which one you are going to wear.

Sitting out in the middle of the ocean like a big ship, the country is at the mercy of the west winds which blow off the Tasman Sea. It can be as glorious in the winter as in the summer . . . and as miserable in the summer as in the winter.

The first impression you get of New Zealand is the vibrant green of the countryside. Green is created by rain and the first thing you would have wanted to pack is rain gear. A plastic, finger-tip parka is ideal. You can buy a New Zealand oilskin, favoured by fishermen, for about $26. It will not win any beauty prizes but is perfect for the job.

The gabardine-type raincoat is not the best clothing item in a wardrobe for travelling when you are jumping in and out of cars, buses and airplanes, especially in really wet weather. For warmth New Zealand makes good sweaters out of its own wool. Sweaters are often called jerseys or jumpers. New Zealand men tend to wear a sweater of natural grey wool which is very handsome.

Business wear is formal although in the summer you will see a large number of males in walking shorts and, *de rigueur,* long socks with short sleeve shirts and a tie.

The older ladies in cities dress formally for shopping.

In the evening, at a private home or good restaurant, the dress is again formal. New Zealanders do not dress in bright colours.

We like to travel in tennis shoes. They are comfortable and light and lend themselves to quick, short hikes. Walking is what you do when you are travelling and bad shoes can spoil any trip. In New Zealand you can buy sheepskin liners to put into your tennis shoes which make them warmer and springier.

We also had San Francisco, water-tight, hiking boots, broken in before the trip, which proved invaluable, not just for the Milford Track but for any occasion when it was wet and muddy. Tennis shoes, once damp, flunk the comfort test.

The climate tables give a spread from Auckland in the north with a summer average of about 76 degrees and a winter average of about 58 degrees fahrenheit to Dunedin in the south with a summer average of 68 degrees and a winter of 50 degrees.

New Zealand has almost completely changed all measuring scales to the metric system: weather temperatures, rainfall measurements, highway distances, golf hole distances, grocery store weights, etc. If you don't have your metric system memorized, you should have a pocket-handy converter with you. You will find a conversion table at the end of this book.

Remember that the New Zealand seasons are the reverse of the seasons in the Northern Hemisphere. Summer is from December through February. Autumn from March through May. Winter from June through August. Spring from September through November.

When should you go to New Zealand? Anytime. The summer time is warmer and more suitable for swimming and water sports. *But summer time is New Zealand vacation time and you must be sure that you have advance reservations.*

What To Do In New Zealand

There is so much to do in New Zealand that the biggest problem facing the visitor is choosing from the number of activities which can be fitted into the time period available.

Certainly the most sedentary traveller can have a marvelous time just sight-seeing. The visual wonders of the country unfold in a staggering variety from bubbling pots of thermal mud to snow-covered mountains.

To the student of flora and fauna New Zealand offers a kaleidoscope of new and old friends.

To the horticulturist New Zealand is a constant delight because botanical gardens, public and private, are simply everywhere.

If the study of a different culture is appealing, the civilization, past and present, of the Maori people, is an absorbing, fascinating experience.

Physical ability is not a criterion for falling in love with New Zealand. There is so much to do, so much to enjoy.

For the outdoors person, the sportsman, the problem of selection is multiplied.

New Zealand is synonymous with trout fishing.

Hunting, some of the world's finest, is without season. There is everything but snake hunting. There are no snakes in New Zealand.

Zane Grey, in 1926, made the deep-sea fishing of New Zealand famous.

There is a two-month season on quail and pheasant and a three-week season on duck and geese.

In New Zealand there is a golf course for almost every filling station. Rub two Scotsmen together and you get a fairway. There are well over 325 registered golf courses in a country about two-thirds the size of California.

When the skier in the Northern Hemisphere is looking at oiled bodies on beaches and dreaming of snow, there are treeless slopes at sizeable ski developments in full swing in New Zealand. There is superb mountain-top ski touring.

With the Southern Alps as a training ground there is challenging alpine climbing, and for hiking . . . there are five-minute or five-day walks at every turn. Take your pick.

Then there is yachting. Go charter a yacht and cruise the islands.

There is magnificent salmon fishing from January to March and surf-casting the year 'round.

Tennis courts are everywhere and lawn bowls and cricket. Many squash courts. Rafting down a river is a growing visitor sport.

If you like spectator sports, learn about the national mayhem called rugby. It is a thriller.

Horses? You can ride them or bet on them. New Zealanders are not bragging people but they do glow over the record for wins set by New Zealand horses in the most prestigious horse race in the Pacific, the Melbourne Cup. (It's the lime content in the New Zealand grass, they tell you.)

Or if your sport is just having a drink in a cool bar, there is a bit of that too.

The Outdoor Life
The sporting life in New Zealand is the finest in the world for its comparative size.

With a little organization you can ski on a mountain and trout fish on a lake in the morning, shoot a red deer in a forest and deep-sea fish on the ocean in the afternoon.

The variety of sports covers every popular pastime. That's good news for the visitor. Better news is that the *quality* level of the sport is so extremely high.

Fishing
Trout fishing in New Zealand is the first fame of the country. In pre-European times there were no freshwater fish of any consequence. The English, who always take their civilization with them, corrected this by importing brown trout via Tasmania in 1867. (The English also imported the rabbit for hunting with disastrous results.)

The ova of the California rainbow were imported from the

Russian River in only one shipment in 1883. This shipment became the progenitor of a pure strain of rainbow which is now sent all over the world, especially to the United States . . . and back to the Russian River in California we presume.

It is interesting to read how the ova were sent. A captured female (hen) rainbow was stripped of her eggs which were then overlayed with the sperm or sperm glands of the male (jack) fish, and then packed in a living moss cocooned in layers of ice and charcoal several feet thick. The box was cargoed in the ship's refrigeration chamber. The ova, still in a frozen state on reaching Auckland, were hatched and raised in a stream near the Winter Garden in the Auckland Domain.

The superb water and feeding conditions of the New Zealand lakes and rivers proved ideal breeding grounds for the browns and the rainbows and it did not take them long to surpass the size and condition of their ancestors. It was not only the size of the New Zealand trout which gave the country its reputation for trout but the condition of the fish resulting in ferocious fighters made it a mecca for anglers around the world.

The American brook trout did not prove hardy enough to stand up to the competition of the rainbow and the brown and the attempt to introduce the species in Lake Rotorua failed. However a small colony survived and was transplanted to a lake near Taupo (Lake Hinemaiaia) where they have thrived, reaching up to five pounds. Unfortunately the lake has recently been filling with silt, restricting the trout.

The trout fishing season is generally from the first of October to the end of March . . . and lasts two months longer in districts controlled by the Government.

Lake Taupo and Lake Rotorua are open for fishing all year long.

Generally fishing on streams feeding into lakes and 300 yards from the mouths of the lakes is reserved for fly-fishing. (More fish are caught by fly-fishing in New Zealand than by any other method.)

Rainbow trout dominate the waters of the North Island with brown trout available but harder to catch. In the South Island the brown is more numerous but still is a wily bastard.

Fishing licenses can be confusing but the Government makes it easy for visitors by offering a Visitor's License, good for one month which includes all but two unimportant lakes in the North Island.

(There are twenty-six different fishing districts in New Zealand, each with its own acclimatisation society, with separate licenses and separate seasons.)

The Visitor's License costs $4 for men and $2 for women and is a great bargain. *Visitors' Licenses must be obtained from a Government Tourist Bureau.* They are not available through sporting goods stores or acclimatisation societies or guides.

The Government Tourist Bureau is an excellent source for putting together a fishing trip for you including itineraries, hotel-motel-lodge reservations, plane reservations and guides.

A word about guides in New Zealand. If you aren't an expert fisherman but you still want to experience a New Zealand fighting trout on your line, you are probably going to go trolling on a lake or you are going to have to take a boat out on a river.

You have no choice. You have to have a guide. He has all the equipment for you except underwear and socks. He has all the necessary ground transportation from a limousine to a Land Rover. He has a jet-boat or a launch. He probably can sell you a day's license if you didn't get a Visitor's License. He'll have lunch and morning and afternoon tea if you ask for them.

For the novice getting a guide in any fishing country is essential. The guide knows where the fish are, what to fish with, where not to fish and waste your time. He can tell you the best places to go on your own.

For the novice and the expert alike he has another great value. He has keys. He has keys to paddocks of farmers who trust him, knowing he will always lock the gates and not disturb the livestock. He can go where few other fishermen can go. If you want a shot at stretches of river which are comparatively virgin, you need an experienced guide to open the gates.

There are over fifty top professional guides in New Zealand. All guides are inspected regularly by the Tourist and Publici.y Department's hunting and fishing officer.

The cost of a guide runs from $112 to $150 a day. A good guide is worth every penny of it.

Salmon are found only in the South Island and the run up river starts after the first of the year and continues into March.

They come in monstrous sizes.

The salmon are generally fished at sea mouths with heavy gear surf rods using metal spinners on bait-casting reels.

Surf-casting is also productive on any shoreline in New Zealand.

Scuba diving, increasing in popularity around the world, is found throughout New Zealand and the visiting scuba diver is invited to contact one of the many scuba clubs in coastal resort areas. They are listed in the telephone directories.

The shores of New Zealand teem with shellfish and are particularly productive for scuba divers. There are also scuba charters available in the most popular areas.

Big game fishing is at its best in the late summer (February–April). Striped marlin are the most prolific of the swordfish followed by blue and black marlin. An international contest is held in the Bay of Islands in March.

The deep-sea fishing ports are all found on the east coast of the North Island. If you take a map of the North Island, you can locate the popular fishing bases moving your finger from north to south: Whangaroa, Bay of Islands, Tutukaka just north of Whangarei, Mercury Bay on the Coromandel Peninsula, with fine fishing off of Great Mercury Island and Tauranga and Whakatane on the Bay of Plenty, with the principal fishing being off Mayor Island.

Visitors can join individual big game clubs at an average fee of $5 which includes the use of club facilities.

Reservations for charters should be made well in advance of a fishing date.

"Fishing in New Zealand" is a highly useful pamphlet put out by the Tourist and Publicity Department and available through New Zealand tourist offices.

For individual help the fisherman can write to The Hunting and Fishing Officer, Tourist and Publicity Department, Private Bag, Rotorua, New Zealand.

"Angler's Guide to the South Island of New Zealand" is published by the South Island Publicity Association of New Zealand in Christchurch and is another useful information pamphlet.

Golf
If you are never far from water in New Zealand, you are a shorter

distance from a golf course.

There are public courses and private courses everywhere. With a few exceptions, especially as to times, they are all open to visitors.

The normal practice for visiting players is to carry a letter of introduction from their home club. We never found it necessary. Our practice was to call the course we wanted to play and tell the club secretary or the club secretary's secretary that we were visitors and we would like to play their course and could we come out tomorrow? We were always given a hearty "Come right along."

We avoided the obvious members' hours of Tuesday morning for the ladies and Saturdays for the men.

Golfing all round New Zealand is simply a big bag of fun. Not only are the courses interesting variations of golfing layouts but they are inevitably scenic. And the prices by world standards are non-existent. We sometimes paid $1 for a greens fee. $5.00 is about the maximum.

Carts are called *trundlers* and spikes are called *sprigs.*

Professional shops are available at all of the golf courses with any desired equipment except powered golf carts available to rent or buy.

"The only aid the visitor will not find available is the motorized trundler; they are not used, except by the occasional member who has been granted permission to use one, on medical grounds," to quote a Government pamphlet *"Golf in New Zealand".* Nor are there any caddies.

The standard golfball used in New Zealand is the small English ball.

Above all the New Zealander plays golf *briskly.* There is none of this nonsense of sighting, practice swinging, wiggle-waggling, walking away from the ball, etc. You get up to the ball and hit it and charge forward.

A sign before the first tee at the Centennial Course at Taupo says in effect and sums up the New Zealand attitude: *"You should play this course and have an enjoyable game in less than 3½ hours."* It should be an exportable item.

In Taupo a professional lesson costs $5.

We played more than twenty golf courses and inspected an equal number . . . that is less than 10 percent of the golf courses in New Zealand. We wished we could have played them all.

Hunting

Wildlife like the rabbit and the trout has been imported to New Zealand and, like the rabbit and the trout, has found the virgin country a place to multiply in such numbers that some of the species have caused severe depletion of grass and cover, threatening the land with erosion and destruction.

Therefore there is no limit on the big game and no license required. (A permit is required in national parks, State forests, scenic reserves and unoccupied Crown land.)

Deer, elk, chamois, thar, wild goat and wild pigs have no season.

The sale of wild venison to the export market, particularly West Germany, has brought about an increase in professional hunting and there are areas where deer hunting is particularly competitive.

Although the Forest Service offices can supply local information on terrain, hut locations, climate and the equipment necessary for safe, productive hunting, it is best to hire a guide to get the most from your time.

A guide often has the hunting rights to vast acreages where you can hunt deer, particularly, with the best chance of bringing home the venison. The guide can also provide lodges, scope-fitted rifles and food. When required he can call in an airplane to drop the hunters in remote areas and return for a pickup at a designated time. Helicopters are also available. Rates for guides start at about $50 a day and go to $125 a day per hunter.

If I were going hunting in New Zealand, I would write to Rex Forrester, the Hunting and Fishing Officer, Tourist and Publicity Department, Private Bag, Rotorua, New Zealand and lay my ambitions, budgets and time limitations in his lap. He has the immediate knowledge to put it all together for you. Or as the New Zealander would say, "jack it up." Rex has written an excellent reference work, *"Hunting in New Zealand"* and is completing a similar book on fishing.

Note: the importation of firearms into New Zealand has to be declared. It requires an "entry permit" – good for one month at no charge – from the police at the airport. Shotguns do not need to be registered. Revolvers and pistols are illegal and entry is prohibited.

The hunting of duck, Canadian geese, pheasant and quail starts the first Saturday in May. The duck-geese game season lasts three weeks but the pheasant-quail season lasts two months.

Licenses are required and can be purchased at local sporting goods stores.

Opossums, which you will see by the hundreds on the highways, killed by night drivers, wallabies and rabbits, wild pig and hares, are considered pests and a license to hunt them is not required.

You are advised to check with the local Forest Service or Rabbit Board before going hunting, and you should not go hunting on private property without first obtaining the owner's permission. Most owners are highly cooperative and many will offer worthwhile advice on just where to go.

Skiing

New Zealand is a below-the-Equator ski country and that is its primary appeal as a ski center. Location. If the itch in your ski pants isn't satisfied with the itch of your swimming suit, you can go to New Zealand.

Don't expect to find Davos or Courchevel or Aspen or Squaw Valley. The lifts and runs are limited compared to the major international ski centers but there is good honest skiing to be had with some highly unusual attractions.

There are four principal ski resorts, three of these being on the South Island. Coronet Peak at Queenstown. Tasman Glacier at Mt Cook. Mt Hutt outside of Christchurch. The North Island offers skiing at Ruapehu, the tallest mountain in the North Island, on the south end of Lake Taupo.

In the middle of July I flew to New Zealand to explore the skiing which as luck would have it turned out to be too early for the best snow.

At Queenstown a bus takes you to Coronet Peak round-trip for $3.00, eleven miles each way. Metal-clasped ski boots, metal skis, poles $6. All-day lift ticket $6. Cheap.

Signed up for private ski lesson: One hour: $12.

My instructor was Stig Bergman, a blond, movie-handsome Finn, who headquarters in Vail, Colorado. There were thirty instructors on the Coronet Peak instructor list from nine countries: New Zealand, Australia, United States, Canada, Switzerland, France, Germany, Norway and Finland!

We took a three-person chairlift to the top of Coronet Peak and then unbuckled the ski gear and climbed through the snow to a glassed-in lookout which gave a 360-degree panoramic view of the surrounding mountains from the Southern Alps to Ben Lomond and the Remarkable Mountains. Sensational. The morning was magnificent and it gave you that standing-on-top-of-the-world feeling which is a benefit of skiing.

Coming down the snow was thin. Tussocks – thick clumps of grass – were peeking through the snow on every side. But no trees and no rocks. (One of the advertised slogans of New Zealand is to "ski the treeless slopes".)

We traversed over to the top of chairlift Number 2 which was installed the year before giving the area two chairlifts, two poma lifts and two rope tows. We did part of this trail before rejoining the regular *piste* which took us to the top of the final run known as *Shirtfront*. In four inches of snow it was very rugged.

"You can't take beginning Americans on this slope," said Stig. "But in two days you take New Zealanders. Tough people."

A stretcher coming down *Shirtfront* convinced me that I didn't need any more skiing at Coronet Peak so I went to the Alpine Restaurant and had chili and milk for 55c. Overheard in the restaurant, "I've seen skiing last here six weeks and I've seen it last six months."

In order to keep to my travel schedule the hotel had a taxi pick me up at Coronet Peak and take me back to the hotel in time to change and get an airplane to Mt Cook. The taxi came out eleven miles picked me up and took me back eleven miles. Cost: $7. The driver didn't wait for a tip because he didn't expect one.

"Driver, how long does the skiing last here?"

"Oh, four months would be stretching it."

Mount Cook Airlines to Mount Cook National Park in British HS748 prop-jet. Weather closing in.

Checked into Hermitage. Nice hotel. No refrigerator in room. Strange that the Government Tourist Hotels don't perpetuate one of the nicer New Zealand customs.

Checked into the Alpine Guide office. Gavin Wills, the general manager of Alpine Guides, a gentle, bearded, giant of a man. "Yes, we can fit you into a ski group doing the Tasman Glacier tomorrow and we can fix you up with the proper gear but the weather looks rather 'iffy'. Check in tomorrow morning at 8:30 and we'll see."

And for forty-eight hours it rained.

No Tasman Glacier skiing.

Gavin: "It's a mountain situation. People come back year after year. Sometimes they have lousy weather. Sometimes they have magnificent weather. They understand. They have enough flexibility in time to go off to Queenstown or wherever if it's bad and come back when it's good. As I say, it's a mountain situation."

Skiing in the Mount Cook area is the most tingling of New Zealand skiing.

The Tasman Glacier is a wide-sloped classical glacial skiing experience which can be easy or difficult depending upon your ability.

The top of the ski run is at Tasman Saddle at more than 8,000 feet. It is not a place for novices. Glacier skiing means crevasses, particularly in the upper areas, and I'd rather go down a building without any elevator than go down a glacier without a guide.

The cost of glacier skiing is $60 for two runs (with guide) as part of a group. For better skiers Alpine Guides will take you to the Big Three: the Murchison, the Mannering and the Annette Plateau, which adds up to 10,000 vertical feet of downhill skiing requiring six to eight hours. Helicopter skiing costs $80 for one day.

In addition Alpine Tours offers ski touring trips where guides take you to high huts on mountain tops where you climb and ski and never cross another track! The brochure says succinctly: "You've got to be fit."

A week long ski tour which includes hut fees, food and guide services plus the cost of an aeroplane getting you in and out costs $180.

Also, for the really rugged, there are mountain skiing courses: ". . . practical instruction about climbing with ski and skins, the use of rope on foot and on ski, crevasse rescue, route finding, and the special problems of surviving in winter conditions". Courses are limited to groups of six and last six and a half days: $130 includes hut fees, food and instruction.

To an ardent skier Mount Cook is the place in New Zealand where the potential experiences are superlative and unmatched in other parts of the world.

The instructors at Coronet Peak in Queenstown were discouraged by the snow conditions. It was said that some of them were abandoning Queenstown for Mount Hutt.

Mount Hutt was not on my itinerary but it is obviously a ski field of growing popularity.

The resort lies sixty-two miles southwest of Christchurch on good roads.

There are no accommodations at the ski center itself but there are accommodations in Methven, Ashburton and Christchurch ranging from first-class hotels to farmhouses and bunkhouses. All-inclusive packages are available through travel agents.

The lift facilities at Mount Hutt consist of four T-bars which go to the top of the South Peak (6,810 ft.), two platter lifts, a rope tow and two fixed-grip learners' tows. Mount Hutt also has a Kassbohrer snowpacker from Europe which is at present the only one in New Zealand.

Mt Ruapehu (9,175 ft.), which is in the Tongariro National Park, is reached by car from the Taupo airport. You stay at the Chateau Tongariro, a Government-owned hotel and take a four-wheel-drive bus from the hotel to the ski center where you can rent ski equipment for $7, buy a one-day lift ticket for $6, and get a toasted spaghetti sandwich for 25c.

By car Ruapehu is about four hours from Wellington and more than five hours from Auckland . . . within reach of the gung-ho skier who probably belongs to one of the many ski clubs which have bunkhouses on the slopes of the mountain. As a result Ruapehu is the most populated of ski resorts . . . crowded on the weekends but much easier on the weekdays.

There are nursery slopes and expert downhill runs serviced by three modern chairlifts, two T-bars and ten rope tows. Four thousand skiers are accommodated daily in peak season!

A snowmobile operates at the resort and, most appealing, in good weather there is a helicopter that can take you to the top of Ruapehu where you can look down into a warm-water lake . . . they used to swim in it until the water became *too* warm! . . . and if there is enough snow, you can ski all the way back to the Chateau. Marvelous!

I arrived at the Chateau under black skies just as the last light faded.

I inquired into helicopter and a guide and, yes, if weather permitted it could be done but the weather was rather "iffy" and I'd better check in first thing in the morning.

The next morning there was a blizzard. The snow was going from left to right in a white curtain in front of my window.

Damn. I took the four-wheel bus up to the ski center: *Top O' the Bruce.* Couldn't see fifteen feet in front. Impossible. Went back down to the Chateau and brushed the snow off the rental car and drove to Taupo.

The next day at the airport the weather was beautiful and taking off for Auckland the peaks of Ruapehu and its neighbors were glistening in lovely skiable snow.

"It," I said to myself philosophically, "is a four-letter-word mountain situation."

● For a free Guide to Skiing New Zealand's Leading Areas write to P.O. Box 8107, Christchurch.

Hiking and Climbing

There are simply sensational hikes in New Zealand of every description. New Zealanders say "tramping".

The most famous is the Milford Track which we took and is descr bed in detail. The Routeburn, the Hollyford Valley to Martin's Bay, the Heaphy are other three-day to six-day hikes in the South Island. In the North Island a guided tour through Urewera National Park track is just being put together.

But there are walks everywhere. New Zealanders just love to get out in their "bush". Two minutes, thirty minutes, three hours . . . just ask the local public relations office wherever you might be and there will be hikes and walks and tramps to meet your mood and physical condition.

The national parks are particularly rich in good hikes. Trails are well marked and the paths are kept in fine condition. The more we saw of the national parks the more we admired the work of the Park Ranger Service.

Climbing is another matter and for the relatively élite few.

Mount Cook National Park is the scene of the best alpine climbing and the Alpine Guides who offer the Tasman skiing, etc. experiences also have a school of mountaineering alpine guiding with a gamut of courses ranging from basic through advanced. The address of Alpine Guides is PO Box 20, Mount Cook, Mount Cook National Park.

Tennis
Tennis courts are everywhere. There are public courts, private clubs, lawn tennis courts, hard courts. Most private clubs have open hours for visitors for a small fee. The local public information offices will have specific information of the best places and times to play.

Boating
A resident of New Zealand finds his kit complete when he owns his own house, his car and his boat. As a result there are 75,000 pleasure boats or about one in every tenth household, certainly one of the highest per capita figures in the world.

If you make a friend of a New Zealander, the first thing he will do is invite you out in his boat whether it is a sixty-foot yacht or a sixteen-foot runabout.

There is no trouble getting out on the water.

River Rafting
New and growing. Example: Canterbury and Alpine Travel in Christchurch offers a five-day, 124-mile ride down the Clarence River: fare $180.

Spectator Sports and Others
Horse racing is the most popular year-round sport in New Zealand with some of the finest thoroughbred horses bred in the country taking the track. (The annual yealing sales attract Australian, Far East countries, South African and United States buyers and total millions of dollars.)

There are some 260 meetings over 390 days of racing each year. Auckland alone has three tracks: Ellerslie and Avondale for racing and A lexandra Park for harness racing.

Rugby Union, an amateur sport, is the most popular seasonal sport extending from the end of March into October. It is a terrific game.

Cricket is the summer sport and the newspapers' sports sections are full of incomprehensible cricket results. Cricket is as complicated and unexciting to Americans as American baseball is to non-Americans. No, that is not exactly true because there is a lot of softball played in New Zealand.

What else? Water skiing is very popular as is surfboarding. There is soccer and rugby league which are semi-professional.

There is motorcycle racing, midget car (go-kart) racing and Grand Prix racing and many motorboat and yachting events.

Add to the list rowing, lawn bowls, croquet and, oh yes, bridge.

New Zealanders are dotty-potty over bridge and there are bridge clubs and tournaments on every corner.

New Zealand's enthusiasm for sports is reflected in the disproportionately high number of world champions it produces in relation to its small population. Bob Fitzsimmons in boxing. Sir Edmund Hillary in alpine climbing. John Lovelock created a heritage in winning the mile in the 1936 Olympics which has been passed down through Halberg and Snell to John Walker, today's champion miler. Bob Charles in golf, the finest left-hander in the world. World champion rowers. Grand Prix drivers, yachtsmen and, the toughest lot of them all, the New Zealand rugby players.

(Maybe it's the lime in the grass.)

Accommodations, Food, Booze and Time – New Zealand Style

What Should You Buy for Motoring?

The first three things you should do in New Zealand if you are going to drive yourself are:

1. Buy the North and South Island *"Mobil Travel Guide"* books.

2. Join the Automobile Association if you aren't already a member at home.

3. Buy a "chilly-bin".

The best guide books about New Zealand are the two-volume *"Mobil Travel Guides"* compiled by Diana and Jeremy Pope. The two volumes comprise definitive information and we couldn't imagine travelling without them.

The books are published and distributed by Reed in New Zealand and distributed in the United States by Chas. E. Tuttle, but are hard to find in American book stores. If you wait until you reach New Zealand, go to a Whitcoulls' store, a nationwide book store, and buy your copies. They will cost half of the American price.

Incidentally, Whitcoulls' has an excellent library on all New Zealand travel literature. If you are going to be in Auckland for any length of time, it would also be worthwhile buying Whitcoulls' *"Map Directory of Auckland City"*.

The Pope books have interesting introductions which will add to your visit. The books are arranged alphabetically by town so it is not a road-map type of guidebook. It is well cross-indexed.

For your road information you should join the Automobile Association. If you are not a member in your home country, you should join in New Zealand. The cost is only $4.00 initiation, plus $13.00 for annual dues.

Besides providing an emergency breakdown service, the AA has a super library of maps. First of all you can get a map of each island in its entirety. Then you can get colored sectional maps of each island. These sectional maps then can be had in sub-divided black-and-white route maps.

It doesn't stop there.

If you go into an AA office and say, "We want to take a tour going from here, to here, to here," they will compile a folio of strip maps specifically for you, stapled together, which will contain time and mileage charts for each section of your trip. On the back of the maps is historical and points-of-interest information.

For the North Island the AA will provide you with an *"Outdoor Guide"* with listings for camping grounds, trailer (caravan) parks and cabins. There is also boating information including sites of boat ramps. The *"Outdoor Guide"* gives a listing of golf courses and even suggested picnic areas. Very handy. Also for the North Island there is an *"Accommodation Guide"* with information on hotels and motels. All of the information regarding the South Island is combined in a single AA volume, the *"South Island Handbook"*.

The courtesy of the AA personnel is as good as their information. Cheerful, helpful people.

Armed with all of your AA literature together with the Pope books, you have all of the information you need.

You are almost ready to take the road.

But not quite. Besides an engine, wheels, petrol, maps and guidebooks, you can't really move in New Zealand without a *chilly-bin.*

A chilly-bin is a polystyrene picnic hamper which will keep ice, cold drinks, cheeses, sandwiches, chicken etc. cold up to ten hours, dependably. Oh, yes, this should be accompanied by at least one large thermos bottle, to hold your tea.

Morning teas, noon picnics and afternoon teas alongside the road are a way of life in New Zealand.

You'll note quickly that a New Zealand "tea" isn't just stopping, pouring a cup, drinking it down and pressing on. "Tea" means spreading a tablecloth, putting out cookies, cakes and tomato sandwiches. Highly civilized. This custom has its dangers and it should be discussed in conjunction with accommodations.

A Place to Stay and a Place to Eat

A four-star motel in New Zealand will give you a full kitchen, completely equipped including the first day's milk and a supply of instant coffee, tea and sugar. Living room. Separate bathroom. Separate bedroom. (Request twin or double.)

In Auckland, for example, on a return trip we had all of the above plus colored television and a newspaper placed at our door every morning. $18 a night for two.

Such accommodations together with your chilly-bin create a temptation to start "living-in", to do a steak or an omelette for dinner, and then you start to carry eggs and salad oil and vinegar, and pretty soon the whole thing gets out of hand.

On one of our first shakedown side trips from home base in Taupo, we were stripped down to one golfbag, one suitcase and one handbag. *And three bags of food!*

Our New Zealand friends roar at this story and reply in one voice: "You took too many clothes!"

So there is an argument for forgetting the chilly-bin, taking your tea in tearooms (there are thousands of them) and staying in hotels where you are waited on. You avoid the danger of becoming a do-it-yourself servant. If you do so, however, you miss a rare food experience.

Buying is another food experience.

The best food buys in New Zealand are milk . . . 10c a pint . . . lamb and beef, butter and cheese . . . which are half the price of anywhere else in the world except Australia . . . and fruit in season.

Oh, God, the memory of huge bowls of strawberries and peaches floating in buckets of thick cream!

Beef is pasture-fed and not finished in stockyards and marbled and aged like American beef. It is better for you. The veal is not pink veal.

Lamb is a great buy, of course. "Hogget" that you'll see labeled is not a small pig but a year-old lamb.

Bakeries sell mostly cakes, pastries and hot bread. Some small grocery stores reserve bread for customers and when there is a surplus you'll see a sign outside saying "Spare Bread".

There is a great commercial bakery in Auckland, Klisser's Farm-house Bakery, which makes a brand called *Vogel's Swiss Style Mixed Grain Bread.* It makes the most superb toast you've ever tasted.

Another brand put out by the same bakery is Reizenstein's which comes in an almost-black variety. It makes an outstanding rich bread for picnics or with grilled meat.

Eating out in New Zealand takes a little knowledge.

There are two kinds of restaurants, licensed and unlicensed. The licensed restaurants will be boldly advertised and not seeing such signs outside of a restaurant you can safely assume that it is non-licensed.

A restaurant which is licensed can sell you cocktails, beer and wine. An unlicensed restaurant cannot serve any alcohol; however, you can take your own beer or wine to many of them. (Ask beforehand if you are in doubt.) The law says you can't bring beverages after 6 p.m. but people do, and only the licensed restaurants complain. (An unlicensed restaurant, ironically, can serve you an Irish coffee filled with Irish whiskey because it has been *cooked.)*

New Zealand is basically an agriculture, meat-and-potato society, much like the American mid-West, which is reflected in the restaurant menus. Steaks dominate the menus. Surprisingly, you don't see much lamb (often listed as *hogget* or *mutton).* If there is fish on the menu, you can be sure it is fried.

In the principal cities there seems to be a wave of more sophisticated new restaurants coming on stream and it is worth asking around and doing your own exploring.

Chinese restaurants in any city around the world are usually worth trying. The menus in many New Zealand Chinese restaurants seem to be restricted to chop-suey and chow mein and a choice of Continental food.

Another major area of food in New Zealand is the "take-away" where you can get hamburgers, milk shakes, French fries ("chips"), cooked chickens ("seasoned" chickens mean they are stuffed) and a variety of sandwiches. There are also lots of "fish-and-chip" shops.

The colloquial word for chicken is "chooks".

Your Bar Needs Help or You Need a Little Drink

The stand-up bars in New Zealand are found only in hotels or taverns. There are no cocktail bars *per se.*

Licensed restaurants may have a lounge where you can find a drink before eating.

The hotel or tavern bar will have a public room on one side where you will find the serious drinkers, mostly drinking beer in sizeable quantities. On the other side you will find the private bar, or lounge, which isn't private at all, where the mood and crowd are a bit more genteel.

In between there is usually a bottle store where you can buy a bottle of whiskey or other spirits, cold beer or wine from any country, and mixes.

A "wholesale" liquor store has a larger stock of everything and will offer better prices. A minimum purchase of two gallons or more of alcoholic beverages is required by law in wholesale stores.

You can buy alcohol by the bottle in a "wine store", but a wine store can only sell wine and may sell only New Zealand wine. It is not uncommon to sample the wine in wine stores. You'll often see New Zealanders going into these stores with empty half-gallon flagons. They are going to get the flagons replenished with sherry or lighter red or white wine.

Wine in New Zealand is becoming a more important industry and the result is better wines of more consistent quality.

However, there is often lacking anything resembling ageing. "If it is bottled it is ready to drink" used to be the slogan, but date-labelled wines two to three years old are coming on the market.

One major Australian vintner, McWilliams, has moved into the New Zealand wine market, as has one major United States liquor company, Seagrams, which has a 40% share in Montana.

About Driving in New Zealand

The first thing we did in New Zealand was to buy a Japanese-made station wagon, high yellow, right-hand side drive, of course, with radio, heater and reclining seats. We called it the "Yellow Rose of Tokyo".

It was a used car, looked like a Tinker Toy inside the hood, but it drove 12,000 miles and the most trouble it gave was to cough once on a high hill on a cold morning.

The station wagon model was necessary.

Although we travel constantly we can't seem to shed a basic insecurity in leaving anything at home.

In the "Yellow Rose" we packed three tennis racquets, one golf bag stuffed with two half-sets of clubs and a canvas golf bag for the Lady Navigator plus two sets of golf shoes.

There was a metal caddy holding five fishing rods, two fishing tackle boxes, one canvas picnic hamper, one "chilly bin", two large suitcases, two small suitcases, one shoe case, one portable radio, one typewriter and six minor pieces of hand luggage.

The poor "Yellow Rose" rear wheels splayed out like a wounded horse when it received all of the gear.

You really had to get the car wound up to pass anything on the road.

The first thing to remember is that the driving in New Zealand is on the left hand side of the road. Very important to remember. A lapse of memory can lead to all sorts of disastrous endings.

Drivers in New Zealand are polite. They don't honk their horns at you like New York taxi drivers. They don't scream at you and call attention to your parental derivation like Italians. They don't drive paint-job to paint-job like the Japanese.

There is a tendency to tailgate – largely, I suspect, because most of the roads will be two-way roads which call for a quick pull-out and a quick cut-in.

You are expected to keep your seat belt attached because that is the law.

Throughout the country there are a number of one-way bridges. They will be posted. If the sign on your side of the bridge says "Please Give Way", that means the other fellow has the right of way. Do so.

This was brought to my attention in a most definite manner when a milk truck in Northland went by my right ear in the other direction doing fifty miles an hour at my first one-way bridge. It pays to be polite for one very good reason – you live longer.

You don't have to run out of gas ("petrol") to go to the bathroom. The New Zealanders are conscious of what road travel does to one's kidneys, particularly with all that tea. You will see little block houses in even small villages. They are labeled *"TOILETS"*. No mistaking their meaning. Most of them, for some reason, will be labeled *"LADIES"*. I don't know why this is.

In addition to toilets for ladies there are frequently seen *"Plunket Rooms"*. The Plunket Society was founded in the South Island by Sir Truby King, (1858–1938) a medical reformer who was determined to fight the high infant mortality rate through education of mothers and by the supply of trained nurses in Plunket Rooms. The Plunket Society (or, more correctly, The Royal New Zealand Society for the Health of Women and Children) is highly successful and is an important part of New Zealand's health program.

Yes, visiting ladies can use their rest rooms.

In Bluff I saw a man with an obvious problem dashing madly into a Plunket Society house and I thought men could also use the facilities of the establishment, but it turned out that the house was also a district's voting place and the dashing man was only trying to vote before the polls closed. No, there are no Plunket facilities for men.

When you see little tearoom places labeled Morning Tea, Take-Aways, Afternoon Teas, Hot Pies, it usually means there is a bathroom thrown in.

It is foolhardy to try and translate your usual mileage to New Zealand travel. Don't count on making more than 250 miles a day and still have your tea stops, etc. The roads are winding, two-lane, lots of truck traffic and, besides, you are on vacation. Where are you going?

If you are going to be on the road all day, make sure you have your hotel or motel space booked ahead of you.

The post office is where you can bank money, mail letters and send telegrams. It is also a place where you can make long-distance ("toll") telephone calls. The person at the counter will take your number, call it for you, direct you to a private booth and you pay for the call afterwards.

With the AA accommodations book, you can call ahead from the post office for reservations when you are on the road. Most post offices are closed on weekends. Longdistance telephone calls are modest in cost.

If you aren't pushing, driving in New Zealand is superlative. You are never far from water, be it river, ocean or lake. The roads are interesting and directions well marked. There are abundant *"REST AREAS"* clearly marked where you can change drivers, take a stretch and have tea.

Also you will frequently pass signs pointing to a roadside house saying *"FIRST AID"*, which means there is a qualified first-aid person inside or the sign will say *"FIRST AID KIT"* which means there is some equipment but no trained personnel.

New Zealand's road signs follow the familiar international pattern, but you will need to remember that speed restrictions are shown in kilometers, not miles. A "50" sign means that you are entering a built-up area and must not exceed thirty miles an hour. A "70" indicates a limit of forty miles an hour, and an "LSZ" sign warns you that you're in an area where you should slow down to thirty if the weather conditions are bad, or traffic is dense, or there are children about.

On the open road you are restricted by law to a maximum of fifty miles an hour (80 km/h) . . . a gas-saving idea imposed during the international oil crisis. It is not generally respected, but the traffic police are on the lookout for infringers, particularly during public-holiday times when traffic density builds up. (At such times, too, they are out in full strength with breathalysers at the ready, and a drunken driver will get scant sympathy in the courts.)

The Kiwi traffic cop is usually gentle in manner, but he has a hard center. His ultimate boss is the Minister of Transport, and the Ministry (branches in every town) issues free copies of the *"Road Code"*, which is clear and helpful. It pays to get and study a copy.

A Thumb Nail Review of Early History

"Where did the people come from and when?" the visitor to New Zealand asks.

Carbon-dated campsites indicate there existed a nomad civilization of Polynesians in New Zealand before AD 900. No one knows where the people came from specifically or when. These nomads lived by hunting an ostrich-like, wingless bird, sometimes as high as ten feet, called the *moa*. The people became known as the *Moa-hunters*.

The first Maori to come to New Zealand after the Moa-hunter, word-of-mouth history says, was a Polynesian explorer named Kupe who came to New Zealand in AD 950, sailed completely around the islands and then returned to *Hawaiki* safely.

According to Maori traditional history, two canoes came from Hawaiki in the mid-part of AD 1100 and stayed. These first Maoris were joined by others in the Great Migration of 1350. Seven canoes are identified by name and Maori tribes in New Zealand today trace their ancestry back to the name of the canoes of their forefathers.

What necessitated the journey and even the location of Hawaiki is still a matter of debate.

If you pause for a moment and think about the successful navigation of Kupe and his followers . . . without a written language . . . obviously inheriting by word of mouth the route to New Zealand over a 400-year period, it is unbelievable. But it happened.

In any case the new Maoris absorbed the Moa-hunters and built in place of campsites the *pa,* or fort, and *kainga,* the unfortified village.

In 1642 Abel Tasman, a Dutchman from the Dutch East Indies, sailed across what was then an unknown ocean, now the Tasman Sea, to be the first white man to see the new country ... which he called "Staten Landt" and which, after having several names, finally became known as New Zealand after the Dutch maritime province of Zeeland.

Tasman was twice thwarted from making a landing, once by unfriendly Maoris, once by unfriendly seas. He was never to set foot on his discovery.

It is remarkable that New Zealand was not seen again for 127 years. Captain Cook in 1769 on the first of his three voyages came to New Zealand and made the first white-man landing at what is now Gisborne.

In the late 18th and early 19th centuries sealers and, later, whalers were to establish stations along the coastline and slaughter the sea animals for fur and oil.

Missionaries came to the North Island in the early part of the 19th century.

The first New Zealand Company was unsuccessful in establishing a colony of immigrants in 1826 but a second New Zealand Company in 1840 and successive years established immigrant communities in Wellington, Wanganui, New Plymouth and Nelson. Two subsequent companies set up immigrant settlements in Christchurch and Dunedin.

These six colonies, largely made up of carefully screened applicants from England and Scotland, were the first bases for an established European society.

At one time in American history the Indians watched an almost endless line of wagon trains streaming across the Dakota plains. They said, "The white man is emptying whatever country he came from." With the rapid increase of the white man, the Maoris wondered out loud if "the whole tribe" was coming from England.

In 1840 in the Bay of Islands the Maori chiefs signed the Treaty of Waitangi which was the Magna Carta of New Zealand. The treaty not only established a policy of dealing with Maori land but also established New Zealand as a British colony.

In the early 1860s gold was discovered and thousands seeking fortunes poured into New Zealand from the goldfields of Australia and California. Large numbers came from Ireland and China. Many settled permanently in New Zealand.

In the 1860s the wars with Maori tribes brought British military. To strengthen the militia, the retired British military known as "the Fencibles" were recruited. Both groups stayed.

The term "Fencibles" comes from the British word for military who could be used for home duty only. These militia men were brought to New Zealand in exchange for seven years duty. They received free passage, and the title to the cottage and land on which they lived.

Earlier in the 1800s the mighty kauri tree gave New Zealand its first industry: timber. Later, the fossilized gum from the kauri was found to have great merit in varnishes and in the 1880s another wave of immigrants, mostly from Dalmatia, brought another tide of new citizens to dig for gum in Northland.

During this entire period the Maori population was slowly being decimated. First of all they eradicated themselves in large numbers through inter-tribal wars. Then wars against the Pakeha (Europeans) further reduced their number. Finally the white-man diseases proved an almost fatal blow. By 1896 the Maori population was down to around 42,000.

It was not until 1909 that the entire population of the country reached one million. Today there are just over 3,000,000 people in New Zealand of which about 250,000 are Maori.

The Media

It is a common fault of the traveller in a new city or country to complain to the local resident, "I can't find any *news* in your newspaper." The traveller is actually saying he cannot find the familiar format of news that he is accustomed to finding in his hometown newspaper.

The complaint can be heard in New Zealand where the mass circulation newspapers are most concerned with local and national issues and are light on the coverage of international news.

The New Zealander is fond of reading. *The New Zealand Herald,* a morning newspaper, has a circulation of 225,000. The evening *Auckland Star's* circulation is 125,000. In a country of just over 3,000,000 people there are thirty-eight daily newspapers with a combined circulation of over one million.

A visitor is also impressed with the high number of bookstores.

The broadcast media is owned by the Government with the exception of a few private radio stations.

The Government radio which provides the most coverage on international news is the national non-commercial network which also broadcasts cultural programs which were our favorite listening. (New Zealand is the ideal country to drive through while a symphony or opera is background music on the radio. Not Sibelius or Smetana because that is pastoral whipped cream on top of pastoral whipped cream but best counter-pointed with the lacy designs of Mozart or Bach or Haydn.)

Commercial radio stations, Government owned, operate regionally and locally.

There are two Government-controlled television networks broadcasting in color and in black and white.

As in Europe the daily newspapers do not publish on Sunday but there is an active weekend and Sunday newspaper industry of about the same depth and tone one finds in Europe.

There is a large number of magazines but not a national news magazine. The closest thing to a national magazine is *The New Zealand Listener,* owned by the Broadcasting Council. It lists the coming week's radio and television schedules and contains a large selection of articles which reflect the attitudes and concerns and the general happenings in the country. There are two or three national weekly magazines specialising in feminine affairs.

Advertising is heavy throughout the country. There are fifty-four recognized advertising agencies. One advertising technique which smites the visitor is the use of signs outside of retail stores. It can best be described as the *splat* school of sign language. The signs are large, the more boldly painted the better, the colors are often faded. We decided this was all very camp and awarded points to the most blatant cluster of signs.

I questioned the use of signs to an Auckland advertising executive. "Yes, I know what you mean," he said. "It reminds me of the same impression I had when I was driving from the airport into Los Angeles."

Touché.

There are very few billboards in New Zealand and even those are obviously of a restricted size and mostly confined to railroad right-of-ways.

A Personal Word of Caution About Time and the New Zealander
I belong to the "Uptight About Time" Club. The Lady Navigator says that I am the president. Lots of husbands belong. For some reasons wives don't belong.

As a matter of habit our family never leaves for a party earlier than the time we are supposed to arrive. This habit creates bowel rumblings and stomach ulcers and lion roars from the male mate when the family is trying to catch an international flight.

Now the Lady Navigator, even minus a mental clock, is the greatest person in the world. We are deeply, affectionately, openly in love. In a grand compliment a friend said, "Watching you two just sitting together is like watching an X-rated movie."

To see us arrive at an airport for a take-off is to witness a couple enacting the Ice Age. We are never speaking to each other. Unfortunately it becomes twice as intense because we always catch the airplane. Fortunately we are always hand-holding friends by the time we land. Even on short flights.

If you belong to my club and have the good chance to travel with a New Zealander, you need advance advice.

The idea is *not* to get from here to there in the shortest possible time with a minimum time for pit stops, bladder breaks ("I told you to go before we left the hotel!") or picture stops ("Buy a postcard when you get there!").

To travel with a New Zealander is an education.

Stop for morning tea. Stop for beer. Stop for roadside picnic lunch. Stop for ice creams. Stop for peanuts. Peanuts make you thirsty. Stop for beer. Stop for afternoon tea.

You just learn a new, relaxed way of living and stop.

As a bus driver said to the crowd when a visitor, an American, pointed out the tardy time to him, "What's time, Mate?"

Or as a hairdresser in Auckland said to the Lady Navigator, "People who watch their watches die ten years earlier!"

The New Zealand way is not bad. You laugh a lot, chatter a lot and you eat and drink your way up and down the country.

Oh yes, one other interesting time factor: There is only one unit of time in New Zealand – it is ten minutes. Ask a New Zealander how long it takes to get from here to there? – "Oh, ten minutes." How long does it take to get a boat out of the water on to a trailer? – "Oh, ten minutes." How long does it take to catch a trout? – "Oh, ten minutes."

If you are a clock-watcher, adopt the New Zealand style, forget the watch and the time factor and live ten years longer.

The average New Zealander with an agricultural heritage is straightforward, friendly, honest. He will go out of his way to help a stranger but he has a strong respect for privacy and won't intrude himself into a stranger's company.

Being an islander ... a remote islander ... he accuses himself of provincialism and indulges, indeed makes an art of self-belittlement. Whatever you do, don't agree with him. He is sensitive. (As we are from Hawaii, we understand this "island" attitude. You can insult us. You can question us. But, please God, don't be condescending towards us.)

The average New Zealander is gentle.

American: "He is a dirty wop and ought to be hung!"

New Zealander: "Well, he does come from the Mediterranean, doesn't he, and they are different from us, aren't they? But it doesn't mean that he should go unpunished, does it?"

This gentle speech habit we called the "non-didactic New Zealand agreement question".

How does the New Zealander look at himself? Listen to James McNeish in a few lines from the book *"Larks in a Paradise"* featuring photographs by Marti Friedlander: "... kind to strangers, careless of wives ... worshippers of fair play and fellowship with an uncontrollable fear of Communism and garlic ... precise in flora, clumsy in pants".

Clever words, witty words, zingy observations, words of pride and, there you are, self-belittling words.

A "Where-Is-That?" Map

Maori place-names can be terribly confusing. Many sound alike. Taken syllable by syllable, Maori names are fairly simple and pretty to pronounce. But still defeating for the visitor.

Weather reports and news reports use a mixture of names. Sometimes just a city. Sometimes a local area. Sometimes an area that covers an entire province.

An unoriented visitor won't know if it is going to snow or rain in his backyard without a preliminary briefing.

A map of basic place names is at the beginning of this chapter. Here is a map of the weather regions:

2. Auckland – The Challenging City

**A Funny Airplane . . . A Glorious Playpool
. . . A Cracked Skull . . . A Wine Crawl . . .
The World's Largest Yacht Racing Day . . .
And Good Eats.**

Finding the charm of Auckland is easy.

You have a New Zealand friend who picks you up at the airport. First he takes you out on the lovely harbor in his lovely yacht.

He takes you to the Members' Stand at Ellerslie and you watch the beautiful New Zealand horses run at one of the most handsome race tracks in the world.

He takes you to his manicured golf club, gets you a guest membership card, lines up a tennis pro for the Stanley Street courts.

His wife gives you the city tour of the vast green parks, the flowered gardens and museums, and vistas from drive-up mountain tops.

They entertain you at a cocktail party looking at the twinkling lights of the city and you meet a cross-section of New Zealanders who above all are individualistic and freshly witty.

You think "What a charming city. How I love Auckland."

The other side of the coin is arriving in Auckland in the rain. It is Sunday. You are alone.

What do you do on a rainy, lonely Sunday in Auckland? You cut your throat.

The streets are bare. The shops are shut tight. Queen Street, the center of Auckland civilization with its bald signs and Victorian-railroad-station architecture, looks like a bad dream.

You go back to your hotel room and watch New Zealand television. Old American reruns.

You slash your wrists.

Finding interesting alternatives is the challenge. There's a fine city out there. How do you discover it?

We played a game with our Auckland friends called "What do you do on a rainy Sunday in Auckland if you are a visitor and you are alone?" The answers varied widely from the expected, "I'd get a blond and a bottle of Scotch and –" to a blank-wall, stunned silence. One person said quietly, "Go to church."

The consensus was that a commercial bus tour was the best way, even if it is rainy, to see the city and its environs and some of its indoor attractions including the War Memorial Museum. You can take a city tour in the morning and a country tour in the afternoon which includes a visit to a vineyard and a tasting room . . . except on Sunday. Sorry.

Or you can take an all-day trip up the Hibiscus Coast and take a dip in a thermal pool and come back through orchard land and visit the Museum of Transport and Technology. Terrible name for such an interesting place.

You can skip the bus tour and take off on your own in a taxi and see the War Memorial Museum in the Auckland Domain (when you read "domain" think "park"). Read first a little background on Maori culture if you can (the Pope books will give you a good briefing) because there is an excellent collection of Maori carving and decorating which is highly sophisticated and your background reading will help you enjoy it that much more.

Besides much of everything like most museums, the War Memorial Museum has a collection of native canoes of the South Pacific which is the only one of its kind we remember seeing.

Also the Museum contains the Planetarium which gives demonstrations on Saturday and Sunday afternoons.

Besides the Museum the Stanley Street courts where major tennis matches are held are located in the Domain. There also are the headquarters for the lawn tennis association and if you have a question about tennis in New Zealand, this is the place to drop in or inquire by telephone.

The botanical gardens include the Winter Garden, two giant hot-houses with indoor plants . . . we saw a breathtaking display of begonias . . . and there's an outdoor fernery there too.

By all means visit Auckland's two major observation hills: Mt Eden and One Tree Hill.

You should visit them twice. Once when you first arrive and your guide will point out downtown Auckland, the two harbors of Auckland and various other landmarks which in the confusion of a new city are incomprehensible. The second time you visit the observation hills you say, "Oh, that's where so-and-so is." Go twice.

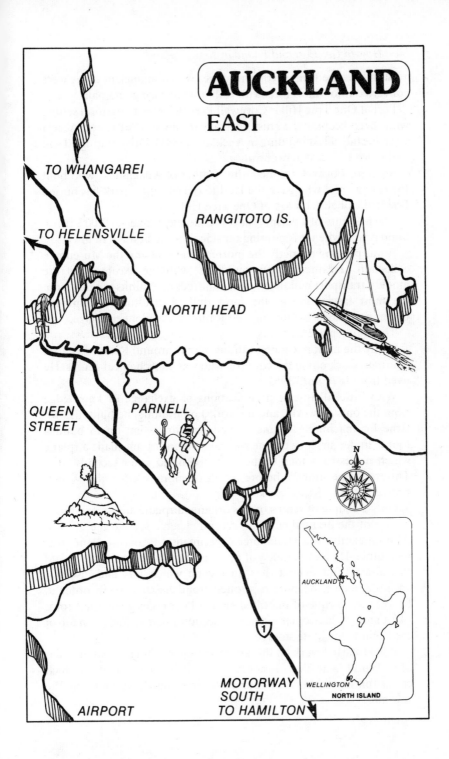

Both hills are former volcanic cones which in ancient times were converted into Maori forts with elaborate terracing and palisades.

Part of One Tree Hill is Cornwall Park, a 300-acre pastoral setting with sheep keeping the grass neat, a tearoom, of course, and Acacia Cottage, the oldest building in Auckland (1841). Drive through Twin Oaks Drive . . . a stately entrance.

Sir John Logan Campbell, the "Father of Auckland", who built the cottage and who gave the land to the city for a park lies buried beside the obelisk on top of One Tree Hill.

The Museum of Transport and Technology is open at 9:00 a.m. on Sunday and when it is pouring outside, it is the best bet in town.´

It was pouring properly the morning we went and the Museum, a collection of rather scruffy buildings, with the exception of the modern transport building, offers hundreds of exhibits ranging from the most fascinating to the most dull. Agriculture. Computers. Communications. Steam engines. Railroads. A pioneer village.

The whole place was ours.

Easily the most intriguing exhibit centers around Richard Pearse, a farmer, stuck out in the country, who was a mechanical genius. He lived from 1877 until 1953.

With little, if any, communications or exchange of knowledge from the outside world, and no workshop training, he built his own lathe for machining engine components and went on to build a four-cylinder airplane engine which he put into a self-made airplane which successfully took to the air but crashed a few seconds later. This was nine months before, or three months after, the Wright brothers flew at Kitty Hawk!

Only a couple of scraps of this original airplane are on exhibit. A replica of the original craft has recently been added to the display. Also on exhibit is a much later experimental Pearse airplane. It is incredible. He had the idea of an airplane which would hover and this aircraft, on exhibit, has an engine which *tilts* and also has variable pitch propellors controlled from the cockpit. In order to balance the torque of the tilted engine Pearse designed a tail rotor like a modern helicopter's. The rear section could be folded on top of the cabin to facilitate storage.

Pearse started work on this aircraft in the 1930s and abandoned it after World War Two. It never flew, but its Pearse motor (which could run as two-cycle or four cycle) was run occasionally by the inventor.

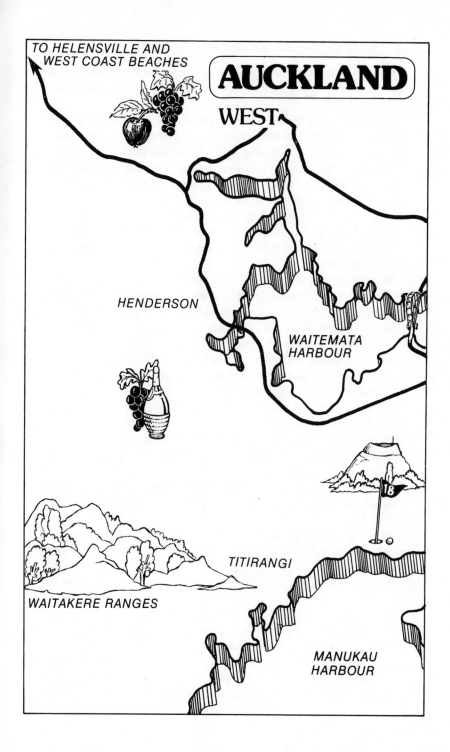

TO HELENSVILLE AND
WEST COAST BEACHES

AUCKLAND

WEST

HENDERSON

WAITEMATA
HARBOUR

18

TITIRANGI

WAITAKERE RANGES

MANUKAU
HARBOUR

Pearse also built a sound-producing machine, a four-speed bicycle with reciprocating pedals, a motorized plough and, also on display, a motorcycle.

There is a lot of nostalgia for World War II aviation buffs at the museum including a Lancaster bomber and a mission control hut.

In contrast to the technology part of the Museum is the Village. Fortunately, the Sunday morning was a "working" Sunday. The colonial houses, the blacksmith shop, the church, were alive with people in costume recreating their "daily" chores. At one "Fencible cottage" a woman was baking bread. The blacksmith was drinking tea. In the tiny church an elegantly dressed lady kindly played for us "Onward Christian Soldiers" on the antique organ. We thanked her and felt very holy.

What do you do on a rainy Sunday in Auckland? Go to church.

Also open on Sunday afternoon is the Auckland City Art Gallery which has a wide range of art including the first art dating from Captain Cook's visit in 1769 to Frances Hodgkins (1870–1947), New Zealand's most outstanding painter of international status.

There is a fine collection of sculpture and also an exhibit of colonial Victorian architecture and as you are going to see a great deal of this architecture in New Zealand, it is worth studying.

Sunday at the Zoo is not a bad idea, even in the rain, and Auckland's Zoological Park has a magnificent setting, housing animals for the most part in their natural setting, including a *kiwi* house (the flightless nocturnal national bird). The zoo is open every day from 9:30 a.m. to 5:30 p.m.

You'll find that most public buildings in New Zealand offer some kind of catering service with at least tea and sandwiches on the menu.

There are other museums, churches, buildings, historic houses which you can take in on Sunday afternoon but the above can keep you occupied and covers the best of the lot.

A rainy Sunday in Auckland doesn't have to be a terrible experience.

On a weekday first visit the Auckland Public Relations Office near the Harbor on Queen Street. A city public relations office in New Zealand is not a place for placing publicity, writing annual reports, taking pictures of the president of the company or writing speeches. A public relations office of this sort in New Zealand is a center of information where a visitor can pick up literature, ask questions, even book tours and get help with accommodations.

Become familiar with what they have to offer.

Start by picking up *"This Month in Auckland"*. It is loaded with good tips – airlines, churches, exhibitions, liquor laws, maps, rental cars, sightseeing tours, sporting and other up-coming events.

One of the best ways to get a feeling of Auckland is to get out on the water. At the bottom of Queen Street is the Ferry Terminal and, if nothing else, you can catch a ferry to Devonport which runs every forty minutes and for $1.20 for a roundtrip ticket you get a splendid ride and an idea of Auckland from the Harbor.

Not *the* Harbor really because there are two harbors. The principal harbor is on the Pacific side of Auckland and is called the Waitemata Harbor. The second harbor, on the Tasman Sea side of Auckland, is the shallow Manukau Harbor. When you come into Auckland from the south, you cross an isthmus where the two oceans are separated by only a mile of land.

If you are in Auckland between the end of October and Easter the most entertaining part of your New Zealand visit could be an excursion to one of the resort islands in the Hauraki Gulf, just outside of the Waitemata Harbor. You can go for a day or for a week.

What Do You Do About Auckland Shopping and Dining?

If you, as an international shopper, walk the length of Queen Street you're going to find the experience a little thin. As you would expect there is a strong presentation of sheepskin rugs, seatcovers, slippers. A few Maori carvings. Some pottery. Good blankets and sweaters.

If you need to buy any emergency clothing, you can find anything you want.

On Queen Street the sidewalk is divided by a white line. "They do it on highways, don't they?" was the answer when asked why.

Less than a $2 taxi ride away from your hotel is an expanding shopping experience in the fashionable residential area of Parnell. Parnell boutiques are constantly increasing in number. Antique stores. Kinky clothes stores. Knicknacks. Crafts.

This shopping-area development is largely due to the restoration efforts of one gentleman, Les Harvey, who can be seen wandering Parnell wearing a sweater inside out, in sandals, greyhaired. He doesn't believe in automobiles and the parking is awful.

You can make a pleasant morning of shopping in Parnell.

In Parnell is Antoine's, one of the best Auckland licensed restaurants. It is expensive by New Zealand standards but the food is good. A fairly extensive wine list.

Other Parnell restaurants worth a visit are La Trattoria, which is licensed (mainly Italian food) and Hobson House (open only at night) where you take your own wine.

At all three it is wise to reserve.

For the more adventurous the Ponsonby Road area houses several good restaurants. Among them Ponsonby's Council and Fire House (housed in an old fire station) and Raffles (St Mary's Bay Road) are licensed.

Oblio's and The Deerstalker (both in Ponsonby) are unlicensed but, because of quality, among the most popular restaurants in town. Take your own wine.

The Deerstalker specialises in venison and other game. Especially good are the mussels which grow on the oyster beds in the Bay of Islands.

Ponsonby is about a $2 cab ride from the centre of town. For daytime shopping (if you're interested in junk) several junk-cum-antique stores are scattered along a dozen blocks.

The best downtown restaurant is Clichys which is licensed. A fun place with French provencal-type cooking.

If full there is a good wine bar and food service upstairs. Good quiche, cheese and pate and wine. No reservations and it is popular.

The best fish restaurant is Pelorus Jack run by a former Air New Zealand chief steward. It is in Rutland Street, 100 yards from central Queen Street. The fish of the day is always fresh. Extra good are the mussels and the smoked eel. The restaurant is licensed but doesn't mind if you have a special bottle of wine you want to bring with you.

For good steaks Tony's downtown (licensed) is recommended. We found there the best prepared steaks in Auckland. No reservations but be prepared to wait.

If you care to cross to Devonport, on the North Shore (ferry or car) The Flagstaff is one of the best unlicensed restaurants in town. Take your own wine and reserve.

Food shopping in downtown Auckland is comparatively limited but in the suburban areas are the same modern shopping complexes with the same modern supermarkets you find everywhere in the world today. So if your timid little heart has fears that this frontier country won't have "Baggies" or aluminum foil or frozen dinners, rest easily. They have it all.

Good shopping, particularly if you are interested in handicrafts, can be found in several "street markets" run by the owner-operator-craftsmen.

Open on Fridays and Saturdays are the Cook Street Market, near the Town Hall, the Downtown Market, 104 Fanshaw Street, and the Mill in Durham Lane.

The Kiwi Bangtails

Horse racing is a year-round spectator sport in New Zealand. One of the known visitor attractions in Auckland is Ellerslie Racecourse which is within minutes of downtown and just off Highway 1, the southbound motorway.

The first attraction at Ellerslie is the thirty acres of formal gardens. The second attraction is the number of magnificent New Zealand horses running on the flat or steeplechasing ... both running clockwise. The third attraction is the number of characters you can savour in the Members' Stand, all out of Central Casting. You can't get in without a guest card.

The setting is first rate and local guidebooks tout it as "the finest in the Southern Hemisphere" or "one of the world's most attractive". Okay. As a collector of race tracks I would give it a first-class rating for floral decoration and ambiance, particularly at the Spring Meeting when all of the colorful spring flowers are in bloom.

The track itself is slightly bowlish, being lifted at both ends. At the end of the backstretch the steeplechase course rises to the height of the grandstand and it makes a splendid sight when the horses reach the top and come thundering down like a charging brigade reaching for the last turn home.

In some races there are so many horses entered that the race is divided into two divisions.

There are $1, $2, and $10 windows. You bet to win or place. There are also combination bets – doubles, trebles, quinellas, jackpots – but difficult to translate without a guide.

The first meeting at Ellerslie was held in 1857 and I think some of the first horse bettors (punters) are still there, which is the reason that you must make every effort to get a guest ticket to the Members' Stand.

Here is where tradition holds court. The men are in coats and ties, some even wear hats.

The women are mostly in tweeds in winter and soft silks in summer, adorned with Queen Mary hats, fur in winter, silk in summer. They are tailored. And they twinkle all over the place. It is anything but stodgy.

At Santa Anita in California you can't tell the difference between the stable jock and the owner's wife, denim on denim, uniform on uniform, unisex on unisex, boredom on boredom. The Members' Stand at Ellerslie provides a tidy relief.

Oh, yes, at Ellerslie we could get a roast beef sandwich for 33c, a tot of whisky for 42c and a glass of beer for 55c which is a handy economy, especially after losing seven races in a row.

Note: You are never far from the horses in New Zealand. Between year-round racing and trotting there are about thirty meets in the winter month of June and about sixty meets in the summer month of January. There is no racing on Sunday.

We picked up a complimentary schedule of all meets at all New Zealand tracks published by the *Auckland Star* from a bottle store counter.

You can also lose your money on ponies without having to go to the track. In every city and town there is an office marked *"TAB"* (Totalisator Agency Board) which is a legal off-track betting shop. You can place your wager on any race going on in the country.

A Small Sip-Trip in the Country

Part of the Auckland experience is to organize a "wine crawl".

Surprisingly there are over fifty wineries in the Auckland district ranging from the small family vineyard of five acres to Corbans, one of the country's top four producers.

Each vineyard has a retail salesroom where you are invited to sample products of the vineyards. They pour a generous sample.

If you try a dry red, a dry white, a sherry, and a port at each vineyard for example, and visit, as we did, eight in one morning, it leaves you in a winey fog by lunch time.

The *N.Z. Herald* in the past has published a poster called *"Wine Trails"* showing the location of the vineyards in Henderson Valley, about fifteen minutes to the west of downtown Auckland and the Kumeu district to the north of Henderson Valley.

Drives in the wine country alone are worth the trip. The country is rolling, sunny, and the vineyards in leaf have singular beauty of their own.

Part of the fun of the "wine crawl" is to find those vineyards whose output is too small to reach the retail market but whose product is outstanding. The price is always reasonable. An example is the Sutton Baron Vineyard on Lincoln Road where the Collard brothers make a dry white wine "private bin" which was selling for $2.40 a bottle. It is pale white in color and clean, dry in taste. An ideal luncheon wine. You can't buy it in the market. We bought a case.

The New Zealanders are becoming more and more proud of their wines with good reason. Generally we found the reds to be uneven and underaged . . . unless you go to the home of a wine writer like Michael Brett who opens bottle after bottle of gorgeous red wine for dinner. In the retail store it is more difficult.

The level of dry white wines is more consistent, we found, and of more enjoyable quality.

To the west of Henderson Valley is the Waitakere Range of mountains and part of the scenic drive which also leads to the west coast beaches. One of our photographer friends says that this is the one spot she always takes guests because "it is truly New Zealand".

In our last visit to Auckland we stayed in the Waitakere Park Lodge, a small tree-top motel overlooking the lights of Auckland. With a swimming pool and a sauna and a squash court, the Lodge is a bit of Mediterranean luxury on top of a mountain, an ideal place for honeymooners and for people looking for a retreat. However, it is a forty-five-minute drive from the city and if you are doing any nightlife, the mountain drive home is punishing.

A Yacht Trip and the Largest Yacht Racing Day in the World

The Hauraki Gulf is a formidable name for what is in reality a frontdoor playpool for Aucklanders, sprinkled with islands near and far to suit the taste of the sailor.

You can realize why in New Zealand golf is a winter game. In summer everybody is out on the water.

Friends of friends asked us to join them on their 43-foot sloop one Sunday morning for an all-day outing and we tasted the marine life of Auckland. It is a hard life to beat.

That Sunday morning at dockside was somewhat overcast and the weather had been so "patchy" that no one was sure if the day was going to stay glued together or not. The fact that it just got better and better and better made it that much more enjoyable.

Our boat was a classic sloop with a long overhanging fantail of a pre-war vintage but stepped out with an aluminum mast and boom. A beautiful boat.

Our hosts were Ray Thorpe, an architect, and his wife, Betty, an attorney.

The popularity of boating in Auckland is reflected in the fact that in one year a new yacht of over 25-feet was launched for every day in the year . . . 365 boats! Until the Harbour Board stopped the practice, a slipway at the Westhaven Marina was adding $10,000 to the price of a boat.

Our day was ideal. We sailed out past the harbor entrance but in protected waters without any wave action but a steady breeze. To the north was Rangitoto Island, a perfect cone, the last of the extinct volcanoes in the Auckland area to have been active. Ahead was Browns Island and as we tacked around the island the lead boat of the Dunhill Racing Series came boiling through the waters with her spinnaker set and surrounded by admiring launches bringing the victor home. The winning boat was the international racer *Kialoa,* out of Wilmington, Delaware, which we had seen in Honolulu following the Transpac Race.

We proceeded on to Motuihe Island where we anchored and swam and drank before lunch. Lunch on board was cold cuts and salad and cheese and white wine. Included in the cold meats was a "Scotch Egg" . . . a hardboiled egg packed in sausage meat and deep fried. Delicious.

Motuihe Island is a perfect one-day destination. There were something over seventy boats on the beach and in the harbor but it wasn't crowded. There were many skiffs and launches and water skiing was popular.

After lunch we were rowed over to the island and took a leisurely stroll along the beaches and through the trees.

There are many such islands in the Gulf which can be reached by private boats or public launches or even by amphibian aircraft. The Gulf has to be one of the outstanding attractions of Auckland and a visitor in the summer should share in its pleasures one way or another.

The wind picked up a few knots but the sea was still calm and we sailed back to the yacht club in one straight reach without tacking. Perfect.

The only misadventure was cracking my head on an overhead hatch spilling blood in the cabin of a guest boat . . . bad form . . . and requiring stitches. This again, proved educational. First the kindly surgeon didn't charge anything for his services because I was covered by the national policy of free medical attention for accident and emergency treatment and, secondly, the surgeon was a mine of information about fishing at Taupo.

One of the advantages of sailing on the Waitemata Harbor was to experience the waters which the following day would be churned by the feverish activities of the "world's largest regatta".

For 136 years Auckland has celebrated its "Anniversary Day" with a regatta, a tradition started by the Royal Navy in 1841. The popularity of the event combined with the popularity of sailing in New Zealand eventually grew to include more than 1,000 boats ranging from dingies to million-dollar racing machines. Forty-three classes now race on Anniversary Day.

Fortunately we didn't have a boat on regatta day because the wind came up a stiff northerly puffing to forty knots. Conditions for the small yachtsman couldn't have proved worse.

The weather kept the entries down to around 700 boats. Still the harbor was alive with sails as races began at 11 o'clock in the morning from six starting and finishing points ... a different event from those earliest days when visiting ships in the harbor would put over longboats to race Maori war canoes for a keg of beer.

The shores of the harbor were lined with cars. To watch the races, there are many excellent vantage points. We went to North Head, a former military base with gun emplacements guarding the harbor, where we could see from the Harbor Bridge to the islands in the Gulf.

From the beginning it was obvious that the little centerboard boats were going to have a busy day ... and so were the rescue craft.

More than thirty yacht club patrol boats and an Air Force helicopter were in constant action. Seventy-seven boats were in difficulty during the day, including six at one time.

The spectators consisting of picnicers, lovers, children, dogs, grandmothers, were kept alive pointing out on the water and saying "Look at that one! Look at *that* one!" It was a day for a spectacle and it certainly proved to be one.

If you are going to be in New Zealand the last Monday of January, mark it a day for Auckland's Anniversary Day.

Anybody for Golf?
There are three public golf courses in Auckland and twenty-nine private courses.

The most popular public course is Chamberlain Park Golf Course near the center of the city, and it can be reached by bus or taxi. What you spend on transportation you will save on greens fees: $1.70

weekdays, $2.40 weekends. You can have a hot lunch at the clubhouse and you can also rent clubs. It is open every day of the year.

Another public course, also on a bus route, is the Takapuna Municipal Golf Links across the Harbor Bridge. Green fees are $2 week days, $2.50 at weekends. The course is next door to the Poenamo Motor Inn, which is useful if you're hungry or thirsty after your game.

We played Titirangi which was one of the more expensive courses in New Zealand. Greens fees: $5 for men, $4 for women. 50c a trundler. Titirangi is a nice, interesting course. The clay-based fairways tend to crack in the summer but the greens are true and fast. Many bunkers which you don't see at country courses.

We were joined by a delightful doctor who helped keep us out of trouble. (If a boy comes out of the bushes and tries to sell you a ball, he is to be instructed to take the ball to the club pro. If a member buys a ball from a retriever, he is subject to instant dismissal!). "You have to understand. If we didn't have such a rule, the urchins would be all over the place pinching the members' balls," the good doctor explained.

The Auckland Golf Club is known as Middlemore because that is the club's location . . . not too far from the international airport. It is Auckland's most prestigious club, which is proven by the antiquity of its clubhouse. Ties and jackets are necessary in the upstairs lounge. Visitors are welcome only if introduced by a member.

The course is fairly flat, heavily bunkered around the greens and when the rough is allowed to grow, narrowing the fairways, a tough test off the championship tees.

The club staged the 1971 British Commonwealth Amateur Tournament (the only time the event was held in New Zealand) and has held the New Zealand Open Championship several times.

The three New Zealand members of the foursome were good golfers, instant and repeated betting men and merciless in their comments on their opponents' talents. They were most enjoyable.

After golf and a shower, we retired to the men's lounge upstairs where we helped ourself from a huge refrigerator full of beer. For harder spirits there was a buffet table covered with bottles and mixes. Take the bottle of your choice to the table along with the mixes and pour your own drinks and fill in an accounting chit as you drink. Neat.

In New Zealand where there is no serious unemployment to speak of and a dearth of help, you find do-it-yourself service stations, do-it-yourself cafeterias, etc. The Auckland Golf Club was the first do-it-yourself bar we found.

If Auckland is your introduction to New Zealand it should also be your introduction to *pavlova,* the national dessert. It is a fluffy meringue covered with fruit, covered with whipped cream, and covered again with fruit. Properly made, it is feather-light and like a good rum punch is much more lethal than it tastes.

Angela Brett's Perfect Pavlova
4 egg whites
8 tablespoons castor sugar
1 teaspoon cornflour (cornstarch)
1 teaspoon vinegar

Beat whites until *very* stiff and gradually add sugar, one table-spoon at a time, still beating. Mix cornflour and vinegar together and fold into mixture. Make a round of the mixture (about 10" diameter) on dampened greaseproof paper on oven tray. Preheat oven to 300F, put pavlova in oven and turn heat down to 250F. Leave in oven about 3/4 hour.

The pavlova should be slightly crisp on the outside and soft as marshmallow on the inside. Cover the pavlova with whipped cream and sliced fruit – strawberries, kiwi fruit (more generally known as "Chinese Gooseberries), passionfruit etc.

Warning
"Does she or doesn't she?" is a question in New Zealand which doesn't pertain to the color of a woman's hair or to her bedroom behavior. Rather it is a question to whether a woman can turn out a successful pavlova or not because a pavlova is that peculiar kind of dish which demands a touch of delicate talent.

The Lady Navigator, who is a lady of natural ability in the kitchen, tried all of the recipes in the book. She tried the pavlova. Several times.

"Does the Lady Navigator or doesn't she?"

She doesn't.

While on the subject of eating, we will repeat the New Zealand daily eating cycle. Breakfast. Morning tea. Lunch. Afternoon tea. Dinner. Supper.

Morning tea, afternoon tea and supper consist of coffee or tea and cookies (biscuits in New Zealand), thin sandwiches and cakes. Sunday-night tea takes the place of dinner and is made up of whatever is around the house.

The cakes, which are part of the teas, are scrumptious. Here is one of the best we found:

Rita Bookman's Apple Cake

4 oz butter	2 tsp baking powder
1 cup sugar	2 cups flour
2 tsp cinnamon	2 eggs
2 tsp spice	2-2½ lbs stewed apples (drained)

Cream butter and sugar, add eggs and dry ingredients. Roll out in two pieces and put into 9" cake pan with layer of stewed apples in between. Bake 1 hour at 350 degrees.

A visitor to New Zealand is perplexed in a supermarket . . . or even a corner grocery store market . . . to see the disproportionate amount of space given to the cookie (biscuit) section. We didn't understand it until early in our visit, we were introduced to Chocolate Wheatens, a smooth combination of wheat cookie and dark chocolate.

It was like an alcoholic getting the first drink.

Soon we were into Cameo Creams followed by an intense but short devotion to Tartan Shortbread. Then it was a dizzying succession of Gingernuts and Chocolate Creams and Fruit Puffs. We levelled off for a while on Peanut Brownies and Hokey Pokey and Orange Wafers until the fatal day we discovered Toffee Pops. For the rest of our stay, we remained loyal to this rich candy-bar-cum-cookie with occasional exploratory forays into sugary pastures.

Like all New Zealanders we picked up the habit of passing the cookie (biscuit) section very slowly, muttering slowly to ourselves, with much dipping in and putting back and changing of mind, wishing the section were twice as large.

3. Northland: Cradle of the Nation

The Birth of a Nation ... The Flagpole War ... Zane Grey Waters ... 90 Mile Beach ... A Pet Dolphin ... A 2,000-Year-Old Tree

The country north of Auckland is known as *Northland*. It is not heavily promoted in tour packages, yet it is the birthplace of the nation, an international mecca for deep-sea fishermen, and a major tourist destination for holidaying New Zealanders.

It is country with an intriguing past and it is delightful scenically. To miss Northland is to miss New Zealand. It has no counterpart.

Driving out of Auckland on a spring day full of sunshine is to find the country at its best. The fields are deep green, like a lush fairway on a golf course and you feel you could play the whole trip from Auckland to Cape Reinga with a nine iron and a putter.

White sheep, like golfballs, dot the countryside, beef cattle and milk cows are interspersed. The views are peaceful, pastoral; in a frantic, crowded world, these soul-satisfying scenes of New Zealand will be often repeated. You never grow tired of them.

In the spring your first look at New Zealand will be further enraptured by a countryside full of Easter lilies growing wild by the stream beds. Thousands upon thousands of them.

"Good heavens," you say. "I can't stand it."

"Right," says your New Zealand guide. "Time for morning tea."

Onward, Northward

Travelling north from Auckland takes you through "Hibiscus Country" through beachside resorts, through the country towns of Warkworth and Wellsford, to the capital of Northland, Whangarei, with a population of about 35,000. Whangarei is a deep-water port. By New Zealand standards it is industrialized. It has a refinery, a glassworks, a cement plant.

To the tourist the three-star attraction in Whangarei is the Clapham Clock Collection with over 400 clocks of every size, shape, and description, the oldest dating back to 1636.

To the sportsman the three-star attraction is Tutukaka, a beautiful little harbor eighteen miles to the north which serves as a major deep-sea fishing base. Charter boats are available. There are also sight-seeing boats and other marine activities.

The turn off to the Bay of Islands is Kawakawa, population 1500, whose claim to fame is that the railroad line runs down the middle of the main street.

It is worth a picture. And if you are lucky enough to pass by on a Sunday when the Kawakawa Bowling Club is in action, you can capture the spirit of the country in one lucky photograph. White uniforms on a bowling green. Peaceful. Pretty. Quietly sporting. That's New Zealand.

We quartered at the Bay of Islands Motel, just south of Paihia. Separate cabins. New. Bedroom. Bath. Kitchen. Living room. $18 a night, double.

The Bay of Islands
In this magnificent harbor is where it all began.

Kupe, the original explorer, came into the Bay in AD 950; 200 years later he was followed by another Polynesian, Toi.

In 1769 Captain Cook discovered the harbor for the Europeans and gave it the name, *Bay of Islands.*

For good reason. One guidebook says there are eighty-six small islands. Another guidebook says that there are over 150 islands. We won't count. There are a lot of islands. The largest is only 555 acres. The Maori Reserves own many. Many are privately owned. (In Kerikeri we saw a fifteen-acre island advertised for sale with a two-bedroom house on it, electricity, telephone. *Rowing distance to the mainland* was a feature. The price: $75,000.)

The population around the Bay is small. The four population centers total only 3,000 residents.

But be cautious. In the summer-Christmas-school-holiday peak season lasting from Christmas Day to the end of January, over 40,000 New Zealanders come to the Bay of Islands on holiday! They come with 3,000 camper-caravan-house trailers and towing 1,000 boats. Plus the yachts that come in from the sea. What a sight to behold.

Besides the schools, many factories and shops close during the national vacation period. *Don't go anywhere in New Zealand during this period without a reservation.*

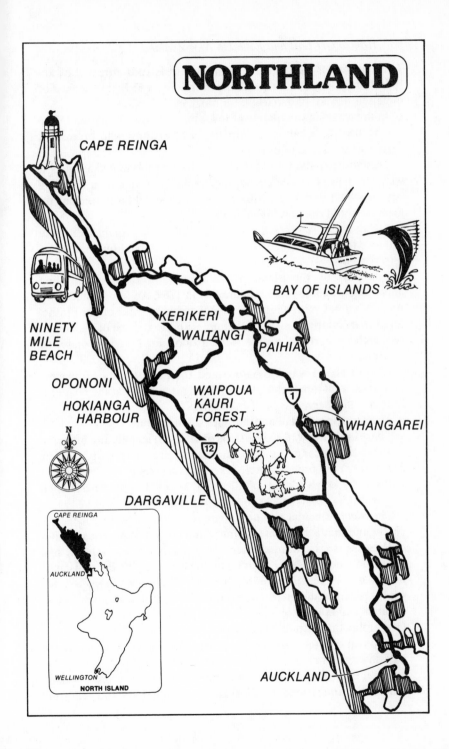

NORTHLAND

CAPE REINGA

BAY OF ISLANDS

KERIKERI

WAITANGI

PAIHIA

NINETY
MILE
BEACH

OPONONI

HOKIANGA
HARBOUR

WAIPOUA
KAURI
FOREST

1

12

WHANGAREI

N

DARGAVILLE

CAPE REINGA

AUCKLAND

WELLINGTON

NORTH ISLAND

AUCKLAND

The majority of visitors come to the Bay of Islands attracted by the sparkling blue sea water twinkling in the sun, and Paihia, a mass of motels, is a point of departure for much of the action.

At the wharf in the middle of town there is an Information Office and is also the location of four travel companies who promote a variety of marine action.

The most popular tour of the Bay of Islands and touted as the best water tour in New Zealand is the *Cream Launch Trip,* a day-long voyage which retraces a former servicing of island farms, picking up farm milk and distributing mail and supplies.

Today's tourist takes the pleasant sixty-mile trip in calm safe waters with the added comfort of having available liquid and solid refreshments.

You pass by the island where Captain Cook made his first anchorage when he came into the Bay in 1769. And this island, with Assassination Cove, where the French explorer, Marion du Fresne, three years later was murdered along with twenty-five of his sailors. A searching party of twelve went to look for him and only one returned.

A third island was the base island for Zane Grey's fishing expeditions. You lunch and swim in the right weather at the beautiful little bay that served as his fishing camp.

The servicing of mail and supplies still continues.

There are other water excursions of different lengths and interests. The fares are comparatively modest, as are most costs in New Zealand. (You order a pre-packed picnic lunch for the Cream Cruise. The lunch consists of filled roll, assorted sandwiches, boiled egg, fruit, cake and a package of raisins. The cost is about $2.)

The other principal marine activity is, of course, famous in fishing circles and that is big game fishing. Zane Grey, the American writer of Western stories, was an ardent deep-sea fisherman. After he had fallen in love with New Zealand and the fishing at the Bay of Islands he wrote in 1926, *"Tales of the Angler's El Dorado, New Zealand"* which added to the international popularity of the deep-sea fishing grounds which were only ten minutes away from his base camp at Otehei Bay on Urupukapuka Island.

You can charter boats at Paihia and Russell for a whole day or half day or share a boat and cost with others.

Big game fishing is from December to May with record-breaking blue, black and striped marlin available. Tuna, shark and yellowtail also attract the anglers. The yellowtail continue to run through September.

It is a great temptation.

I have never gone deep-sea fishing in my life. I can get seasick looking at a marine map. My friends call me Admiral Upchuck for good reason.

But here you are in this world-famous fishing ground and you can't buy a postcard and pass it by.

It was October. Absolutely the wrong time of year. But we chartered a nifty little jet-powered boat with driver-guide after a long discussion about being able to fish in calm waters and we could go just where we wanted and for how long we wanted, etc.

The next morning, early, after taking an anti-motion pill, we were in a powerboat and moving away from the dock.

"Where are we going?" I asked tremulously, hoping that we were going to have a long, thoughtful discussion about fishing in waters where the waves never reach more than six inches.

"WE ARE GOING WHERE WE CAN CATCH FISH," roared the skipper and, *whooosh,* the jet-powered boat took off and aimed at the mouth of the Bay.

In a matter of minutes we were in blue water, deep water, tall-moving water.

"What are we going to fish for?"

"We are going to bottom-fish for red snapper," said the skipper.

In the waters famous for blue marlin, mako shark and giant tuna, we are going to bottom-fish for red snapper? Would this be better than a postcard?

It was. Within fifteen minutes we had our first red snapper. Pretty fish. Two pounds. No giant but mine – all mine.

And we fished and moved and followed the birds and bobbed in the waves. And didn't get ill. That was the best part.

The fishing even for red snapper wasn't too good and the skipper asked, "Would you like to tour the islands?" Affirmative.

We wooshed off again and in thirty minutes practically did the whole Cream Cruise. Lovely, isolated beaches. A few vacation houses on private islands. Six-inch waves.

We stopped and fished again with better luck. An even better experience was watching a squadron of gannets diving for their lunch.

The gannet is a graceful, handsomely marked bird with a yellow head, a white body and wings aerodynamically marked in black. He heads for the water like a divebomber, from high up, and hits the water with such force that it sends a fountain of spray several feet in the air. To see a whole covey feeding is a dramatic air show.

At noon we returned to the dock. The skipper cleaned the fish, took our picture and sent us off happily. The cost was about $50 for the morning. A good investment.

We had red snapper and white wine and green salad for lunch. Admiral Upchuck, mighty sailor, famous deep-sea fisherman, slept all afternoon.

At the Bay of Islands you can do what you want on the water for as much or as little as you want to spend. You can rent a dingy with oars for $2 an hour and a jet boat for $15 an hour. Bait, rod, handlines are available for about $2.

A four-hour fishing trip in a group costs $7.

Or you can charter a big game fishing boat for $168 for the day.

The Bay of Islands is a fine place to play.

Adjacent to Paihia is the Waitangi Hotel, the famous Treaty House and the Waitangi Golf Course.

The golf course offers good golf, some of it spectacular. It is a 72-par, 18-hole course, 6,144 yards long. The front nine is par 37 and offers the best golf. The back nine, par 35, offers the better scenic golf with most of the holes overlooking the Bay.

Cost is modest: $2.50 in an envelope at the little unmanned golf shack. (They have since built a new club house.) Or you can pay the pro at his office at the Waitangi Hotel where you have to go to rent a *trundler,* a hand-pulled cart, for $1.

Even though we had a few rain squalls, we had a most enjoyable morning of golf. Birds were singing everywhere.

Lamb chops for lunch. Four for a dollar. Huge, fresh eggs, 95c a dozen.

Lady Navigator: "Here, let me hold the eggs while you get the keys to the car."

Driver: "Oh, I can get the keys to the car without any help. You think I'm stupid?"

Dropped the eggs on my left foot.

Fried lamb chops *and* scrambled eggs for lunch.

For tennis at Paihia there is the Paihia Tennis Club consisting of two asphalt courts, not in great condition. Visitors pay $1.00 per court for forty-five minutes of play. There is an honor box in the wall of the minute club house where you drop your money.

At Waitangi Bridge there is a floating museum, the *Tui,* the Museum of Shipwrecks. The owner and operator is a professional diver who is making a career of exploring the shipwrecks of New Zealand Northland. Many relics and treasures are on display.

Cradle of the Nation

Although Paihia is a touristy town today, it was an important community for the European in 1823 when the Rev. Henry Williams established a mission station on the town's present location.

The first ship built in New Zealand, the *Herald,* a mission ship, was built in Paihia.

In 1834 William Colenso, a pioneer-printer, arrived from England and set up the first press. A year later he printed the first Scriptures in Maori. Press run: twenty-five copies.

Little of interest of the missionary-pioneering days remains to be seen in Paihia except the tree-shaded graveyard of the Paihia Church which contains a memorial erected to Henry Williams by the Maoris. "He came to us in 1823. He was taken from us in 1867."

Across from Paihia on a one-way bridge is the most symbolic building in New Zealand. The Treaty House of Waitangi.

In 1832 chaos was developing in New Zealand by the British taking advantage of the Maoris in land dealings and, in turn, the Maoris harrassing the would-be peaceful settlers. The British response was to send James Busby (1801–1871) to the Bay of Islands as *British Resident.* He was without arms or men. He was to represent the flag and that was *all* he had.

He did however have to have a residence and at Waitangi he built his house overlooking the Bay. It was a prestigious residence of the gracious Georgian lines favored by both Australians and Americans of the same period. Originally three front rooms were built and some store rooms. The wings were added later. Local and Australian materials were used in the building. Iron nails were hand wrought. The roof was shingle. The frame and the floor were of imported Australian *jarrah* wood and the paving was dressed Sydney sandstone.

Busby's flag and Busby's residence were not enough to establish order and in 1839 Britain responded to pleas for action by sending a naval man, Captain William Hobson (1793–1842), to New Zealand to establish British sovereignty with the consent of the Maoris.

Assisted by Busby he drafted a circular letter printed by Colenso in Paihia calling for an assembly of the Maori people and the settlers and on February 5, 1840, the front lawn of the residence was crowded with 2,000 Maoris who had responded to the letter.

Assisted again by Busby, Captain Hobson explained the proposed treaty: that the Maoris couldn't be deprived from their land or fisheries without their consent, and even the Crown couldn't divest the Maoris of land without a mutual agreement. In addition the Maoris were promised the protection of the British under British sovereignty.

Speeches by the attending chiefs for and against the proposal followed. An influential chief, Tamati Waka (the Maori form for Thomas Walker) Nene, who became known as the "Peace Chief", spoke eloquently in favor of the Treaty and the following day, forty-five chiefs signed the Treaty of Waitangi. Later the Treaty was signed by 120 leading chiefs of the northern tribes and approximately 230 chiefs of the southern tribes. The British Colony of New Zealand was proclaimed on February 8, 1840 and was celebrated with the hoisting of flags and the firing of guns.

Hobson, who was later to be Governor, prematurely appointed himself Lieutenant-Governor and established the capital across the Bay at the old site of Russell where it was to remain but nine months.

Today the Treaty House of Waitangi serene in its setting of spacious lawns and tall growing trees is a museum. Nearby the Treaty House is a Maori meeting house, a *whare runanga,* built in 1940 for the 100th anniversary of the signing. A little background reading on Maori art, particularly as it relates to the *whare,* will make the intriguing art form more enjoyable.

In every Maori community there is a *whare* which is used as a meeting house. The carvings in the house record the history of the tribe and serve as a symbol of the tribe's pride and strength. The Waitangi *whare* is unusual in that it represents all of New Zealand with each tribe's notable ancestors carved in that particular tribe's style.

A launch from Paihia takes you to Russell across the Bay in ten minutes.

Peaceful Russell (then called Kororareka) is a far cry today from its early history when twenty hotel-grog shops operated along the waterfront and it was known as "the hell-hole of the Pacific". The Duke of Marlborough Hotel on the Strand postdates those days but the hotel is said to have the oldest liquor license in operation in the country. A good place to stop in and have a beer.

Two buildings are of special interest in Russell.

Christ Church was built in 1836 by settlers after a two-year fund drive which included a contribution by British naturalist Charles Darwin. Being the only hall of its kind in town, the church not only served as a place of worship but also as a meeting hall and a courthouse. During the Flagpole War and the sack of the town, the building came under fire, and cannon and bullet remains can still be seen in the building, which was spared by the victorious Maori warriors.

In 1871 the building was renovated. The roof was raised and the original high, boxed pews were taken apart and used for panelling. The churchyard holds the graves of Nene, the Peace Chief, and members of the Clendon family, Clendon being the first honorary United States Consul in New Zealand.

The second building and a popular postcard subject because it is so picturesque is the two-story Pompallier House. Jean Baptiste François Pompallier (1801–1871) was the first Catholic Bishop to come to New Zealand and the present Pompallier House was not his residence but was originally a simple structure made of mud-packed walls and used as a printery. A classic *Gaveaux* printing press is still part of the exhibits on display in the house along with other memorabilia of the period.

The garden is enchanting filled with rambling flowers framing the building with color. In back of the house is an observation hill where you can look out over the calm harbor where in the 1850s as many as twenty whaling, sealing, trading ships would be anchored.

During the Christmas holiday period Russell explodes with boats being a favorite destination of yachtsmen from Auckland.

The museum in Russell, the Centennial Russell Museum, is good fun.

It is filled with all sorts of odds and ends including an antique apple corer, much gum from the kauri tree, including a sample of beautiful kauri silk. We were to see kauri in every museum from one tip of New Zealand to the other tip, but this was the only example we were to see of kauri silk.

Also it was the first time we were to see a stuffed kiwi bird, the national bird, also a standard museum item with its gigantic egg beside it, one quarter the size of the bird.

Museum director: "The kiwi bird only lays its egg once a year."

Woman bystander, with feeling: "Oh, I'd hope so!"

The most important part of the Russell Museum is the quarter-sized reproduction of the *Endeavour* which was built to commemorate the 200th anniversary of Captain Cook's arrival in 1769. The large model is a sailing vessel and was taken throughout New Zealand and Australia during the anniversary year and then brought to Russell where a special appendage was added to the one-room museum to accommodate it. Although the model is supposed to be seen from a distance on the water, it is just as satisfactory to inspect it close at hand.

A favorite observation point is Flagpole Hill, the focal point for the famous Flagpole War.

The Flagpole War

Hone Heke was a warrior chief who was the first to sign the Treaty of Waitangi. He was also the first to break it four years after the signing. More than any other Maori chief Hone Heke captures the imagination.

He was a chief of the Ngapuhi tribe and a nephew of the powerful chief, Hongi Hika. Besides being clever and attractive, he possessed great mana which, to the Maori, was not just an air of prestige but a psychic force.

In his youth Hone Heke was a pupil of the Church of England and schooled with the missionaries at Paihia. It was a factor which probably saved the church buildings in Russell.

At Russell Heke had his own Customs duty of charging $5 a ship but then the capital was moved to Auckland and to discourage ships from utilizing Russell the British imposed their own Customs. The port business declined and so did Heke's income.

The situation became explosive.

Then an unlikely incident started a chain reaction which led to war. A former Heke slavegirl, the common-law wife of a white-man store owner, referred in public to Heke as a "pig's head". The remark was passed on to Heke, who considered it a reflection on his mana which would not be the same until the insult was revenged.

He raided the white man's store, carried off the woman and in a final sign of rage chopped down the hilltop flagpole above Russell used to signal ships. To emphasize his revolutionary act, Heke went to Paihia and danced a war dance before the surprised missionary bishop.

The British responded by bringing up the frigate *HMS Hazard*, along with 170 officers and men and two six-pounder cannon. A conference was called and Nene, the peacemaker of the Treaty signing, promised that the Europeans would be protected and Heke would be kept in order. The fumbling Governor FitzRoy, who had replaced Hobson, promised in turn to abolish the unpopular Customs duty.

There is a suggestion in history that at this time Heke called upon the United States Consul, who told Heke about America's revolutionary success against these same British. Thus encouraged, he cut the flagpole down again, put an American ensign on the stern of his canoe and paraded across the Bay singing war songs.

A third flagpole was erected and guarded by friendly Maoris but so great was Heke's mana that he personally marched through the guards and cut down the flagpole the night after it was erected.

The situation grew more tense. More military assistance was called for from New South Wales and two companies totalling 207 men were sent.

A fourth tree was prepared as a flagpole but an old chief claimed he had been born under the tree and one night he and his men stole the pole.

The British, probably weary by now of the whole exercise, bought a mizzen mast from a foreign vessel in the harbor and it was erected with a blockhouse around it manned by British soldiers.

Such a challenge couldn't go unmet.

Successfully using a diversionary tactic, Heke cut off the soldiers from their blockhouse and cut down the flagpole for the fourth time.

Meanwhile his colleague chief, Kawiti was carrying out an offensive against the town. British women and children were put aboard ships for safety. Then a workman's pipe accidentally ignited the military powder magazine and blew it up. Without ammunition the military cause was hopeless and they too abandoned the town. The Maoris moved in and looted it and set fire to all the buildings except the church buildings.

However the Catholic Bishop Pompallier's house was partially looted. Heke was furious and was set to execute the thieves. Pompallier, hearing this, went to Heke's camp three miles away and asked that the thieves be spared and only that his goods be returned. Heke agreed to the request and showed his respect by providing the bishop with an escort of thirty warriors to his house.

With the British it was war.

Governor FitzRoy declared an award for Heke's capture. Heke, not to be outdone, declared an award for FitzRoy's capture.

The Maori warriors had a sense of gamesmanship that was hard to match. One story of the Flagpole War is that Heke refused to intercept a British food line because he feared the British would be unable to fight without their beef.

The first battle was joined at Okaihau when the British made a badly planned frontal attack on the Maori fortress or pa. The British suffered fourteen killed and forty-four wounded. It was a major defeat for a relatively small force without medical aid to speak of. What could they do with forty-four wounded? Heke was wounded in the thigh.

The Maoris correctly assumed that the British would bring up guns so they retreated to a stronger pa at Ohaeawai. This time the British brought up 500 soldiers plus eighteen sailors, two six-pounders, two 12-pounders and one 32-pounder.

And again the British made a frontal assault. The result was forty British killed and seventy wounded. A catastrophe. The triumphant Maoris ceremoniously cannibalized one of the officers. It was the only such incident of the war.

Even before England knew of such results the time for FitzRoy had run out. He was sacked. In his place as Governor came George Grey, a military officer who, at the age of twenty-eight, had been appointed Governor of South Australia. He was to prove to be a tough foe but a good friend of the Maori people.

The final battle took place ten miles south of Kawakawa. On a hilltop Kawiti, the same chief who had raided Russell, had a strong pa called Ruapekapeka, or "the Bat's Nest". When you visit the Treaty House at Waitangi you will see a model of this fortress. It is a most sophisticated structure with double outer walls of tall timbers, angled so that if the walls were breached, the enemy faced angled lines of fire. There was also a moat. Inside there were bombardment-proof shelters and even an internal water supply.

A tough fort to crack.

The British brought up 1,100 soldiers plus another 400 friendly Maori warriors. The fort's force numbered 500. The British arrived on New Year's Eve 1845. In ten days they put up earthworks and aligned their mortars and cannons. On a Saturday they opened fire. Successfully they were able to partially breach one wall. Governor Grey was in personal command and was urged to charge. Knowing the bitter experience of such past actions he continued with firepower. That night he offered an armistice. It was turned down.

Heke urged his colleagues to abandon the fort for the safety of the forest, where the British cannon would be useless.

Kawiti refused to move.

The next day was Sunday. The Maoris inside the fort were Christian and assumed that a Sunday should be a universal day of rest and prayer, so they retreated outside of their pa for services. The Maoris with the British heard hymns, guessed correctly what was happening and conveyed the information to Governor Grey. Quickly he ordered a charge. The pa was taken and the Flagpole War was over.

Although taking advantage of the Maori during prayer might be questionable from a sportsman viewpoint, Governor Grey was ordered to put an end to the war as fast as possible. This he did. More important was his gesture of pardoning Heke without condition and sending the Maori warriors back to their families without punishment.

In the future years Governor Grey and the Maoris were to share a mutual admiration for each other.

Should you decide to visit Heke's last stand Ruapekapeka Pa is only ten miles south of Kawakawa, and three miles off the highway.

A diversion en route is the Waiomio Caves, two and a half miles south of Kawakawa and a mile off the highway.

Here are interesting glowworm caves and limestone formations but in the total New Zealand scale of glowworm caves, Waiomio wouldn't rate very high. Of special interest is the fact that the caves are owned by the Kawiti family, descendants of Heke's fellow chief. Also the legend of the runaway wife who hid in the caves for ten months until found by a tribe of Maori warriors. They must have given her the worst punishment imaginable: they sent her back to her husband.

Ruapekapeka is on the northern slope of a hill that has a commanding view of the ships at Russell. You park your car underneath the trees and you are squarely in between the earthworks of the British and the 20-foot palisades of the pa. You walk up the hill inside the fence to the right of the road and you are in the remains of the massive pa which was 100 yards long and 70 yards wide.

To walk the grounds of the former fortress is like walking over any famous battleground. You tend to walk slowly and speak softly.

There is not a great deal left to see. An exploded gun used by the Maoris inside the fortress, remaining holes of cannon-proof pits, wells which supplied water.

Although the rebels lost, the battlefield statistics are the best testimony to the success of the pa. The British suffered thirteen killed and thirty wounded. The rebels had twenty killed and thirty wounded.

The First Missionary

If Hone Heke was the symbol of flags, war and rebellion in 1845, we must turn the clock back to 1807 and the Reverend Samuel Marsden, who became the first symbol of Christianity, peace and agriculture.

He became known as "the Apostle of New Zealand" and as we became familiar with his missionary work we found it difficult to reconcile his New Zealand Christianity with his reputation in Australia for persecution and brutality while he was chaplain at a convict station at New South Wales for twenty years and later as Magistrate of New South Wales.

During his time in Australia he became interested and friendly with New Zealand Maoris who served on ships trading across the Tasman Sea. Two of them were important Ngapuhi chiefs who later were responsible for his success in establishing the first missions in the Bay of Islands.

Marsden saw the potential of extending Christianity to the new land and applied for a missionary branch of the Church of England in 1807 to include New Zealand in the sphere of missionary work.

In 1808 the application was approved but a year later a terrible incident a few bays north of the Bay of Islands delayed any immediate expansion into the new country. The convict ship *Boyd* with a complement of about seventy men put into the New Zealand harbor to pick up a supply of kauri wood for spars. The party of sailors put ashore to gather the wood were massacred by the Maoris who donned their uniforms and returned to the *Boyd* in the evening, overcame the remainder of the crew, killed them and put the *Boyd* to the torch. The ship burned to the waterline and sank, her remains still resting today at the bottom of Whangaroa Harbor.

It was not until 1814 that the restrictions to expand to New Zealand were removed and on December 22, 1814 the missionary ship *Active* anchored in the north end Bay of Islands and on Christmas Day at a place called Oihi Bay, Marsden spoke from the Bible: "We bring you good tidings ..." The place is marked with the Marsden Cross which you can see from your pleasure boat when you take the Cream Cruise.

Three and a half years later Marsden returned with a second band of recruits to the Bay of Islands, went to the Kerikeri inlet and proceeded up river to a river basin just below some gentle waterfalls.

When you visit the Kemp House at Kerikeri you'll see yachts tied up in the river basin and you can imagine Marsden and his band coming up the river and anchoring for the first time. What a restful haven.

The Kemp House was completed by the missionaries in 1822. It is the oldest standing building in the country. Interestingly it was used by a number of missionaries as a residence until, ten years later, James Kemp, a carpenter and an original member of the pioneering band, moved into the house. It remained in his family for over 140 years and only lately has been taken over by the New Zealand Historic Places Trust.

The two-story building is constructed of kauri wood. Obviously it has been added on to over the years. Adjacent to the house is the Stone Store which was completed in 1835. In its time the Stone Store was to serve as living quarters, a library and an ammunition dump. Today it is a quasi-curio store and museum.

The Kemp House and the Stone Store are interesting because of their antiquity. The surroundings are superb. Flowers upon flowers in the colorful garden. A sweet flowing river a few yards away across green lawn, fruit trees in blossom, and a thumping waterfall at the front door, complete an ideal scene.

Across the waterfall is a reconstructed pre-European Maori village called a kainga. As opposed to a fortified pa the village was the place where Maoris lived and farmed in peace. In the time of trouble they retreated from the kainga to the pa.

If you visit the Rewa Kainga, you might like to stop at Keri Park on the right hand side driving back to the town of Kerikeri. Here is a post-European kainga. Also a good picnic spot alongside the river.

The first plough in New Zealand went into the ground at Kerikeri in May 1820. The word kerikeri is supposed to come from the words the Maoris used when they first saw the plough in action: "to dig, to dig". The missionaries found good digging. They didn't make many converts but the agriculture was outstanding.

Today Kerikeri is made up of miles and miles and rows and rows of citrus trees.

And it's "pricey". A modern house with over 4,000 feet under roof, five acres of garden, twenty-two acres of trees: $210,000.

Kerikeri is a likeable place. Americans are finding it. South Africans are finding it. Artists are finding it.

We pulled into an orchard and bought a twenty-pound bag of tangelos, a cross between a tangerine and an orange, wildly juicy, for $4. We had morning tangelo juice for weeks.

We visited *The Black Sheep* on, wouldn't you know, Hone Heke Road. A rundown barn with first-rate pottery, weaving from the wool of black sheep, jewellery and other crafts for sale.

We also had lunch at a place on the road from Paihia to Kerikeri, on the left hand side of the road before reaching the Kerikeri junction: *Jane's Place.* It doesn't look like much but the Englishwoman in the kitchen has been kissed by a culinary angel. Take your own wine.

Don't Miss Waimate North

In 1830 the Reverend Marsden set up the third missionary station and the first inland station, believing that the spiritual virtues of Christianity should be properly blended with the practical virtues of agriculture. The first attempts at agriculture were successful and when Charles Darwin visited the station he wrote that it had been placed there "by an enchanter's wand".

Alas, the agriculture was to fail and the missionaries after Heke's War lost their influence. British troops stationed at the mission destroyed the gardens and all but the mission house and the church.

What remains is delightful.

The Georgian-styled, two-storied building was built by George Clarke, probably out of an architectural book which is on display in the house. (He built a bridge out of the same book.) The center of the structure is a winding staircase which was a successfully ambitious beginning. On one side, downstairs, is a dining room where Grey and Heke shared breakfast after the war, an inside kitchen, unusual for the time, a master bedroom with a dressing room, also unusual for the time and place. On the other side a parlour, a guest bedroom, a den and another bedroom.

Upstairs are three bedrooms for servants, children, students or whoever needed sleeping space in that time of the house's history.

The house is made of kauri wood and it is in Waimate North that you learn to love the golden tone and texture of kauri. It was built entirely by Maori carpenters and workmen except for the hearth-stones and blown pane glass which came from England. A few panes of the original glass still remain.

Fortunately the Historic Places Trust took over the house in 1959 and has done an excellent job restoring and refinishing the house to its original design and character. If you like antiques at all, you'll whimper with envy at many of the furnishings.

The little church next door, St John the Baptist, is the third church to stand on the site.

Because the first bishop to come to New Zealand, Bishop Selwyn, established residency at Waimate North, the modest mission house automatically became a *Palace* and the little church a *Cathedral*.

At the Bay of Islands you can take tours to include all of the points of nearby interest. You can rent cars and do it yourself. Also, not to be overlooked, you can take air tours of the area. Posters at information centers will give information where you can find particulars.

Mount Cook Airlines, through A. E. Fuller & Sons at Paihia, offers three flightseeing packages. Also Mount Cook Airlines offers a day's excursion from Auckland to the Bay of Islands leaving just after eight in the morning and arriving back just after five in the afternoon. It is not what the Bay of Islands deserves but it is better than not going at all.

A Day's Trip to the North End of Northland – A Ride Back on Ninety Mile Beach

Cape Reinga is not the furthest point north of New Zealand. Kerr Point is.

Cape Reinga is not the furthest point north accessible by car. Hooper Point is. If you use a four-wheel jeep.

But Cape Reinga is where the currents of the Tasman Sea and the

Pacific Ocean meet visibly and in a collision of spray. And Cape Reinga is where the Maori spirits disappear down the roots of a twisted pohutukawa tree into the ocean-entrance to the underworld. The spirit reappears on the largest of the off-shore islands called The Three Kings where it takes a final look at the mainland and then journeys on to *Hawaiki* from whence the Maori came.

And Cape Reinga is accessible by bus and has a post office where you can mail postcards home saying, "Hey, look where I am!"

The bus tour of Cape Reinga departs from Paihia about eight in the morning and returns around seven at night, give or take an hour. ("What's time, mate?")

The trip is broken up by frequent stops. Mid-morning tea stop. Bus breakdown stop. Museum stop. Luncheon stop. Photographic stop. Cape Reinga stop. Te Paki Stream stop. Ninety Mile Beach stop. Afternoon tea stop. Mission House stop. And there might be a swim stop, any number of photographic stops, etc. according to the weather and the driver and the desires of the passengers who, being predominately New Zealanders and Australians, are a congenial, happy lot.

Don't take your car. Don't even take somebody else's car. It is a tough road, in many parts even dangerous, and for about $14 it is easier to let an experienced bus driver take over all the worries.

Much of the land on the way to Cape Reinga was once famous for kauri gum.

Once upon a time, it is said, the land from Hamilton, in approximately the middle of the North Island, to the tip of Cape Reinga was covered by giant kauri trees. After the trees died and collapsed they left massive pools of kauri gum which were covered over with earth during the passage of time and became fossilized.

As long ago as 1819 the Reverend Samuel Marsden picked up pieces of gum exposed to the surface and correctly identified them. Gum was sent to England as a curio from the new land and by accident it was tested and found to have outstanding elements for making varnish, particularly fine varnish required by painters.

It led to a gum rush. By 1880 there were over 2,000 Europeans working in the gumfields of Northland. Most of the gumworkers were Dalmatians from what is now Yugoslavia. After the gumfields were exhausted they stayed on to become successful farmers and in their own tradition made sherry and port which in turn led to the wine industry which is growing so successfully in New Zealand today.

Like the goldrush, the gumrush produced grog shops, gambling, shantytown living, etc. It is an important part of history in this part of the country and the museums you visit will feature kauri gum displays, gumdigging tools, gum carvings.

The first sights on the Reinga tour are the orchards of Kerikeri and the continuous farmland and sheep pasture.

You pass by Whangaroa Harbor where the *Boyd* still rests at the bottom and on to Doubtless Bay, which can be appreciated as a vacation area because of its lovely, gentle sloping, golden-sand beaches at Coopers Beach and then Cable Bay.

Real estate is expensive here also.

There is fine fishing in the area including big game fishing at the mouth of the bay.

Kupe, the Polynesian explorer who first saw New Zealand in 950, was reputed to make his first landing at Doubtless Bay. He was the only Polynesian who was said to have returned to his homeland; 400 years later his descendants landed at the same place.

Doubtless Bay is interesting because it was named by Captain Cook who sailed by in 1769 and concluded it was "Doubtless, a bay".

Only eight days later, the French explorer, de Surville, who had passed by Cook unseen in a hurricane at sea, landed at Doubtless Bay and named it after one of his syndicate members, Bay of Lauriston.

You are at the base of the Aupori Peninsula. The land is thin but the Government is experimenting with Santa Gertrutis cattle developed in Texas to withstand the heat and the lack of summer water.

The farms and ranches are owned and run by Maoris and by war veterans rehabilitated into agricultural projects.

Look at the landing strips for the fertilizer airplanes. The landing strips are built so that the planes land going uphill. Makes for a *short* runway. The planes are loaded with fertilizer at the top of the hill and take off on a downhill ski jump.

Thanks to the fertilizer and the planting of marram grass much of the left-over gumfields and sand dunes are being brought into productivity.

About a third of the way up the peninsula is Houhora, a popular vacation ground. Here is also the Wagener Museum. At one time the homestead of a family of Polish nobility, the Subritzkys, the original house has been restored and a descendant of the family has built a modern, 5,000-square-foot museum next door to it. The museum holds a vast collection of relics from New Zealand's past, from Maori carvings to antique washing machines.

You can buy a bauble of kauri gum for a high-fashion pendant for less than $1 – but take care, the gum is brittle and shatters easily.

As you continue up the peninsula you'll see Parengarenga Harbor where the dazzling white-on-white sand makes up the second largest silica deposit in the world. Thousands of tons of silica are removed annually for glassmaking in New Zealand.

Also every year starting at the end of February or the beginning of March, *godwit* birds gather at Spirits Bay until they cover the beaches. On a signal from a leader they take off in a mass formation that almost blots out the sky and start an incredible journey north to Siberia.

You then enter Te Paki station, a 40,000-acre, Government-owned domain, formerly a private tung-oil project which failed. Today it is both a sheep and cattle station and a park. Shooting is prohibited. The pheasant walk down the middle of the road with bored confidence but wild pigs proliferating the countryside are hunted with Doberman Pinschers and knives: the wild pig kills and eats young lambs and is hated by the farmers.

By early afternoon, you arrive at Cape Reinga . . . a cluster of little white buildings holding a year-round weather station, a post office and the living quarters for both operations. The lighthouse, no longer manned, is a five minute walk from the parking lot. Makes an excellent background for pictures.

You can see the two ocean currents meet. You can see the sacred pohutukawa tree.

There is a signpost pointing out different mileages in different directions. Australia. Ecuador. Bluff, at the south end of the South Island. Another good photo prop.

To the west you can see Cape Maria van Diemen named by Tasman in 1642 for the lady of the Batavian Governor.

Ahead, on a clear day, you can just see the tips of the Three Kings Islands or to the east across Spirits Bay to Hooper Point.

To the right and to the left are both magnificent beaches. Grungy cars with surfboards on top are here, as everywhere, you'll find the young chasing the perfect wave and the endless summer.

Back in the bus, past Te Paki station, you drive down Te Paki (literally a stream bed) Stream which is your entrance road to the Ninety Mile Beach. The bed of the stream is quicksand. Not quick-quicksand but slow-quicksand. If you stop a car or a bus it will sink . . . but only up to its undercarriage. The bus driver tells you a proper number of fear-building stories and you enter the shallow stream bed and head down through the water and sand shelves. Halfway down the stream he pulls to the side on a safe bank and you can climb the mountainous sand dunes. You then continue the short drive to Ninety Mile Beach.

Ninety Mile Beach was named obviously by one of New Zealand's first advertising copywriters. (No one knows how it got its name.) It is fifty-six miles long. At low tide it offers a hard, smooth, sand-packed super highway. After the jolting ride to Cape Reinga, it comes as a pleasant relief. There is not much to see but the ride is unique and you find it soothing.

The bus stops halfway down the beach and you get out and pick up a shell for a souvenir and take off again.

If, by chance, you are a surf fisherman, then it is different. The Beach offers outstanding surf fishing and there is an annual surf-casting tournament in January with prizes running in the thousands of dollars. For information write the Public Relations Office, Kaitaia.

The area is well known in New Zealand for a shellfish called toheroa, the country's finest fishfood. The season is limited, the catching is not easy and the restrictions are well regulated.

Mid-afternoon you return to Awanui for another tea stop.

Because of the mid-morning, bus breakdown stop, we were obviously not going to get back to Paihia in time to clean up and get to a restaurant. We ducked the tearoom and ran down the street to a meat shop just about to close and from a bright-smiling butcher we ordered a huge sirloin steak for $1 and then up the stree to buy a pint of milk for 12c. Eight cents for the bottle: four cents for the milk. (The price of milk has since been increased to ten cents.)

The bus rolls through Kaitaia. A sign says "Hello" in Yugoslavian. A mission station was established here in 1833 by William Mathews who explored the country with a friendly Maori guide. However he was captured by a Maori tribe which was not only unfriendly but hungry. He would have been killed and eaten but for the intervention of a chief who admired his bravery. The Church thought less of his bravery because his expedition was not properly authorized and therefore his report does not appear in the Church Missionary Society's records.

South of Kaitaia is the Mangamuka Scenic Reserve of lush-green forest. There is a spring where you can drink soda water. The fern trees are outstanding. Down the highway is the scene of Heke's first victorious battle and then to the Mission House at Waimate North and back to Paihia. It makes a long but memorable day.

Note: The Cape Reinga-Ninety Mile Beach Tour is extremely popular. There are seven buses in the current fleet taking care of over 25,000 passengers a year. If you go anywhere near the December-February season, be sure and have a reservation.

Return to Auckland via the Home of the Pet Dolphin and the Giant Trees

Leaving the Bay of Islands and travelling on Highway 1 you reach Ohaeawai where the second battle of Heke's war was fought and where the British lost a third of their number. A Maori church on Highway 12, which is the highway we followed all of the way back to Dargaville, north of Ohaeawai, marks the site of the pa. Nothing remains to be seen of the original fortress.

Near Kaikohe there is a pretty golf course on the left with a new club house, the Ngawha Hot Springs Golf Course.

A mile and a half off the highway are soda mercury springs with a reputation for curing skin and rheumatic problems. The Domain Pools is a neat and tidy little complex offering a series of milky pools of different temperatures.

Not until you reach Omanaia do you sight the waters of Hokianga Harbor which is a long ragged harbor stretching halfway across the North Island.

There is much history attached to Hokianga. Kupe, the original Polynesian explorer, was said to have left here on his return home. One of the first groups of settlers came here. The first shipyard was here.

The harbor attracted more than its share of characters. One was a ship deserter, *"Cannibal"* Jacky Marmon, who was notorious for becoming more Maori than the Maoris, including participation in the cannibal ceremonies. Another was the incredible Charles Baron de Thierry, an expatriate Frenchman who declared himself

"Sovereign Chief of New Zealand". Claiming some 40,000 acres around Hokianga, he brought with him a band of colonists but his grandiose schemes collapsed as his followers deserted him and the Hokianga chiefs said that no land deal had been made.

Baron de Thierry however did succeed in spurring the British to take more positive action as the eccentric Frenchman's endeavors were promoted as an attempt by France to annex the colony.

Perhaps *Opo* should be included in the cast of Hokianga characters. Opo was a friendly dolphin who appeared in the waters at Opononi, a tiny, seaside resort not too far from the entrance to Hokianga Harbor. For two summers, 1955 and 1956, Opo appeared at the beach and would give rides to the local children. The dolphin drew international attention and was the cause of two books and countless newspaper and magazine stories. He was killed needlessly and tragically the day before a law was to go into effect to protect him. There is a memorial to Opo opposite the hotel, a child with a dolphin, which rests upon the famous dolphin's grave.

Actually Hokianga Harbor should be approached from the south because from that direction you come over a rise and dramatically the harbor is in front of you.

The sand bar guarding the harbor has claimed over fifteen ships since 1823.

At one time Northland was known as the *Roadless North*. Today there are many roads but not all are first class. Much of the road to Dargaville is a *metal* road, that is a coarsely gravelled road. Don't count on fast driving.

Today Northland promotes itself as the *Winterless North*. You'll still need your sweater. As a matter of fact what we really missed in our spring tour was our ski jackets.

The Waipoua Kauri Forest is beautiful.

At one time the kauri tree grew everywhere in the north. It is a noble tree, growing straight and tall, shedding its lower limbs as it grows taller leaving it virtually knot-free. One can imagine how happy shipbuilders were to find such a perfect timber for masts and spars and what a world market awaited.

At the Kemp House and the Waimate Mission House built of kauri, the long-lasting virtue and quality tone of kauri can be appreciated.

The timber boom grew in proportion to the number of settlers coming to New Zealand, and the rape of the giant forests, whose slow growth couldn't possibly keep pace with the demand, was completed before the end of the century.

The Waipoua reserve is one of the few pockets of original kauri remaining. Two giant trees give the visitor the sense of awe of the kauri. One of the trees is 1,200 years old and the other 2,000 years old.

Tanemahuta means "God of the Forest" and lies only a few yards off of the road, where there is also a picnic area and toilet facilities. The tree looks like the giant stump of a giant elephant. Its midgirth is 44 feet.

The largest tree is *Te Matua Ngahere* which means "Father of the Forest". It lies about fifteen minutes further down the road where you make a small detour for a half mile and then walk in for a quarter of a mile. This brute is 53 feet through.

You just have to weep inside of yourself at man's insatiable greed. On the other hand you are thankful for the public attitude in 1952 which resulted in the establishment of the reserve, which covers almost 28,000 acres.

We ate a huddled-against-the-wind picnic lunch at the detour to Father of the Forest. Across the bridge is the beginning of Kauri Ricker Track which is described as a pleasant, 15-minute walk through young kauri trees known as "Rickers". It was just too cold.

Nearby also is Maxwell's Cottage. James Maxwell was the first supervisor in the forest and the cottage where he once lived is now an exhibit of a kauri bushman's life.

The ten mile drive through the forest is a worthwhile trip. Shortly after leaving the forest you come to a sign taking you off Highway 12 detouring through Trounson Kauri Park, a reserve of smaller but thicker kauri. The detour rejoins Highway 12 about eight miles down the road.

The road back to Auckland takes you through Dargaville. Its museum features a 185-lb specimen of gum. Of more curiosity is the building itself which was originally the Dargaville stables, built out of bricks brought from China as ship's ballast.

We were back in Auckland by dusk.

4. Three Roads South From Auckland To Rotorua-Taupo

Vegetable Stands ... Summer Playgrounds ... Deep-sea Fishing ... A Bit of Southern California ... Victorian Mineral Baths

A visitor to New Zealand with even a minimum amount of time will want to go to Rotorua to see the thermal phenomena and the fisherman will want to go to the mecca of rainbow trout at Lake Taupo.

To reach this central lake district there is a delightful choice of three motor routes offering a wide variety of scenery and activities which we call: the Farm Route, the Spa Route and the Pacific Route.

The Farm Route is the most western route through rich agricultural land and for much of the time following the beautiful Waikato river. The Spa or Central Route takes in a rare thermal wonder and a Victorian spa of yesteryear. The Pacific Route includes the playgrounds of the Coromandel Peninsula and historic goldfields and then follows the coast to the summer beaches at Tauranga and Mount Maunganui. To leave Auckland by one route and to return via another gives the visitor a double-rich experience.

The western route or Farm Route is a fast route, going down Highway 1 through Hamilton and Cambridge to Tirau. Here the highway separates and Highway 5 goes east to Rotorua and Highway 1 goes south to Taupo.

Leaving Auckland on Highway 1 you get free of the city on the easy-driving motorway almost to Bombay. After the Bombay Hills you drop down into typical New Zealand vista land. It is lush. It is the richest farm land in New Zealand. It breathes butterfat.

Selling farm produce at roadside stands is a national cottage industry and in the Waikato Valley these stands dot the highway causing the Lady Navigator to try and stop at all of them. Paradoxically, when you include the antique stores in Cambridge, the western route for us was a slow route south.

71

In addition to the pastoral vistas, the gentle Waikato river which originates in Lake Taupo flows through the valley offering quiet river scenes which are tea-stop inviting.

The center of all this bounty is Hamilton. It is the largest inland city in the North Island with a population of 85,000 and boasts a university, a teachers' college and a farm-animal breeding institute whose reputation for research is international.

The city has a St Andrews Golf Course, a pretty lake, an art museum and several parks and tennis courts.

Founded by the military as a base of operations against the Maori in the bitter Waikato Campaign (1863–64), the city was named after a naval officer killed on the east coast in another battle.

The past history of strife and bloodshed seems incongruous to Hamilton, so fat-cat and peaceful today.

The main highway to the famous Waitomo Caves is through Hamilton. Highway 3 goes directly south of the city forty-five miles to Waitomo but we are going to leave the caves for a later venture.

Staying to Highway 1 the road continues along the Waikato river until Cambridge (population 7,000) which prides itself on its trees and its antique shops. "More antique shops than any other New Zealand provincial town," boasts the literature. It was too bad we weren't travelling with a dog because then the dog could stop àt all the trees and the Lady Navigator could stop at all the antique shops and they'd both be in heaven.

Cambridge shares the military history of Hamilton and is also an agricultural center. From here it is a short drive to Tirau and the Rotorua-Taupo junction.

If you take the Taupo road and don't plan on retracing the highway, you should consider a detour . . . only fourteen miles off the highway . . . to the Orakeikorako thermal valley. Watch for the signs eight miles after Atiamuri pointing to the east.

The valley is famous for its multi-colored silica terraces. There are also bubbling mud pots and geysers and a sacred cave (Aladdin's Cave) where Maori women used to do their make-up in the mirror pools. When the conditions are right, evening visitors can take a hot swim in an adjoining cave with the roof of the cave lighted by glow-worms. Wow!

The jet-boat over to the terraces costs $1.50. The detour and the price are worth it all. As the AA map says, "It is now one of the most rewarding visits of its kind available."

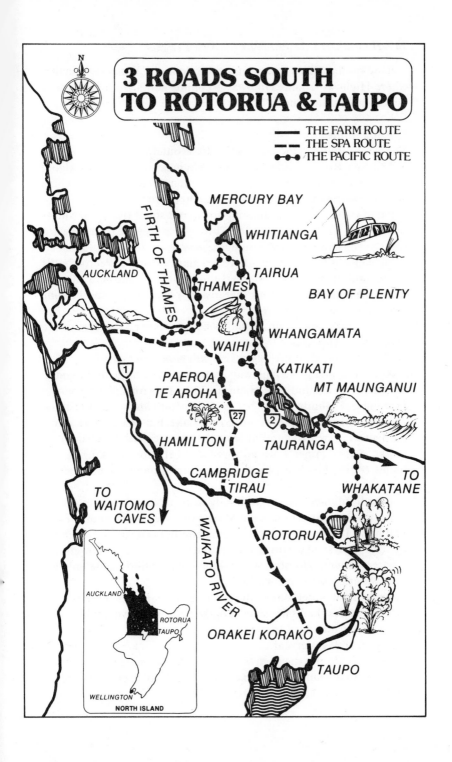

Back on the highway it is a short drive to the Wairakei junction where Highway 1 joins Highway 5 coming south from Rotorua, a fast scamper into Taupo.

The Spa Route
The central route to the lakes is the Spa Route.

The Spa Route follows the same Highway 1 out of Auckland. After the Bombay Hills, there is a junction with Highway 2 which you take to the east, coming eventually to Paeroa.

Paeroa was once a goldmining town and small river port and is now known for its mineral water. Throughout New Zealand a visitor will see constant signs promoting *Lemon & Paeroa,* a national soft drink which is bottled here. There is a giant Lemon & Paeroa bottle in the middle of town and you'd think there would be a mineral water drinking fountain but there isn't. You can visit the bottling plant during working hours.

Goldminers used to drink the Vichy-type water as a cure for the night-after hangovers.

The river, incidentally, is stocked with good trout.

At Paeroa, you leave Highway 2 which goes over the mountain to the Pacific Coast and take Highway 26 to Te Aroha. This is now a farming community center but in the early 1900s it was a fashionable spa where people would go to "take the waters". Victorian gardens were created and Victorian bath-houses with Victorian-type kiosks where mineral water spouted freely for drinking. Lawn tennis courts, bowling greens and croquet grounds completed the domain.

It is all still there although slightly worn around the edges.

An unusual attraction is the Mokena Geyser which spouts every half hour. It is not a natural phenomenon but was created when the mineral waters of the spring were found to have curative powers and a bore was sunk. *Hot* soda water fountained forth! It is the only hot soda water geyser in the world.

The quaint hotel across the street from the park entrance on Whitaker street looks like a hotel of the early 1900s where the guests taking the waters used to stay.

It is all very yesteryear.

From Te Aroha the highway heads straight south to Matamata and then to the junction at Tirau where the traveller goes to Rotorua or Taupo.

The Pacific Route

The Pacific Route is the eastern route south and should be considered as two destination areas because it encompasses (1) the Coromandel Peninsula, considered by many to be one of the most beautiful parts of New Zealand and (2) further south, Tauranga and Mount Maunganui, a seaside city and resort famous for citrus, bathing beaches and fishing.

The route to Coromandel follows the same eastern swing as the road to Paeroa via the motorway to Bombay Hills but stays to the east by taking Highway 25 into the city of Thames, which is called the "gateway to the Coromandel Peninsula". The Peninsula is a vast vacation ground for New Zealanders who come to swim, play golf, deep-sea fish, hunt for pigs, hunt for gemstones, eat the crayfish and sleep in the sun.

Divided by the Coromandel Range, the Peninsula stretches further north than Auckland with the Firth of Thames and the Hauraki Gulf on one side and the Bay of Plenty and the Pacific Ocean on the other side.

The town of Coromandel and the Peninsula were named after a naval ship, the HMS *Coromandel,* which put into the harbor in 1820 to load kauri wood for spars and timber.

Thames is rich in history.

Captain Cook landed near here and explored the Waihou River by longboat. He named the river *Thames* as well as the bay. The name of the river was later changed but the name Firth of Thames remained. Cook later remarked in his journal that if colonization was considered, he would recommend the Bay of Islands and the River Thames.

Thames' modern history was started in the 1850s by a problem facing the New Zealand Government. The country was being de-populated by the people leaving for the goldfields of Australia and California. In an effort to encourage mineral exploration, the Government offered a $1000 reward for a workable find.

In 1851 a Coromandel lumberman, Charles Ring, went to a nearby stream to take a drink of water, the story goes, and when he put his cup into the stream, he saw flecks of gold dust in the stream bottom. He took the dust to Auckland to claim the reward and 2,000 miners were soon in Coromandel. But the expense of mining the gold proved too great and the miners evaporated and Charles Ring's award was denied.

It was not until 1867 that W. A. Hunt stumbled on a river bank and uncovered gold which led to a mine that paid fantastic dividends. Again goldminers poured into the area and within a three-year period, Thames had a population of 20,000, twice the size of Auckland which had been denuded by the transfer of the capital city to Wellington.

The alluvium gold in the streams was quickly exhausted but quartz was then mined and stamped into dust from which gold was extracted. The hills were honeycombed with mine shafts. The Long Drive in 1867, the first Thames bonanza, went 160 feet into the mountain. A roadside sign marks its entry. Another roadside sign marks its exit. Another roadside sign points to the Duke of Edinburgh mine which in a ten-year period paid the equivalent of half a million dollars a share.

The thump of the gold batteries has long gone but many of the Victorian buildings remain. The population is now about 6,000 and the town is semi-industrial with a car-assembly plant, a clothing factory and two foundries.

The first expedition from Thames might be north on Highway 25 which runs along a coast road to Coromandel. Along the highway are many little holiday villages facing the Firth.

Coromandel once so booming with gold mining activity is now a center for the surrounding dairyfarms. A few Victorian-colonial buildings remain.

The Coromandel School of Mines Museum is a small two-room museum which is opened on request. It is full of interesting little knicknacks of its past including a photograph of the gold finder, Charles Ring.

Country roads lead all the way around the tip of the Peninsula for the adventurous driver.

The other road from Thames, Highway 25A, takes you across the base of the Peninsula through reforested hills. At one time much of the land was covered with kauri but these disappeared under the axe and saw of early timbermen.

Highway 25A and Highway 25 form a junction just below Hikuai in a remarkably peaceful valley. You think to yourself, "Could I live here?" And you reply, "With a great deal of pleasure." It is that kind of a spot.

Soon after a patch of gravel road you come to the east coast and the upper tip of the Bay of Plenty. Here is the attractive resort of

Tairua featuring girls in bikinis, crayfish for sale along the road and deep-sea fishing.

Across the little harbor is the new resort town of Pauanui with a golf course, holiday homes, even an airport.

The highway then crosses a mountain range. The summit peak gives a sweeping vista of the Bay of Plenty.

We stopped at a cowshed roadside stand, Wilderland, where the members of a nearby commune offer their home-grown produce for sale. Fresh fruits and vegetables and delicious honeycomb honey.

Further on is the popular seaside resort of Whitianga. The overseas visitor would be attracted to Whitianga for its deep-sea fishing. It is possible to leave Auckland in the morning and be in a boat by that afternoon and out to Great Mercury Island where there are marlin, mako shark and yellowfin tuna.

The season is January, February and March. Reservations for a boat should be made well ahead of time.

Whitianga, on Mercury Bay, is also a pleasant harbor for pleasure boats.

There are miles of white sand beaches, rugged coastlines and golf, squash, bowls and a gun club. (The Mercury Bay Tennis Club, two asphalt courts, 25c a person per half hour. Night lighted. Keys across the road at the Peninsula Hotel.)

For information regarding boat charters, check the Public Information Office on the main street. The Mercury Bay Game Fishing Club has a membership of 800 and holds several world records.

The Whitianga Hotel was cited by Robert Morley, the English actor, in a *Punch* article as being the finest example of "country-fresh" food in New Zealand. We tried it and it wasn't. But the ambiance was near perfect overlooking Mercury Bay with a swimming pool immediately in front and palm trees framing the boats at anchor. We were the only people at lunch.

We also bought a fresh crayfish from a local store for dinner and it was excellent. $1.80 a pound.

There is a small passenger ferry which shuttles visitors to the other side of the harbor where walks can take you to Front Beach and Cook's Bay. Here the good captain anchored in 1769 and took a sighting on the planet Mercury, hence the name of the inlet.

Further south on the Coromandel Peninsula is another seaside resort of Whangamata which also booms with summer visitors and is known for outstanding surfing.

Leaving the Coromandel Peninsula you pass through the little town of Waihi, the last gold producing town in New Zealand until its famous Martha Mine closed down in 1952. At its time Martha Mine was one of the world's richest goldmines and during its sixty-six-year history produced $360 million of gold. In 1909 it was producing $5 million annually and was paying 80 per cent annually to its investors.

Today the mine shafts are flooded.

Nearby Waihi is Waihi Beach, a major beach and surfing resort. Here you pick up Highway 2 again and follow the coastline to Tauranga, which has a Southern California charm of its own. The streets are wide and palm-lined. The sun sparkles off of the harbor waters. The air is soft and temperate.

The countryside grows citrus, fruit and exotic subtropical fruit. If you can, try the kiwi fruit (Chinese gooseberries) and the tamarillos. Delicious over vanilla ice cream.

There is not a lot of special activity in Tauranga other than the big-game fishing although there is the usual golf, tennis, etc. Big-game charters can be arranged through the Commercial Boat Owners' Association.

We stopped at a roadside stand and bought nectarines as big as peaches and peaches as big as small cantaloup. And we stopped by a riverbank and had sherry and chicken and played backgammon and let the world go by.

One thing to see in Tauranga is the Mission House, known as *The Elms.* The gardens are open to the public but the buildings can only be visited by private arrangement.

The Elms consists of a mission residence, one of the oldest in the country, and a chapel and one-room library set in an extensive garden facing the harbor.

The main building was erected between 1838 and 1847 and, seen from the front, it is irresistable for the photographer with its classical colonial lines, perfectly framed in tall trees. In one corner of the property is an English oak planted in 1838 and in another corner, two towering Norfolk pines which were used by sailors as navigational aids for entering the Tauranga Harbor. The trees were known as the "Archdeacon's Sentinels".

A poignant story revolves around the folding table in the chapel. The head of the mission had as his dinner companions a number of officers on the eve of the battle of the Gate Pa. Within the next two days he was to bury all but one of his guests.

Not far from The Elms is an old military cemetery which was built on an ancient Maori fort overlooking the harbor. Buried here are many of the dead from the Maori Land Wars including Captain John Faine Charles Hamilton after whom the city of Hamilton was named. It seems very old in the surrounding trees. Very quiet. Sadly peaceful.

Gayness and youth, however, are not far away. Across the harbor and serving as a harbor head is Mount Maunganui, a popular beach resort filled with hamburger stands, oil-glistening bodies, body surfers. There is much rock music in the air, which smells nicely salty like ocean air should smell.

Mount Maunganui has recently become important as a deep-water shipping port but on the ocean side it is all fun and games. Known simply as *The Mount* it is one of the most popular beach resorts in the North Island, probably due to its miles-long Ocean Beach of golden sand. It was interesting to us that even in the height of the summer season the beach didn't seem to be at all crowded.

The Mount itself was a former Maori fort and, like Mt Egmont at New Plymouth, is the scene for a traditional New Year's Eve dash to the top. The walking path to the summit is rewarded by superlative views.

There is a Marineland on Ocean Beach. You've probably seen better.

In back of The Mount are golf courses, tennis courts, launch trips to nearby Motiti Island and far out Mayor Island. Sight-seeing trips are booked at the nearby airport.

Leaving the Mount Highway 2 goes through Te Puke and shortly thereafter reaches a junction with Highway 33 which you take to the south. After going through more "ho-hum-isn't-it-beautiful" country – how soon we get spoiled – you come to the corner of Lake Rotoiti and then you are at Lake Rotorua.

From there you have a straight dash south to Taupo.

5. Taupo – Rotorua

Lake Country ... Heavenly Scones ... Tame Trout ... Trained Sheep ... Maori Culture ... Famous Fishing ... Mother Nature Huffing, Puffing, Bubbling and Blowing Steam

The approach to Taupo from Wairakei is a never-ending joy.

The highway is wide and sweeping with green forests and lawns on either side.

Picnic tables invite the traveller to stop and rest. He never does. The traveller prefers to take tea along the shores of Lake Taupo.

The highway rolls invitingly onward and you have a feeling you are in a glider.

Then you see the tips of the trinity peaks of Tongariro National Park. First Mt Ruapehu, over 9,000 feet, the tallest mountain in the North Island, always snow-covered, and Mt Ngauruhoe, 7,500 feet and always puffing smoke from its volcanic top, and then Mt Tongariro at 6,500 feet standing sentry of the south end of the lake.

Abreast of Lookout Point the lake suddenly unveils itself before you. A huge stretch of blue, the largest lake in New Zealand.

For our New Zealand adventure, we set up base camp in Taupo. Why?

For the same reasons Taupo has grown from a post-war population of 750 to a population today of over 10,000.

Geographically it is in the center of the North Island. A traveller can reach Auckland in the north or Wellington in the south in a half day ... or Hawke's Bay to the east or New Plymouth to the west in less time.

Within a fifty-mile radius are eight golf courses, four of them in the backyard of the town, many tennis courts, a wide selection of mineral baths and swimming pools, a dozen important lakes and another dozen minor lakes, a multitude of rivers and streams and some of the best fishing in the country.

Lake Taupo is probably the most famous lake in the world for rainbow trout, and the Tongariro River, its principal tributary, the most famous fly-fishing stream in the world.

They measure the annual take of fish out of Taupo by the *ton*.

The rainbow was brought to New Zealand in 1883 from the Russian River in California and hatched in the Auckland Domain . . . near the Winter Garden.

But Taupo, being practically inaccessible in those days, didn't see the rainbow until 1897 although the European brown trout had been introduced in 1886.

The tremendous expanse of the lake, 238 square miles with long sunshine hours, produced a high volume of plankton for smaller fish which provided food for the larger fish. The clear waters of the mountain streams, eel-free, were natural waterways for the rainbows to revert to their Pacific Ocean custom as steelheads of going up river to spawn.

By 1910 it was not difficult to take 20- and 25-pound trout from the lake. The number and the size of the fish led to a decline in their quality as the food supply became strained, so the Government then started a control program.

Today the fish are still giants by world standards. Three and four and five-pound fish are run-of-the-mill. But a ten-pound fish is the cause of exclamation.

Let me tell you about my first trip to Taupo.

I was attending a travel conference in Sydney, Australia. Having attended dozens of such conferences, it doesn't take much urging to leave early. You miss the departing crowds and that is all you miss.

I had written a friend in Auckland telling him that one of my life's ambitions was to catch a New Zealand trout and how did one go about it?

This friend, Bermey Bookman, is one of those people to whom a hint is a military order for itineraries, maps, costs, schedules, alternate suggestions, hotel reservations, plane reservations. Ticket counters light up at the mention of his name.

One evening I was in Auckland from Sydney and the next morning I was off to Taupo.

At Taupo I was met by Tony Jensen, a year-round fishing guide who gathered my bags and took me to Turangi, his home base, at the south end of the lake, ensconced me in a motel and then drove me to a nearby Maori-owned lake, Rotoaira.

I am not a good fisherman, not having the natural "touch" or instinct or concentration that makes a good fisherman. I don't *think* like a fish.

In two and a half hours I had caught the limit of ten fish, all over

14 inches long! It was stunning.

You know the greatest feeling in the world? Sitting in a boat, just bobbing there, not fishing, with the limit already in the bag. And you are wearing slickers because there's a cold wind blowing and black rain clouds are scudding overhead and you're drinking black coffee with one hand to get it warm and then the other hand to get it warm and nibbling on a thickly buttered scone letting it melt in your mouth and you don't say anything and the guide doesn't say anything and there you are with God and silence and beauty all around you and deep hunter-home-from-the-hills contentment.

That's as good as life gets.

The next morning we went on to Lake Taupo and in half a day again had the limit in the boat!

Little wonder that our base camp was to be in Taupo. One of the first things we did after setting up camp there was to return to Tony Jensen. The Lady Navigator caught the first fish and the best fish and the most fish.

It reminded Tony of one of his favorite stories. He had an American client who had been fishing for twenty-five years . . . 90 percent of his clients are Americans . . . and the day was glorious. The sun was full on the waters, there wasn't a cloud in the sky and the lake was pancake smooth.

The American had his wife at boatside, but during his years of fishing she had never consented to go fishing with him despite his pleading. Again he urged her to come along and finally with the beauty of the lake in front of her, she reluctantly agreed.

She caught the first fish.

The husband was delighted. "Now she understands why I enjoy fishing," he said.

She caught the second fish. And the third fish. And the fourth fish.

By the end of the morning the veteran fisherman had caught one fish.

The wife hooked into the eighth and final rainbow of the day and exclaimed with joy, "Oh, look, darling, I have another one!"

Said the husband slowly and grimly: "Just – shut – up – and – pull – in – the – goddam – fish!"

It was to become a slogan for the rest of our trip.

A day on the lake with Tony only costs $9 an hour including his wife's scones. A tremendous bargain.

Scones (pronounced as in *con* man and not as ice cream *cone*) are

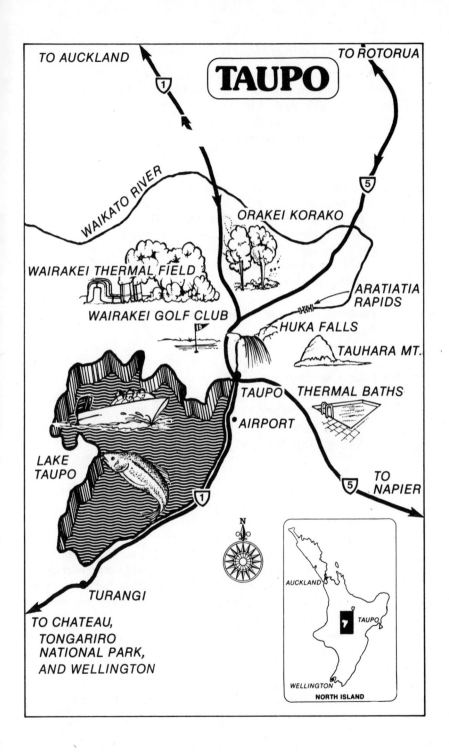

a New Zealand tea staple, a lovely biscuit which can be plain or made with cheese or dates or raisins. Jo Jensen makes a superlative scone. Here is how she does it:

Jo Jensen's Heavenly Scones
(Basic)
 1 cup flour
 1 heaping teaspoon baking powder
 ½ teaspoon salt
 milk to mix – to make a very stiff dough
 2 tablespoons butter (rubbed in gently with fingers)
Pat dough smooth; separate into biscuit-sized segments. Bake at 450°F for approximately 10 minutes. Serve these with jam topped with whipped cream.

For Date, Currant or Sultana Scones
To above add:
 2 teaspoons sugar
 ½ cup currants, sultanas or chopped dates
Bake as in basic recipe.
For Cheese Scones
Eliminate butter from basic recipe, then add:
 1 cup grated sharp tasty cheese
 1 pinch cayenne pepper
 chopped chives if desired

With so many beautiful fish resulting from Tony's guided outings, Jo also shared with us three of her favorite trout recipes:
Bay-Bacon Trout
Clean but don't skin the trout.
For a 5-lb trout, line the body inside with a dozen bay leaves. Salt and pepper to taste. Spread two ounces of butter over the bay leaves. Wrap fish in bacon. Wrap the fish in foil.
Pour one-half cup of dry white wine into bottom of pan. Bake one-half hour at 325°F.
The wine will evaporate.

This is Tony's favorite:
Turangi Trout Cocktail
Clean and steam a trout. Cut into small chunks. Place on

ROTORUA

AGRODOME
LAKE ROTORUA
LAKE ROTOITI
MOKOIA IS.
RAINBOW SPRINGS AND FAIRY SPRINGS
LAKE OKATAINA
ROTORUA WHAKAREWAREWA
LAKE TARAWERA
5
LAKE ROTOMAHANA
WAIMANGU
WAIOTAPU
N
REPOROA
GOLDEN SPRINGS
WAIKATO RIVER
1
ORAKEI KORAKO
AUCKLAND
ROTORUA
TAUPO
TO TAUPO
WELLINGTON
NORTH ISLAND

lettuce leaves. Over the trout pour Turangi Trout Sauce, a home-made spiced mayonnaise:

7 ounces sweetened condensed milk
½ cup melted butter (or salad oil)
½ cup lemon juice (or vinegar)
2 egg yolks
½ teaspoon salt
1 teaspoon dry mustard
dash of cayenne pepper

Place all ingredients in a bowl and beat well until the mixture thickens. Stored in a cool place, it keeps for a very long time.

Spice the amount of mayonnaise needed per serving with equal amounts (approximately) of Worcestershire Sauce and ketchup.

Bottled Trout

What do New Zealanders do with all the trout they catch? They freeze them. They smoke them. They bottle them. *Bottle* them? Yes, and here's how:

Pack fillets (or un-boned chunks) into pint jars. The bones will soften and nearly dissolve. Pour over each jar mixture of:

1 tablespoon vinegar
1 teaspoon olive oil
½ teaspoon salt
½ teaspoon brown sugar

Seal each jar. Place in 300°F oven, in a roasting pan, and cook for two hours. (For faster cooking, place jars in a pressure cooker for 45 minutes.)

A 5-lb trout will fill 4 pint jars.

(First: to make rabbit stew, catch the rabbit, right?)

Tony Jensen has recently written an entertaining, highly readable book recalling his many fishing trips and clients. *"Trout of the Tongariro"* (Reed) is a good gift to yourself or a fishing friend.

More Taupo Fishing

There's good fishing all around Lake Taupo. With Tongariro as one attraction and the tailrace of the hydro-dam project as another attraction the south end of the lake is a popular fishing ground for fly-fishermen and for trolling from boats.

The western bays are difficult to reach except by boat but the waters are heavy with big fish.

The east side of Lake Taupo has popular rivers which are easily accessible by car. There are more than a half a dozen rivers and streams.

In the summer there is not a fish in a river. They have all retreated to the lake, but the fishermen cluster at the stream mouths where the fish come to feed on the insects and to cool themselves in the stream waters. Fishing is restricted to fly-fishing for 300 yards from the stream mouths.

So many fishermen line up in a row at the mouth of the Waitahanui river that it is known as "the picket fence".

In March the trout start their upstream migration to spawn. There is good river fishing until October.

Even with all of the fish in Taupo, you need a guide to introduce you to a few of the better locations, otherwise you could go for days and never see a trout.

If you can't find a guide, go in and chat with the proprietor of a Taupo sporting goods store and buy a few of the recommended local flies and lures and get a copy of *"Taupo Fishing Guide"* by John Sierpinski (Reed) for $1.25. It might save you from being "skunked".

At the north end of the lake, in Taupo town, is a large center of fishing activity. In the pretty harbor there are half a dozen boats for charter. You can rent tackle for about $2. A day's fishing licence costs 75c.

Our favorite operator in north Taupo was Simon Dickie. A well-known sports figure in New Zealand, he was the coxman on the Gold Medal New Zealand rowing eight in the 1972 Olympics and again in the 1976 Olympics team. He is a delightful, enthusiastic guide and companion.

He operates two boats. A small boat with enough power for water skiing which can get the fisherman to a secluded spot in a hurry, and a large boat which is a luxury yacht capable of overnight charters to the western bays. The boat has a head, bar, kitchen and deep-pile carpeting. For the novice it is a luxurious introduction to fishing. $60 covers four hours for a full party, everything included.

One week we had visitors from Cape Cod, Massachusetts, and we chartered Simon's 30-foot launch and went overnight to the western bays.

We left at noon on a handsome, sun-filled day and motored

leisurely over to the mouth of Waihaha river. There were shoals of fish under the cliff. Fish jumping all around the boat. The ladies went trolling with Simon and the men went fly-fishing in the rip of the river.

At the end of the day it was heavenly beyond belief. The soft yellow of the last sun rays slid off Wharawhara Point and spread out over the water in front of us until it gradually melted into pewter and then into dark. The only sound was the occasional bubble of the water in the rip and the singing of the bellbirds and tuis and riflemen (the smallest of New Zealand's native birds) behind us.

One of the advantages of being a mug fisherman is that you have time to appreciate all of the beauty around you.

The next morning five of us got into a dippy-tippy, seven-foot aluminum dingy and went up the Waihaha river, following the gentle curving water path through one of nature's loveliest gardens.

Below us the brown trout darted everywhere. On the riverbank were signs of wild pigs having just come down to wallow in the river mud. And morning glories that belonged in front of someone's cottage. Toetoe, looking like giant ostrich feathers, bent gracefully over the river and yellow broom was in bloom.

Birds surrounded us. Grey heron, fantails, a rare bittern called a matuku swooped from a tree in front of us. Cormorants and kingfishers perched on overhanging tree branches and followed our every move. And the huge cliffs stood on each side of the river and you knew this little lonesome boat was the only way to travel.

After two hours we reached Tieke Falls, a splendid waterfall where we fished for an hour and then went back down river to an abandoned Maori village and picked a hatful of wild blackberries for lunch. The total trip took five hours.

Back aboard the launch, we left Waihaha and went north to Kawakawa Point to the Boat Harbour, an idyllic haven. A small white beach faced the lake and the launch pulled around a little hook in the harbor and snubbed up to the trees.

Simon smoked our freshly caught trout and served bakery bread slathered with thick butter, and a bottle of cold white wine. It was all too good!

Our friends, seasoned travellers, were completing the last leg of a trip around the world. They said it was not only the highlight of their trip, but it was a lifetime experience.

We said, smugly, "Oh, it's like this everyday in New Zealand."

Simon's company is South Pacific Sporting Adventures. The mailing address is PO Box 682, Taupo.

Pre-dawn one morning my Cape Cod friend and I went to Jellicoe Point and fished the rip without success and retreated to Hinemaiaia river and fished for two hours. There wasn't another rod on this beautiful river. My friend couldn't believe it.

He caught an eight-inch trout and dutifully threw it back but then he caught a fat twelve-inch trout. The limit at Taupo is fourteen inches and he threw it back tearfully. "At home that would be a trophy fish!"

Those were the only fish we saw.

The next afternoon he took the car and returned to the same river. Just as the last light was fading he returned. His chest was out to here. "I got one," he said and he pulled out a silvery twenty-three inch rainbow.

When his wife had finally gone through about twelve flashbulbs, he said, "I'd better clean my trout." And he took it into the kitchen and laid it out in the sink and looked at it and looked at it. Finally he turned around and said, "I never saw a trout I couldn't clean with my fingernails before."

If you want a teacher-guide, the locals refer you to Bob Sullivan at Sullivan's Sports Store at the corner of the lakefront and Tongariro, the main street of Taupo.

If you watch fly-fishermen at Taupo, they have a technique of gathering the line in their left hand with a continuing rolling motion of the wrist which keeps the fly steadily moving through the water and I went to Bob and he took me to the lawn across from his store and quickly introduced me to the "Taupo roll". He also gave me hell for my sloppy fly-casting technique and put that right. Good man.

Further up the street is Logan's, another excellent sports store for local fishing knowledge, flies, tackle, licenses and emergency repairs. Ian Logan even fixed a luggage lock for us that in the United States would have had to go back to the factory. Cost 75c. He also rebuilt two travelling trunks inside and out. Cost $5. He and his wife were a constant source of information. Cost? A smile.

More Taupo Action

The scene in Taupo centers around water activities on the lake. There is swimming in the summer time. Much water skiing. You can arrange for lessons at the harbor. There is yacht racing from the Taupo Yacht Club. There are several summer competitive events: power boat racing, water skiing competitions, even raft racing.

There is a floatplane to take visitors on scenic flights and to fishing locations around the area.

Away from the lake there are many other activities. Sky-diving clubs congregate at the Taupo airport from as far away as Wellington. The Taupo Golf Club has two 18-hole courses. $3.50 for greens fee and 50c for a trundler. The older Tauhara course is tree-lined and scenic with many interesting holes. The new Centennial course is comparatively flat and treeless but is longer and more challenging. Taupo has five asphalt-covered tennis courts. Keys to the gate can be had from Logan's Sports Store. 50c fee.

One of the other attractions to Taupo is mineral bathing. On the Spa Road to the Taupo Golf Club is the AC Baths which has modern heated pools for swimming and relaxing and a set of private pools for soaking in solitude . . . but not for more than twenty minutes, the sign warns you. You come out of the water with all the bones melted and all the nerves dissolved. It takes a great deal of effort to start your car afterwards. A favorite spot.

The De Brett Hotel, just south of Taupo on Highway 5, also has thermal baths. Large pools and private pools open to the public for a nominal fee. A magnificent thermal valley setting with walks laid out among steam vents and natural streams.

A little further south on Highway 1 is an AA sign pointing to Botanical Gardens which are about a mile off the highway. The Waipahihi Botanical Reserve is a charming, hill-top garden created by loving, professionally-talented volunteers who have constructed a delightful retreat with picnic tables and short walks. The spring azaleas and rhododendrons are an overwhelming sight.

As you leave Taupo on Highway 1 north you cross a bridge where the water is released from the lake and becomes the Waikato river. A short distance down river is a favorite tour spot, Huka Falls, where the Waikato river, brilliant blue-green in color, funnels through a narrow channel of rock and then surges through a final cleft of stone and falls thirty-five feet into the continuing river below. It's spectacular.

Nearby is the Huka Falls Lodge where celebrity fly-fishermen headquarter to fish this lovely stretch of the river and enjoy one of the best game tables in New Zealand.

Dinner tab for two: $43 including a cocktail before, sherry with soup, wine with the main course and a liqueur after. "Pricey", but one of the more memorable dinners in New Zealand. We had venison soup, asparagus omelette, wild boar chops with home-grown vegetables and a sweet kiss of a fruit concoction for dessert.

Dianne Harland-Baker, the hostess-chef who has been featured in *Gourmet* magazine, did the chops. Here is her basic recipe:

Wild Chops Dianne
Fresh wild pork chops (hung for 2-3 days)
1-2 eggs beaten in a bowl
Mix together:
  breadcrumbs
  garlic
  sesame seeds
  wholemeal flour
  salt and pepper
Dip chops in egg, then in breadcrumb mix, deep fry in oil.
(We tried this recipe with *thick* pork chops. Works fine.)

Five minutes north of Taupo on Highway 1 is Wairakei, a center of activity in itself. The Wairakei Hotel, another Government-owned hotel has bars, a liquor store, a tennis court and swimming pool. Across the highway is a fun-for-novices-and-guests golf course of 15 holes.

Adjacent is the Wairakei International Course, considered by many New Zealanders to be the finest golf course in the country. It is a pretty layout but it is *tough*. Government-owned and operated, open to visitors at all times. $4.50 greens fee. 60c trundlers.

Also at Wairakei is the thermal power station which is the visitor's delight. It looks like a stage set radium plant built by Goldfinger in a James Bond movie. There are miles of huge bright tubes leading everywhere. Steam comes pouring out of vents. There is the sound of wild steam escaping. Even a road sign warns drivers that visability can be impaired by steam blowing across the road. It is all very unusual and nervous-making and satisfactory.

A roadside Information Office describes with charts and three-dimensional displays what is happening under the ground. Most impressive.

For one thing the thermal station supplies 9 percent of the electricity in New Zealand. After you have seen the vast hydro-electric dams and plants throughout the country, you realize what a high percentage 9 per cent signifies and what a huge amount of power is trapped by bores drilled deep into the boiling earth.

Visiting hours for the Information Office are from 9 a.m. until noon and from 1 p.m. to 4 p.m.

Just north of the Wairakei Power Station are the Aratiatia Rapids, two miles off of the main highway. Between 10 and 11:30 a.m. and 2:30 and 4 p.m. the waters are released from the dam and spill through the rapids making a grand sight. During the construction of the dam a farsighted landscaping plan was initiated involving the planting of two million native plants and the creation of picnic spots, lookout points and trails for hikes.

A siren sounds to warn visitors before the waters are released.

Rotorua

In the information office at Wairakei Thermal Station is a display of the thermal zones of New Zealand. They cover the map. But the most intense concentration of activity is a broad swath of red which extends from the south shore of Taupo at Mt Ruapehu through Rotorua eastward to White Island off the Pacific shore from Whakatane. The center can be said to be Rotorua.

Indeed overseas visitors were coming to Rotorua in sizeable numbers before 1886, not only to enjoy the thermal wonders of the area but to enjoy the lakes and scenic beauty.

The primary thermal phenomena were the famous Pink and White Terraces at the foot of Mt Tarawera. The two separate terraces, immense in size, were created by the build-up of silica-laden streams fanning out like giant still-born waterfalls. (A small version of what the terraces must have been like can be seen at the Orakei-korako Valley.)

Then one night in 1886 the most terrible earthquake of the region in memory occurred when Mt Tarawera erupted splitting open like a giant pea-pod spilling volcanic mud and pumice for miles around, destroying a nearby Maori encampment, the tourist hotel across the lake at Te Wairoa and burying forever the Pink and White Terraces.

One all-day tour takes you from Rotorua by the pretty Blue Lake and Green Lake, past the buried village at Te Wairoa and by launch across Lake Tarawera. An easy three-mile walk through the bush to Lake Rotomahana and you board another launch to pass by the sites of the famous terraces and the Steaming Cliffs. At the end of the lake another bus transports you back to Rotorua passing by Waimangu where there is more thermal activity.

You don't have to leave Rotorua to see the most spectacular geyser in New Zealand, however. South on Highway 5, but within the city limits is Whakarewarewa, which looks unpronouncable. Take the word apart and it is easy: "wocka-rua-rua". After you have mastered the easy name you will want to start right in on the full name: *Te Whakarewarewatanga-o-te-ope-a-Wahiao!*

At the entrance to Whakarewarewa is the Maori Arts and Crafts Institute, mostly consisting of carving. Next to the institute is a fort or pa.

The Maoris displaced by the Tarawera eruption now have a small reserve here and they still use thermal steam for cooking, bathing and washing.

The main feature of Whakarewarewa is the geyser activity. There are seven. The most reliable are the Prince of Wales Feathers which erupts to a height of forty-feet and usually serves as a preview for the fountaining of Pohutu, the largest geyser in the country, which can spout up to 100 feet and continue for hours.

A third important thermal area is nineteen miles south of Rotorua on the way to Taupo. Waiotapu is known for the Lady Knox Geyser which spouts when fed with soap! You'll see silica terraces and mud pools at Waiotapu as well.

Another thermal area attracting large numbers of tourists is 11 miles northeast of Lake Rotorua on Highway 30. It is advertised as "Hell's Gate" because of its unusually violent thermal activity with mud pots bubbling and hot water falls and boiling pools of water. More formally on a map it is known as Tikitere.

A Lakeside Maori Village
Ohinemutu used to be the principal Maori settlement in Rotorua and is near the middle of town beside the lake. There is a meeting house and a tourist store with films and postcards and souvenirs and a place where you can stand behind a carved figure and stick your head out the top and have your friend take your picture.

More interesting, photographically, is the bust of Queen Victoria set in a Maori-type kiosk which is lovely in the sunlight. The bust was a present from Prince Albert, Victoria's second son, who was the country's first royal visitor in 1870.

Part of the complex is the Tudor-styled St Faith's Anglican Church, not only photogenic but historically interesting. The grave of the American minister, Seymour Mills Spencer (1810–1890), a founder of the church, is to the left of the church entrance. Spencer travelled widely on his mission throughout this area. He always carried a large umbrella which he used as a tent and he became known as "the parson with the umbrella". He is seen in the chapel window above the organ preaching to a Maori group with his un-furled umbrella by his side.

Another important grave in the cemetery to the right of the church entrance is that of the colorful Captain Gilbert Mair (1843–1923) who twice saved the local community from annihilation with his troops and was the only European to be made a full chief of the Arawa tribe.

Inside the church are the ancient battle flags carried by the tribal warriors during their wars. The church is also an interesting example of Maori carvings and designs. Unique is a window in the right-hand side chapel with a sandblasted figure of Christ wearing a Maori cloak. When you are seated in a pew facing the chapel, it appears that the figure is walking on the waters of Lake Rotorua seen in the background through the glass.

Inviting Things To Do
There are many attractive activities in Rotorua. One of the first things to do is visit the Government Gardens. Enter through the Princess's Gate because it immediately captures the Victorian era of the enchanting complex.

Dominating the gardens is a massive Tudor structure which was the first bath-house created by the Government to give a European-spa atmosphere to the area. On a sunny weekend when the vast green lawns in front are covered with croquet players and lawn bowlers in their meticulous white uniforms, men and women (but in separate arenas, of course), you shake your head thinking you have been time-transferred back to another age, in another country.

The main building now contains a museum and restaurants. Within the grounds are the Blue Baths and just bordering the grounds are the more popular Polynesian Pools with public swimming pools, hot mineral baths and private baths.

One of the standard tour attractions is the Agrodome on the west side of Lake Rotorua.

The Agrodome offers two shows daily featuring the nineteen different kinds of sheep raised in New Zealand. The sheep are in pens inside the arena so you can inspect them individually. During the show they are released from their pens and individually dash madly on stage and take their place on the tiered levels so they can eat the grain meal in a can at their stations.

There is a fascinating demonstration of sheep shearing. The shearer quickly shears a sheep and then does it again in slow motion, explaining as he goes how he keeps the sheep immobilized by a series of ballet movements and wrestling holds while the electric shearing head never stops cutting. Another demonstration consists of a working heading or "eye" dog and a huntaway sheep dog. These animals are so alive, so quick and keen. The dog demonstrations never last long enough.

To the south of the Agrodome are several natural "springs" turned into tourist attractions featuring rainbow and brown trout, some of which are hand-fed. Fairy Springs, Rainbow Springs and Paradise Valley Springs are all within the same area and all are worth seeing. An interesting side-note: near Paradise Valley Springs is the Ngongotaha Trout Hatchery from which over *six million* eggs have been flown to the USA to be released in the Rocky Mountain waters of Colorado.

To the north of the Agrodome are the Taniwha Springs . . . more trout . . . and the Hamurana Springs which display water fowl and pet deer and have a nine-hole golf course.

There are tours to take you on short excursions, half-day excursions or full day excursions to all the sights in the Rotorua area. One of the favorites is a launch trip to Mokoia Island.

Mokoia Island is in the middle of the Lake Rotorua and is the stage for the Romeo-and-Juliet traditional story of all nations. Hinemoa (Juliet) who lives on the shore loves the prince, Tutanekai (Romeo), of another tribe and the tribe lives on the island of Mokoia.

In this love story Romeo doesn't climb a balcony but Juliet goes for a long swim. Frustrated by the removal of the couple's get-away canoes, she makes waterwings of six calabashes, native gourds, and swims to the island and finds Tutanekai's servant at the island's spring. She insults the servant who returns to Tutanekai. He grabs a club and goes to the spring to revenge the insult to his servant . . . and out of the bushes comes his lover. They live happily ever after.

Part of the island trip to Mokoia is to swim in the lover's pool.

Another unhappier story is the sack of the island by the fierce warrior Hongi Hika who portaged war canoes from the ocean to Rotorua. Hongi Hika had previously visited Europe where he successfully traded gifts for fire-arms. With firepower he devastated his enemies. At Mokoia, it is said, his life was saved by a metal helmet given to him by George IV!

Daytime Sports and Nightime Sports

Trout fishing is a leading sports attraction of the Rotorua area. The lakes of Rotorua, Rotoiti, Okataina and Tarawera rival Taupo in their appeal to the angler.

Lake Tarawera, particularly, has a reputation of having the largest fish because the lake is so rich in smelt. The trout frequently go over five pounds in size. (I fished the lake twice, once with a professional guide and one week-end with friends and never had a nibble.)

Stream mouths and streams are reserved for fly-fishing only. The season is October 1 to June 30. Lake Rotorua is open for fishing all year long.

Bird hunting in the season is to be had in the district and there is also not-too-easy hunting for deer and pig.

The national authority for all hunting and fishing is in Rotorua and if you have any questions or want fishing or hunting guides who will provide you with ground and water transportation, equipment and expertize, check into the Hunting and Fishing Office, Government Tourist Bureau at Fenton and Haupapa streets.

With acres of calm lake waters in the area, water skiing is a natural favorite in Rotorua.

For golfers, besides the nine-hole course at Hamurana, there are three other golf courses. The best . . . and good fun . . . is the Rotorua Golf Club called Arikikapakapa. Eighteen holes, par 70. Free lift if you hit in a mud pot. Visitors are welcome during week days but play is restricted to members during the weekends. Tennis courts can be found at the Government Gardens.

One of the advantages of Rotorua being both a center of Maori culture and a gathering place for international visitors is that the two cultures can cross.

Only Queenstown is as visitor-oriented as Rotorua but the South Island with only 6 percent of the Maori population doesn't enjoy the same Maori heritage.

In Hawaii Polynesian dancers constitute a separate industry and the Hawaiian entertainment and the luau are a standard part of every visitor gathering. This doesn't exist in New Zealand. But in Rotorua the visitor can be sure of seeing the vigorous masculine dancing and the intricate feminine dancing of the Maori.

It is like whare whakairo (carved meeting house) art work. The men are the virile, brutish carvings and the women are the graceful, detailed decorations of the walls and ceilings.

In Rotorua you can attend a hangi, which is the New Zealand native feast.

Being a tourist center there is a comparatively large amount of nightlife.

You can even go dancing at night. And that's not too easy to do in New Zealand.

Our Friendly Farmer

One of the problems in travelling the country by car and then retiring to a dark corner and writing about the travelling is that you don't meet enough New Zealanders.

All those people on tour buses have that driver-guide to bombard with stupid questions but we didn't have such a constant source ... until one day a car drove in the gravel driveway of our lakeside cottage at Taupo and a rolling bulk of a man grunted his way out of the car and came to the door.

He stuck out a hamlike hand and said, "My name's Bruce McKinstry. My sister lives behind Bernie Bookman."

We suddenly were blessed with a great source.

Bruce McKinstry, we found out, is a farmer. A farmer in America is a person who grows crops on a farm but in New Zealand a farmer is also a person who grows livestock on a farm. Later I asked a station owner, "What's the difference between a station owner and a farmer?" He answered, "A farmer is a person who grows *more* on *less*".

Bruce McKinstry leases 500 acres about a half an hour northwest of Taupo where he runs 1,600 ewes, 400 pedigreed rams, about 70 head of cattle. He also raises four boys and four girls. Or his wife, Hilary, does.

He grumbled about the growth of New Zealand. "You know what I can see now from my house? I can see the lights of a neighbor . . . maybe ten miles away . . . but still! I call it slum farming."

How many sheep are there in New Zealand? "Depends when you want to count them. If there are about 40 million breeding ewes in New Zealand and each one on an average has one lamb during the spring plus the 15 million other sheep . . ."

"You mean that (at one time) during the spring there are close to 100 million sheep in New Zealand?"

"You might say that."

"How do you get 40 million ewes pregnant?"

"How do you think? There is no artificial insemination . . . at least not yet. The rams do all the work."

"How many rams does it take?"

"About two percent."

"You mean for every hundred ewes there are only two rams?"

"You might say that."

"How long does that ram have to get the job done?"

"About six weeks. Less. Each ewe has a cycle during an eighteen-day period. We expect that after two cycles she will be with lamb."

"My God, that is a lot of work on the ram!"

"Oh," rolling in the chair, "they don't seem to mind."

Later at his farm, Bruce showed us how each ewe and lamb and ram is tagged by number and the production of the ewe is meticulously recorded as to lambing, lamb weight, etc. The performance of the rams is likewise recorded. All of the statistics are fed into a computer in Hamilton and the ewes and rams who don't meet the criteria of performance are culled out.

He showed us samples of wool and how the wool is graded for weight and texture and told us how he communicates with his list of prospects for the annual sale of pedigreed rams. He even had sales promotional gimmicks to promote the name of his farm *Craig Royston*. Key rings and monogrammed tee shirts made in Hong Kong. Slum farming indeed.

The McKinstry family was one of our Taupo delights. Bruce's attitude towards food, meat in particular, was typically New Zealand forthright: "I like mutton. It's better than lamb, you know. More flavor. You don't want to eat those wee little things. I like a good piece of beef. Veal is all right but it has to be red. Not this pink stuff. Like pork that is almost as white as the fat around it. Who would want to eat that? Argh! I like my meat just salted and peppered. Don't need any of those fancy sauces, you know. We have the best meat in the world. Why spoil it? You know why the French have all those fancy sauces, don't you? Cover up the smell of bad meat. That's the truth."

The McKinstry boys use Yamaha motorcycles to work the sheep. The bikes are known as "Japanese quarter horses" in farming circles.

Doug, the nineteen-year oldest son, brought us a Christmas tree and stayed and had a beer and talked about his passion: hunting. Later when we were leaving the farm after a visit he presented us with a side of ribs from a wild pig he had shot.

What do you do with a side of wild pig ribs?

We marinated the meat in wine and onion and garlic and spices for twenty-four hours . . . put it in the oven at 500°F for 15 minutes . . . and then reduced the heat to slightly less than 200°F and cooked it all day. Fantastic.

Everybody visiting New Zealand for more than four weeks should be assigned a friendly farmer.

The Lady Navigator had a tooth problem, went to a Taupo dental clinic. Young dentist, recently graduated from the dental school at Otago University, was enraptured by all the American goldmetal work. The Lady Navigator said afterwards that she didn't know whether she was a patient or a laboratory specimen.

Bridge repair cost $7.50.

I had to have a prescription renewed and the chemist said he couldn't do it without a New Zealand doctor's okay. Went to local medical clinic. Saw doctor. Got advice to lay back on red wine and cabbage and picked up new prescription. Office call: $3. Prescription cost: no charge.

A Maori "Do"

Not long before leaving New Zealand, we were invited back to Turangi at the south end of Lake Taupo to play in a Maori golf tournament and stay for the hangi that followed.

A hangi in Turangi. It sounded like a lynching party in a Colorado cowtown.

The golf tournament was joyous. I played with a 245-pound Maori golfer who hit cross-handed. He drove a golf ball out of sight. There were tents with libations scattered around the course and the participants were never dry. At one point my partner hit out of the woods to the skirt of a refreshment tent and had a fine recovery shot and a cold beer at the same time.

The hangi that followed the tournament was delicious.

The hangi is like the Hawaiian luau with modifications. The luau usually has only pork cooked in the underground imu. In New Zealand the cooking pit with the charcoal fired stones is called an umu and the meat is a combination of pork, lamb and chicken and the three meats add their flavors to each other. Fantastic. There were mussels, raw fish marinated in coconut juice, potatoes, dressing, etc.

After the hangi was finished the golf prizes were awarded.

The Lady Navigator won a tea set. She in turn made a pretty speech and presented the tea set to a young Maori lady who had sat for seven hours out in the sun helping to run the tournament. The Maoris thought this a splendid gesture and stamped their feet and clapped and shouted. She was almost adopted into the tribe.

Speeches were made. More prizes awarded. The beer and other beverages were flowing freely. Music started with a piano accompanied on a single-string base instrument attached to a wooden box. A guitar joined. There was singing and Maori dancing. All spontaneous, loud and raucous.

How late a hangi lasts depends only on the endurance of the guests. We had the drive back to Taupo in front of us and we sneaked out early.

The button on the evening was provided several days later when we returned from a trip to Wellington. There was a package and a letter from the young Maori lady who received the tea set. The package was an illustrated book about New Zealanders with outstanding full-color photographs. It was a book we had seen in all the bookstores but we had never bought. An expensive present.

The letter said . . . "your kind gesture will never be forgotten." And it was signed "Arohanui . . . lots of love. The Lady on the 12th hole."

What do you do?

New Zealanders!

6. Swing To The East

An Exploding Island ... Captain Cook's First Landing ... A Nifty Golf Course ... A County Fair ... and A Vineyard Visit

Leaving Rotorua on Highway 30, you pass by the "Hell's Gate".

Further on in the clean, spring day are the waters of Lake Rotoiti (Little Lake) which are famous for trout fishing. Before you leave the lake you pass by the gates of Moose Lodge where Queen Elizabeth spent a five-day vacation on her New Zealand visit in 1953–54. Across the lake on Highway 33 is Okere Falls and the start of a sightseeing launch trip that includes a lakeside look at Moose Lodge.

The next lake, Lake Rotoehu, is separated from Lake Rotoiti by a rich stretch of forest known as Hongi's Track. The invading warrior chief on a mission of revenge for the murder of a nephew sailed from the Bay of Islands to the Bay of Plenty and portaged his war canoes across land and through a series of lakes to reach Rotorua. This mile-long stretch of forest is a memento of the raid.

About half-way through the track you should be prepared to stop at a fenced-off tree on the north side of the highway. This tree was planted, it is said, by a Maori chieftainess in honor of the place where she met her husband. If you make a speech in honor of the tree and leave a fern branch at its base, you can go on your journey protected against evil spirits.

The last lake in the series is Lake Rotoma, a quiet area, sparsely sprinkled with vacation homees.

The drive into Whakatane is through timber land, orchards and, of course, sheep and cattle pastoral land. Whakatane, with a population of about 7,000, is one of the principal coastal towns of the Bay of Plenty, so called by Captain Cook after having been well provisioned on his first visit to New Zealand, in contrast at his first landfall to the south, where he had nothing but trouble and called the area Poverty Bay.

Whakatane was the site of one of the landings of Kupe and also of one of the *"Great Migration"* canoes in the 14th century. According to the legend, Whakatane derived its name from the daughter of the canoe's captain. The men of the canoe had gone ashore to explore leaving the women on board. The canoe lost its anchorage and started drifting to the sea. Now, the giant paddles of the canoe were tapu (forbidden) to women but the captain's daughter in desperation seized a paddle saying, "Ka whakatane au i ahau" ("I will act as a man"). The other women followed her example and they brought the canoe back to shore.

Whakatane means to be manly. Women's liberation came early to the Bay of Plenty and there is a statue to the captain's daughter, Wairaka, at Whakatane Heads.

We reached the town just in time for morning tea and decided on the seawall as a good spot. To the left in the bay was Whale Island and straight in front –

"Look!"

There was White Island shooting up a gigantic mushroom of white steam just like it probably was doing when Captain Cook named it 200 years ago.

We took it for granted that the island always acted in such spectacular fashion, only to learn later that it had just erupted an hour and a half before we arrived.

Above the town is Puketapu Lookout, a sacred place to the Maori, and you are asked to behave accordingly. On top of the lookout you have a spectacular sweep of the mountain ranges, the fertile valley and the Bay of Plenty. The local Rotary Club has mounted a plaque to remind the visitor that he is facing the ocean called "Pacific" meaning *peaceful* and asks the visitor to pray that the many countries and people who border these waters will live in peace.

In the middle of the town is a high, tumbling waterfall and, in contrast to the frontier-Victorian wooden-faced stores there is an incongruous modern fountain. Also if you have occasion to go out to the airport . . . the golf course is adjacent to the airport and you will see one of the world's most eye-popping, small-town air terminals. It looks like it was designed for Disneyland.

There is a variety of things to do in Whakatane. Besides playing golf and visiting the airport, where you can book scenic flights, there is Ohope, a popular bathing beach, trout fishing on four rivers, hot springs, jet-boat trips up the Rangitaiki river, big-game fishing charters, and good hiking parties. The local Public Relations office has specific information and can help arrange your activities.

From Whakatane you take the road along the ocean beach and skirt Ohiwa Harbor to reach Opotiki, whose name means "the place

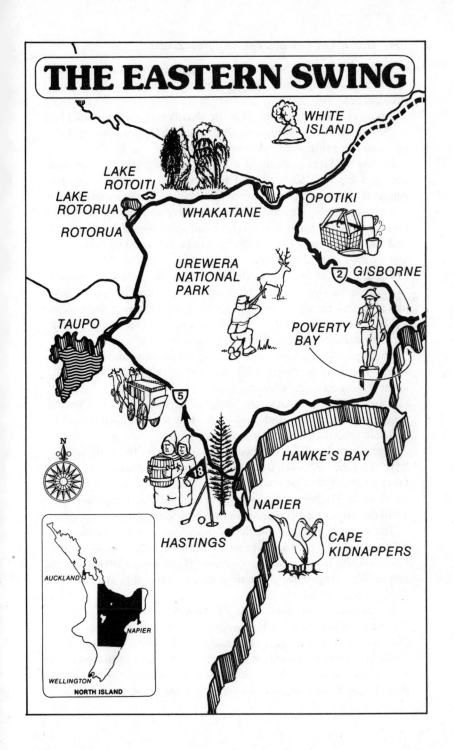

THE EASTERN SWING

WHITE ISLAND

LAKE ROTOITI

LAKE ROTORUA

ROTORUA

WHAKATANE

OPOTIKI

UREWERA NATIONAL PARK

GISBORNE

POVERTY BAY

TAUPO

HAWKE'S BAY

NAPIER

HASTINGS

CAPE KIDNAPPERS

N

AUCKLAND

NAPIER

WELLINGTON

NORTH ISLAND

of many children". It is a pretty little farming town especially with the three Victorian hotels freshly painted. Church Street, the main street, is peaceful.

It is all very much in contrast to the ghastly tragedy that took place in 1865. In 1859 a Lutheran minister came to Opotiki to establish a mission. His name was Carl Sylvius Volkner.

During a Maori uprising of a violent warring sect the Reverend removed his wife to Auckland but returned to be with his parishioners. He was taken prisoner by the head of the rabid sect and was subsequently hanged. His eyeballs were gouged from his head and eaten by the warring chief, his head was severed from his body and the chalice was filled with his blood and the cup was passed among the frenzied warriors.

The Church of St Stephen the Martyr stands in singular peace in the middle of Opotiki. The blood-stained chalice, Volkner's Bible and his colleague's book are on exhibit. Photographs of the time are by the font including a bust shot of Kereopa, the sect's fanatic, who was subsequently captured and hanged in Napier.

More pleasant occupations can be found seaward of Opotiki. There are long stretches of beach safe for swimming, surfing, spear-fishing and skin-diving.

South of Opotiki is Urewera National Park which offers excellent hunting for deer, pig and wild goat. There is a Public Relations Office in Opotiki for visitor assistance.

From Opotiki to Gisborne you have a choice of two routes. If you have the time, the coastal route (the East Cape road) to Gisborne takes in many fine beaches, swimming and fishing, camping and picnic spots. Highly scenic it is just over 200 miles in length and takes a full day. It is a favorite drive among New Zealanders.

The second route is through Waioeka Gorge, also a scenic drive following the Waioeka River to its head. It takes less than three hours to drive from Opotiki to Gisborne if you don't stop for a picnic lunch. We stopped for a picnic lunch because that is what New Zealand is all about.

At the usual well-marked *REST AREA* we turned off and, following a slightly used road, meandered down to a cliff overlooking the river and pulled into the shade of the trees. Out came the chilly-bin. First a cold splash of sherry to take away the dust of the road, then cold sliced chicken eaten with the fingers, hunks of bread slathered with New Zealand butter, hot-house tomatoes, an icy beer.

The sun is warm. The river murmurs. The birds sing everywhere. The day is suddenly sleepy.

"Without looking at your watch, my walking chronometer, tell me what time it is," Lady Navigator said.

"It is exactly one-thirty."

"Now look."

"It is one forty-two."

"You are really going to hell."

And that, in a Year of Saturdays, was the last thing heard before taking a nap.

The First City in The World to See The Sun

Self-disparagement is an art form of New Zealanders. Listen in silence. Never agree.

I remember once being asked after I had played a certain golf course how I liked it. "Oh," I said. "I thought the front nine provided very interesting golf."

"And what was the matter with the back nine?"

You can imagine then the ironic pleasure that the people of Gisborne take with the name *Poverty Bay*. As you roll down into the valley you pass acres of corn fields, rich pastoral lands, vineyards. It is a fat countryside.

Gisborne itself is the market center for the farms and sheep and cattle stations of Poverty Bay. With a population over 30,000 it is a popular recreational center as well as a market center. The limited number of motels makes it advisable to have a reserved room before departing for Gisborne.

There is excellent surfing in the area. Young men with their noses pointed like young bloodhounds towards the waves are everywhere. Besides surfboards they surf in kayaks. Spectacular.

Behind the principal city beach of Waikanae there is Churchill Park which has public tennis courts. Also dressing rooms, a childrens' playground, pool and camping grounds.

Gisborne offers two titles for self-promotion. One is the *"City of Bridges"* because it is situated on three rivers. The other title is the *"First City In The World To See The Sun Every Day."* (Later on when you are in Napier you will see their self-promotional title of "the first *principal* city to see the sun every day".)

But the reason to be in Gisborne is to make the pilgrimage to the spot where Captain Cook made his first landing.

At the foot of Kaiti Hill at Kaiti Beach, there is a Cook Memorial monument. The inscription reads: "This Memorial is erected to commemorate the first landing in New Zealand at Poverty Bay of Captain Cook on Sunday, 8th October, 1769." The date is now considered to be in error; the true date being a day later. No matter.

You have to stand in awe of this man, Captain Cook, who made three incredible ventures into the Pacific from England. You find his mark everywhere in the Pacific. From that day in October in 1769 until February 13th in 1778 in Kealakakua Bay in Hawaii where he was killed, in eight and a half years he literally explored a new world from Bering Straits to the Antarctic.

Kealakakua Bay in Hawaii is a dreamy, tropical spot with amber blue water and coconut trees overhanging the beaches. Such a contrast to the beginning here at raw Kaiti Beach.

Later you climb unwisely to the top of Kaiti Hill. "You could have driven!"

There is a splendid lookout here with a noble statue of Captain Cook with his back to Poverty Bay and, in the distance, Young Nick's Head, so named for the cabin boy, Nick Young, who was first to spot the whitecliffed headlands, the first landfall for the *Endeavour* in New Zealand.

At Gisborne you can play tennis, play golf, and have all of the marine sports. You can go deep-sea fishing and you can take bus or air tours.

The dining is somewhat limited. You ask the motel proprietor about the restaurant with the French name down the road.

"Oh, it's run by a couple of English girls who do different things with food, you know."

Silence.

"Like put leeks on your steaks."

Silence.

"If you like leeks on your steaks."

Silence.

"Personally I don't like leeks on my steaks."

That convinced us we should try the French restaurant but we fell asleep watching Sgt Bilko on television.

In Gisborne a butcher before the Labor Day weekend advertised: "For your weekend barbecue: 5 pounds sausage, 5 pounds lamb chops, 5 pounds steak: $10."

In Gisborne the second-story house on Childers Road is made out of the bridge of a wrecked vessel, *The Star of Canada.* It looks very comfortable there on Childers Road.

In Gisborne you go into an antique store and find out what you already know. People around the world are aware of the value of antiques and there aren't any great bargains any more.

From Poverty Bay to Hawke's Bay

The coastal drive from Gisborne to Napier on Highway 2 is a roller coaster ride.

You pass by Morere Hot Springs and through the town of Wairoa which has a lighthouse by the main street and peaceful rest areas. About 15 miles from Napier you come to a lake lined with weeping willows, Lake Tutira, which is now a bird sanctuary named by a farmer-author, Herbert Guthrie-Smith. The lake has an excellent reputation for fishing.

As you approach Napier sitting up on a bluff you are reminded of Mt St Michel in France which is reached by a causeway. Napier looks like a walled city.

Before 1931 it virtually was an island city almost surrounded by water. But on February 3, 1931 the entire Hawke's Bay area was shaken by a tremendous earthquake that reduced most of the buildings of Napier and neighbouring Hastings to the ground. What the earthquake didn't destroy the subsequent fires did. For ten days the earth continued to shake. But what nature destroyed was compensated by the phenomenon of the bottom of the inner harbor rising as much as eight feet above sea level giving Napier land on which to expand. Over 8,000 acres were reclaimed from the sea by the earthquake.

Napier with a population of 45,000 is a hustling city. Nowhere does the visitor receive more promotional literature than in Napier.

Center of the tourist attraction is the ocean-front mall and highway called the Marine Parade. Flanked by stately Norfolk pines the Marine Parade extends a "golden mile" which really is intended to be walked.

You'll pass by the Marineland where dolphins and seals put on their shows, a kiwi house where live kiwis can be seen, a new aquarium, a floral clock, an outdoor concert park, swimming pools, a boating lake, restaurants, rest areas. An excellent focal point for the visitor.

Just off of the Marine Parade on Coote street is the comparatively new Centennial Rock Garden which features an artificial 75-foot waterfall and attractive rock pools surrounded by many native shrubs and plants.

If you continue up Coote street you will find "Scenic Drive" markers which will take you to Lighthouse Road and to the Bluff Hill Look Out. You'll pass by old wooden residences that survived the earthquake. From Bluff Hill you can see everything from the airfield to Cape Kidnappers. Splendid view.

Napier is a city of parks. One of the more splendid is the hillside Botanic Gardens which forms a natural bowl and you think, "What a great place to hold a concert" and you are pleased to learn that is just what they do. There is also an aviary which holds many gorgeously colored birds, not easily identifiable from the cage inscriptions but enjoyable just the same. Peacocks preen outside their cages unrestrained. A permanent cage of kiwis is kept here but because the kiwis come out only at night and the Botanical Gardens shut their gates at sunset, one doesn't see a kiwi.

Adjacent to the Gardens is a cemetery with the headstones of many prominent people associated with the history of New Zealand.

If you are not a headstone hunter but a rose hunter there is the Kennedy Park Rose Garden with over 3,000 bushes and if you are a model nut there is a Lilliput Village with a working model railway, etc.

One of the principal attractions at Hawke's Bay is the gannet bird colony at Cape Kidnappers, 13 miles south of Napier. The spectacular diving gannet, which we saw in action at the Bay of Islands, comes here to nest starting in October. At one time there are over 10,000 of the golden-crowned birds in the sanctuary. A bus tour visits the colony daily from October to March (minimum 8 passengers). The cost is $5.

Or, as an alternative you can drive about ten miles south of Napier to the Wyfold Riding School and join a Pony Safari and take a conducted ride along the beach to the gannet sanctuary.

We were just a week too early to see the first gannets but, by luck, we were just in time to see what we would call a County Fair, the Hawke's Bay Agricultural and Pastoral Show.

First, however, we wanted to test the local golf and after calling the secretary of the Napier Golf Club we were on the tee of a nifty, tree-lined 18-hole course by ten o'clock in the morning. This course dates back to 1895. The 6,555 yards of fairways are divided into three parcels and you are frequently crossing a road to reach a new hole. It is a pleasant course that demands more skill in placing the ball where you want it than merely hitting the big ball.

The clubhouse is new and there is a unique Maori carving at the entrance showing one figure with a carved golf club and ball on top of another carved figure with golf club and ball. The upper figure represents Kurupo Tareha, whose family owned all the surrounding land and who was an amateur champion of New Zealand, and the bottom figure represents one of his sons, "Cappy", who was also a champion. On display upstairs is a banged up trophy cup which the boys used to use for a chipping target.

We were invited to use the upstairs café and bar service.

The local rules particularly when it comes to natural hazards are always interesting. Here is the (a) ruling for lifting a ball without penalty at the Napier Golf Club:

> *If embedded (sucker) in a wheel rut, on or touching dung, in a rabbit scrape, within two lengths of a staked tree, fixed seat, stile, water tap, hydrant, hydrant cover or grave.*

Green fees are $3. Trundlers: 20c.

Every district in New Zealand has its "A & P" show. The *Agricultural* refers to the farm produce and the *Pastoral* refers to the livestock. Because the economy of New Zealand rests so heavily on its agricultural and pastoral industries, the A & P shows are important events.

The farmer, and his family, come to the show first as professionals to buy and to sell. As professionals they also put forth their products to be judged in competition to their neighbors. Then they put their talents up against their neighbors in sheep-shearing contests, wood-chopping and sawing, horsemanship, even apple-packing contests if that is part of the local industry.

They also put their sheep dogs into competitive trials.

Of course, there are carnival attractions for the tots and the teen-agers but these are unimportant compared to the professional aspects of the show.

If you can find an A & P show in your travels, *go.* Even if you have to change your itinerary or detour or lengthen your stay, *go.*

The day we went to the Hawke's Bay A & P show at Hastings it was People's Day which meant a public holiday. (There are lots of public holidays in New Zealand.) The shops in Napier and Hastings were shut tight. Everybody went to the show.

It was a sunny, spring day and there were thousands of people. Farmers and wives and children. The shop keepers. The school kids on vacation.

Many were having tea under umbrellas in the parking lot. Many of the men were in the bar under the grandstand sloshing down beer in huge quantities. There wasn't a seat in the grandstand to be had.

We arrived just in time to see the last dog go through his paces in the sheepdog finals. What a marvel. You can almost feel the dog thinking as he stops and starts, cat-crawls, darts quickly to one side or the other, constantly moving half a dozen sheep forward through a series of fences and enclosures.

The dog trials were followed by the equestrian events and there were horses everywhere. It was a mammoth part of the A & P show.

We witnessed an apple-packing contest. While we watched a team of two women packed 125 cartons of apples in 75 minutes.

Sheep dominated the show. Different strains of sheep were on display and judged for quality. They were being offered for stud, offered for sale.

There was a display and competition of wool.

There were exhibits and demonstrations of farm machinery, cars, trucks, boats.

We watched sheep-shearing and wood chopping. And we watched the squealing girls on the carnival rides and ate a hot dog impaled on a stick and dipped in mustard.

It was great.

Another thing not to be missed in New Zealand is dinner at one of the local hotels.

We inquired of our hotel proprietress for a dinner recommendation. She said there was a new French restaurant in town "but all they want to do is feed you and turn you out."

She recommended the *Masonic Hotel* on Marine Parade and that was where we went.

My turtle-neck sweater and gabardine golf jacket were out of place. I should have been in coat and tie. But the setting was ideal. High ceiling, bandstand. English decorum. The dinner included soup, salad, fish, main dish, dessert. Coffee and liqueur were served in the lounge after dinner.

Our scurrying waitress of eighteen years old blushed and said, "Thank you" with every sentence.

The golf, the county fair, the "hotel" dinner was all of a period that could have been somewhere in America . . . in the twenties. It was the way the world used to be and it was very pleasant.

Things to Do

At Hawke's Bay there are many active or spectator diversions depending upon the visitor and the time of year.

There are two other golf courses besides Napier. There are a dozen public tennis courts, asphalt covered, at Onekawa Park. There is surfing, swimming, skating and sailing. If you want to go deep-sea fishing or just cruise the bay, it is all available.

And of course city bus tours, and there is a scenic drive which is worthwhile if you don't take a bus tour.

If you really get stuck for something to do, Napier offers you a number of factory tours including a tour of a fertilizer plant.

The district has a number of wineries which are open to the public.

7. A Swing To The West

An Underground Concert ... Homage to Sir Peter ... The Do-It-Yourself 10c Waterfall ... The Home of Blue Vein Cheese ... A Splendid Canoe Complete With Battle Scars

The solo feminine voice quavered on the first notes of *"Some Day We'll Meet Again"*. Then the voice became firmer and stronger and by the end of the first chorus the voice was sure and sweet. At the beginning of the second chorus the audience started to join in and the volume in the underground cavern became wondrously full and by the completion of the song one was tempted to cry and applaud at the same time.

The scene was in *The Cathedral* at the Waitomo Caves, probably New Zealand's leading tourist attraction.

The Cathedral is a natural vaulted cave with a 50-foot ceiling which with its hollowed limestone walls forms a perfect acoustiitti-callal chambeeber. Opera stars, rock artists, world-famous choirs have all come here to perform for themselves and to record professionally in this renown room. A volunteer vocalist in the group following our group had done us the service of singing and providing a memorable moment.

Waitomo, forty-six miles south of Hamilton, is a vast area of limestone formations over millions of years old carved by the seepage of water through lime. Long known to the Maoris, the area was discovered in 1887 by the Europeans and by 1910 there was a hotel catering to visitors who then and now come from around the world.

Three caves are open to the public with guided tours. The most popular cave is the Waitomo Cave with its entrancing Glow-Worm Grotto. Two nearby caves are the Aranui and the Ruakuri which are known for their limestone formations. Colored lighting has been used with theatrical effect to accent the formations in all the caves.

We arrived early from Taupo and had a cup of tea in the sunny parking lot and then joined a tour group of Australians. The young tour guide with walking-stick-cum-pointer led us into the well-lighted rooms and we proceeded from chamber to chamber admiring the formations of stalagmites and stalactites.

In the Cathedral we had our concert and then we descended into a darkened room to allow our eyes to become accustomed to the dark and we heard again about the remarkable New Zealand glow-worm. A member of the gnat family, the strongest survives by eating its sisters and brothers and later on its aunts and uncles. By a bio-chemical process using its bodily content (there is no waste), the glow-worm manufactures a light which it can turn on and off at will. It lowers a threadlike antenna from its body and with its light attracts insects which are floated into the caverns on the underground waters. The insects head for the lights, become entangled with the sticky tentacles and become morning tea.

After several months of this happy existence the larva hatches into a mouthless fly which either dies from starvation or is eaten by its admiring surrounding relatives. The space between glow-worms is the respectful distance given by territorial prerogative.

We descended to the river level and in the semi-darkness were shepherded into a boat and with the guide hand-pulling the boat on overhead wires we floated into black. Overhead became filled with a myriad of lights, a star-filled sky, and in the silence requested by the guide to keep from frightening the sensitive glow-worms we glided on a magic river.

The boat ride doesn't last long enough – but what would be enough?

In a few minutes we were back on land and out in the sunshine.

We drove back to the Waitomo Hotel, another one of the Government-owned hotels. All seem to be blessed by the same graciousness. Why this is we don't know. Internationally, Government ownership of a service business and graciousness never seem to go hand in hand but in the New Zealand hotel enterprise graciousness survives.

Part of the Waitomo's attractiveness is its antiquity. In the center of the hotel is a small two-room museum which is worth visiting if only to see the costumes issued to visitors in 1910 for trips to the caves: smocks, hats, gloves, hobnailed boots and kerosene lamps. The only thing missing was a prayer book. In those days they climbed down on rope ladders.

Outside the hotel is an enchanting little garden where you can take pictures of each other.

The vicinity offers good fishing and golfing which the hotel can fill you in on or inquire at the modern tavern at the bottom of the hill opposite the post office where you also buy your cave-guided tickets if you are not on a tour.

Heading south on Highway 3 towards New Plymouth you pass through the town of Te Kuiti. Beyond the railroad tracks on the left you will see a Maori building which was built under the direction of a famous rebel, Te Kooti, while he lived in the area under sanctuary of the Maori king. If you have now become interested in Maori carving, it is worth a stop.

It was raining off and on. Finally in a break of sunshine we pulled off the road on a green bank on the crest of a hill for picnic lunch. Beneath us was the idyllic pastoral setting dotted with sheep, of course. A green blanket of grass stretched down to a pond of water in the center of which was a small island budding with wild flowers . . . and wild ducks at rest.

To the left, barely seen through the trees, was a white farmhouse, the road leading to it bordered by a deliberate design of multi-colored trees.

We stretched out the wool robe and had our sherry and chicken and cheeses and tomatoes and eggs in peace.

In our travels we have visited castles and chateaux and villas. We've been in penthouses, townhouses and mountain lodges. But the sight of many of the farmhouses or station houses ("homesteads") in New Zealand, situated on elevated heights, backed with the wind-breaking greenery, with a long line of trees curving on the roadside to the mainhouse, looks like a most enviable housing situation. The fact that you might see an adjacent helicopter now and then gives you the idea that the inhabitants are not suffering.

Approaching the coast from the north you enter the Awakino Gorge following the Awakino river to the coast town of Awakino. There is good fishing here and in the rivers further south.

Only 20 miles from New Plymouth, a sign at the left of the highway says "HISTORICAL SITE".

You are at Urenui, once a densely populated area of the Maori, a place of many battles and bloodshed.

Towards the beach is swimming and picnicing. Towards the hills is the resting place of one of New Zealand's most known citizens, Sir Henry Peter Buck. Born with the name of Te Rangi Hiroa this

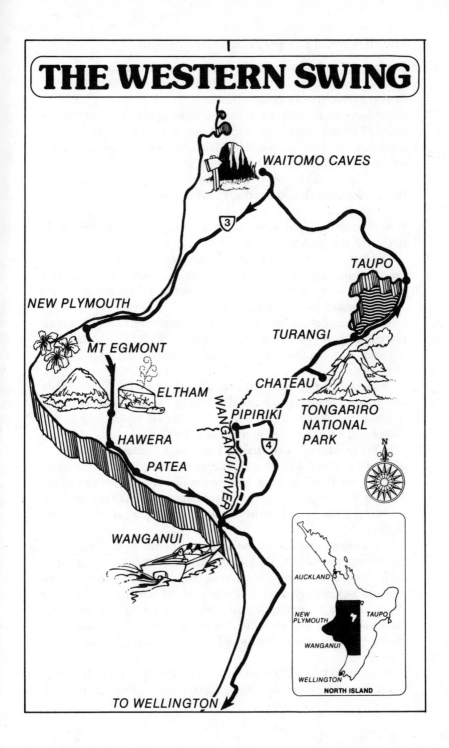

THE WESTERN SWING

WAITOMO CAVES

③

NEW PLYMOUTH

TAUPO

MT EGMONT

TURANGI

ELTHAM

CHATEAU

WANGANUI RIVER

PIPIRIKI

④

TONGARIRO
NATIONAL
PARK

HAWERA

PATEA

N

WANGANUI

AUCKLAND

NEW
PLYMOUTH

TAUPO

WANGANUI

TO WELLINGTON

WELLINGTON

NORTH ISLAND

handsome combination of Polynesian and Caucasian became in time an outstanding anthropologist and was the Director of the Bishop Museum in Honolulu, Hawaii.

His ashes lie at Okoki Pa. From the highway it looks like there is a white flagpole erected at the site but as you drive to the hillside you see the 20-foot concrete symbolic canoe-prow painted white and red. At the bottom of the memorial is Buck's tombstone.

From here you look out over the countryside and the Tasman Sea. It is a most unusual and impressive memorial.

New Plymouth is a port town . . . the largest cheese exporting town in the world, the guidebook says.

The beauty of New Zealand is in its country. There is not much beauty in the cities or towns of New Zealand except what the New Zealanders bring from the country into the city. That is why we are always heading for the parks.

This is particularly true in New Plymouth where early residents placed two parks back to back, Pukekura Park and Brooklands, and adjoined a race course for good measure – all in the middle of the city.

Brooklands has a giant puriri tree reputed to be 2,000 years old and a giant chestnut tree planted by one of the first pioneers.

The Rhododendron Dell and the Azalea Dell were both in full bloom and a stunning vision of multi-colors.

In the middle of Pukekura Park is a large boating lake which is divided by *The Poet's Bridge*. The name came from a racehorse called "The Poet" and the money for the bridge came from the winning bet on the horse. The donor later committed suicide from the bridge which gives you the thought that he later bet on the wrong horse.

The Fernery and the Begonia House connected by tunnels are highly recommended by the local residents. Best of all is the genuine, do-it-yourself, ten-cents-for-ten-minutes, thirty-foot-waterfall-complete-with-changing-lights. At the foot of the boating lake near the main entrance is a dry, high wall of stones set on different descending levels. On a tree at about five o'clock from the wall is a red machine. You put in ten cents and turn the handle and marvels on marvels . . . .

Water starts cascading from the top of the high wall and bouncing down the different levels, colored lights come up from underneath the shelves of water and the lights change from yellow to pink to green to orange. It's your own personal, do-it-yourself waterfall. Glorious.

The Pukekura Park with Brooklands has a reputation of being one of the best, if not *the* best in the country . . . and in a country where parks are superior it is a must-see for a visitor.

We went from one end of New Plymouth to the other. At the northern end is Fitzroy Beach with surfboarders in rubber body suits. At the south end is Centennial Park with surfboarders in rubber body suits.

Halfway between is Kawaroa Seaside Park which has a pool complex, squash and tennis courts.

We went from one lookout to another lookout, four lookouts in fact, and there wasn't really that much to look at.

Adjacent to the New Plymouth Power Station Lookout however is a pinnacle rock with paths leading up the sides and a sign advising that climbers may do so at their own risk. We didn't care to risk.

The New Plymouth power station is fed by natural gas which is an important economic factor in this part of the island. There is information and explanations at the lookout site if the visitor wishes to explore it further.

We visited St Mary's Church on Marsland Hill. Founded by Bishop Selwyn in 1842 it is the oldest *stone* church in the country and has a charming garden setting. Behind the church is a short walk lined with cherry blossom trees which were in full bloom. Along the walk are white, three-seater ornamental, wrought-iron chairs. Perfect in their place.

Beside the church is the original church bell which had been in continuous use since the church's founding until the weekend before our arrival a choir boy used it too vigorously and the clapper fell out.

Behind the church is another lookout.

In back of New Plymouth is Mt Egmont, a snow-capped, perfectly-shaped volcanic cone rising over 8,000 feet. (On New Year's Eve the local caper is to climb the peak and light a bonfire.)

In our motel room there was a picture of Mt Egmont with a bromide caption: "It is said if you can see Mt Egmont clearly, it is going to rain. If you can't see Mt Egmont, it is raining."

From all the lookouts we couldn't see Mt Egmont.

The next morning was spring-clear, the air was fresh-washed and the sun was sparkling on picture-postcard pretty Mt Egmont. We called the New Plymouth Golf Club, one of several in the city, and asked if we could play. The morning was too good to resist. "No trouble at all," was the response.

In a few minutes we were on a park-like golf course with Mt Egmont beaming on us on one side and the Tasman Sea smiling at us on the other.

It was a splendid morning of exercise and easy sightseeing. The water holes on two, six and fourteen were memorable, particularly on fourteen where a pair of grey heron took off across the fairway and landed on a nearby tree and, after we had played through, flew right back to the pond again.

The clubhouse at New Plymouth is a two-story, white gracious relic. It smells. It creaks. It is filled with a million memories.

The secretary at the new clubhouse at Napier had said, "We bit the bullet three years ago. You'll find most golf clubs in New Zealand facing the same decision. Destroy what is dear . . . and inefficient . . . and start over again. Or hang on for a few more years." New Plymouth is hanging on.

We finished our round, changed shoes and headed off around the mountain towards Wanganui.

There are several optional routes around Mt Egmont. The longer route, 111 miles, takes you around the coast with an option of visiting Pukeiti Rhododendron Trust fifteen miles from New Plymouth.

The Pukeiti Rhododendron Trust is a 900-acre reserve started by a handfull of nature lovers twenty-five years ago. Today it has a membership of over 3,000 and people come from all over the world to enjoy its flowers and streams and birds. If you are in the Taranaki area which is the New Plymouth–Mt Egmont district, in October or November, you can see Pukeiti at its peak.

The shorter route and an excellent straight road from Waitara to the coast town of Hawera takes you through Inglewood, Stratford and Eltham all of which are entrances to the Egmont National Park.

The attraction of the Mount Egmont National Park is in its bush . . . being an isolated peak it has an unusual variety of local flora and fauna . . . and there are many interesting hikes or walks. These start at Stratford Mountain House, Dawson Falls Tourist Lodge and the North Egmont Chalet.

During the winter months of July through September the Stratford Mountain House is a popular base for skiers who go to the

Manganui ski fields.

The hike to the top of Mt Egmont is not considered difficult but changing weather conditions can make it perilous. Experienced hikers make the climb without guides. But overseas visitors should not climb without a guide provided from the membership of the Taranaki Alpine Club. For details get in touch with the Egmont National Park Board.

All of the above is written with a certain feeling of guilt because we didn't go to Pukeiti and we didn't climb Mt Egmont.

All of the North Island was abloom in stunning displays of rhododendrons and azaleas from the simplest home garden to the most formal parks, and while we should have seen what must be a dazzling display of hundreds of different varieties together putting on a show at one time, we passed.

The reason was gastronomic. When we were in Kerikeri at the Bay of Islands we were introduced to an outstanding blue cheese. It is called simply Blue Vein and it comes from a dairy town, Eltham, thirty-three miles from New Plymouth. Eltham was on the short route of our map.

Bypassing the other attractions after golf at the New Plymouth Country Club we hastened towards Eltham where we had lunch at a take-away restaurant. "Steak sandwich: 50c. Tomato sandwich: 45c" said the wall menu. Gives you a quick economic picture of the relationship between meat and vegetable prices. Lady Navigator often spent more at the greengrocer's than at the butcher shop.

There are all kinds of fanatics in the world and we are priviliged to have among our acquaintances several cheese fanatics who die in loud pleasure at the proper marriage of the right cheese with the right wine. We haven't entered that lunatic circle but there is a touch of heaven in, say, a Stilton cheese with a pile of walnuts, a cut of cold apple and a bottle of good port, isn't there?

We asked the proprietress if there were a place in town where we could find samples of the Eltham cheeses and she directed just around the corner.

We wandered all over "just around the corner" not knowing what we were looking for until we found the offices of the New Zealand Co-operative Rennet Company. In a display case outside the office was a variety of their novelty cheeses and a red-haired, blue-eyed lass to help us.

We bought a three-pound round of Blue Vein, the last of their

Swiss-style Gruyère for a fondue, a delicious Danish Havarti, a wedge of Gouda and a wedge of Romano. The whole packet cost less than $5.

It was in this area of Taranaki that the export dairy industry of New Zealand was born, not, as one would expect from an immigrant English dairyman, but from a Chinese gold digger who came to Otago in the goldrush of 1866 and expanded into exporting of scrap metal to China. In the Taranaki district he found an edible fungus and bought it from the local farmers who still refer to the fungus as *Taranaki Wool*.

The fungus is the base for the Blue Vein cheese which is not as strong as the Italian Gorgonzola or the French Roquefort but is creamier and has a more delicate tangy taste.

Chew Chong, the Chinese exporter, first sent Eltham butter to England. The venture was a financial failure but it established in time the quality and the price of New Zealand dairy products.

It was a fine lunch hour.

Two outstanding attractions in Wanganui are the Maori church and the museum.

St Paul's Anglican Memorial Church, a block off of Highway 4 is a white, simply-steepled church from the exterior. Its interior is a classic example of modern Maori design and carving. Each wall panel and rafter pattern has to be studied to be appreciated. The infinite precision in execution and the detail in color and line plus the abundance of it all makes the church, referred to as Putiki, a fulfilling part of the New Zealand experience.

In the vestibule of the church is a prayer composed during World War I by the English poet Rupert Brooke:

> *They shall grow not old*
> *As we that are left*
> *Grow old.*
> *Age shall not weary them,*
> *Nor the years condemn,*
> *At the going down of the sun*
> *And in the morning*
> *We shall remember them.*

Further down Highway 4 is Durie Hill. You have two ways of going up to the Lookout Tower. Either drive or take a unique elevator at the Highway level opposite the Wanganui Bridge. The elevator takes you up through the hill. In either case climb the few winding steps to the top of the tower for a sweeping view of the sea, the river, the city and the hills beyond.

Behind this tower is the War Memorial Tower rising another 100 feet which you can also climb. Little boys were throwing fire crackers down the stairs the evening we were there which made a proper loud, echoing sound for the little boys but discouraging for visitors.

The Durie Hill Tennis Club is in the same vicinity.

Still further down Highway 4 (Anzac Parade) is the riverfront James McGregor Memorial Park or Kowhai Park with a children's playground full of wildly imaginative playground equipment. You wished you were a child so you could go play on them.

There is a deer park in Wanganui with deer which, according to the guidebook, will feed out of your hand. They must have been well fed because we couldn't find one to feed.

In the middle of the city is Queen's Park which is given over mainly to public buildings of cultural interest. Here is the public library, an art gallery, a modern convention hall and, best of all, a happy museum.

The Wanganui Public Museum merits three stars. Not only does it have interesting material of local history and Maori culture and natural history but the style of presentation is outstanding and sets a standard not equalled by many museums.

The front room of the museum is devoted to a look back at yesterday in New Zealand. There is a section of a Victorian village reproduced in scale with store-front windows displaying articles of the time. Much intriguing stuff. Great background for antique-ing! A colonial cottage is reproduced with furniture and properly dressed dummies. (Reproducing colonial cottages seems to be a patriotic duty of New Zealand museums.)

Two lovely musical instruments are on display. One is the first organ to be seen in New Zealand. It was given to the missionary brothers Henry and William Williams at Paihia in the Bay of Islands. The organ, vintage 1829, doesn't have a keyboard but plays five hymns from a rotating cylinder, like a player piano. The other instrument is a polythron which rotates a flat, punctuated metal disc by means of a spring. You buy a token from the museum attendant, insert the token in the machine, and the room is filled with a melody by Rossini and in remarkably good tone.

In the second room, a modern addition, is the Maori collection, dominated by a splendid war canoe. Built in 1810 the canoe saw battle action in 1865 and still bears bullet holes in its side. It is named after Hoturoa, the captain of one of the original immigrant canoes, the *Tainui*. This war canoe held seventy men. Although its purpose was functional, the canoe nevertheless carries elaborate carvings and decorations.

Three displays which caught our attention were those showing how the Maoris trapped birds and rats, the magnificent feather cape collection, and a miniature display of the machinery the Maoris used to move giant timber for fortifications and canoe building.

Upstairs in the natural history section is a stunning display of butterflies. Also there is an interesting exhibit of the skeletons of the extinct moa birds which resembled the ostrich and were the initial staple source of food for the earliest arrivals in New Zealand.

The Wanganui Public Museum gets full marks. Leaving it we climbed the steps to the Sarjeant Gallery, a handsome art gallery indeed.

There are three golf courses in Wanganui including a municipal course practically in the middle of town.

The Wanganui river plays an important part in the history of the area and we were determined to take a ride at least part way up the river.

There are several jet-boat rides offered, lasting from one hour on the river to a full day going fifty miles up-river to Pipiriki.

In contrast to the jet-boats, the same company operates a paddle-wheeled river boat which takes you to a picnic park twenty miles up the river. Sounded appealing.

However the day dawned black and rain started to fall so we cancelled any idea of river exploration by boat and settled for the museum and art gallery visit and headed up the river by car and on to Taupo.

You follow the historic river by car as far as Pipiriki. Before the Europeans came the river provided food and a means of transportation for canoes including war canoes such as the one on display in the museum.

The Europeans also found the Wanganui river a logical means of transportation and at one time river boats with a capacity as high as

400 people took the three-day, two-night journey between Wanganui and Taumarunui, a distance of almost 150 miles.

At Pipiriki you can take a jet-boat trip up the river for twenty miles ... the most beautiful stretch of the Wanganui ... and visit the *Drop Scene,* which has the appearance of a mountain dropping into the river as you approach it. Also taking the jet-boat trip you can visit the underground cave behind the waterfall.

Both the river road and the short-cut on Highway 4 to Raetihi provide beautiful scenery. Coming north on Highway 4 towards Lake Taupo you enter Tongariro National Park, one of the three national parks in the North Island.

In a country of contrasts, Tongariro is a contrast within itself. Tall peaks, often white-tipped with snow rise spectacularly out of a desert plain.

These mountains were sacred (tapu) to the Maoris. Their chiefs were buried in the slopes. To protect the venerated ground the land around the peaks (6,500 acres) was given by the Maori chief, Te Heuheu Tukino IV of the Tuwharetoa tribe, to the Government to create a park. This was in 1887, fifteen years after Yellowstone, the first national park in the world. Later the Government added land to the park and it now covers 166,500 acres.

Chateau Tongariro, a Government-owned hotel, is the center of the park's activity with the National Park Headquarters being near the hotel. The hotel itself, a gracious hostelry now being modernized, offers the country's highest golf course (nine holes), tennis, bowls, a putting green.

Featured in the winter time is skiing on Ruapehu.

In the summertime there are a variety of walks to waterfalls (Taranaki Falls, Tawhai Falls), silica springs and mountain streams. Summer mountain flowers dot the landscape.

Permits to hunt red deer and Japanese sika deer are available at the National Park Headquarters.

A good highway connects the Chateau with Turangi on the south shore of Lake Taupo in less than an hour's drive.

8. A Swing To The South

Chocolate-Box Scenery . . . A Parade of Roses . . . the Railroad That Was Thrown Out of Town . . . Masterton . . . The Golden Shears . . . A Farmhouse Holiday . . . A New Sweater, Size Tight

Among the confusing weather report names are *Taihape* and *Manawatu*.

South of Taupo on Highway 1 is the town and area of Taihape. Further south is the river and valley of Manawatu. Palmerston North is the center of the valley and this was our first destination of a southern swing.

After leaving the south shores of Lake Taupo and following the famous Tongariro River into Tongariro National Park, you climb steadily until you reach a desert plateau. It is the only desert of its kind we experienced in New Zealand. To a cattleman in Arizona, the desert of New Zealand would look pretty handsome but it is comparatively barren by New Zealand standards and carries no stock.

It is a fast trip across the tussock-covered plateau with the snow-covered mountain of Ruapehu to the west. After the military camp of Waiouru the desert scenery starts to disappear and in its place from Taihape to Bulls appears a constant presentation of views of delicate beauty.

A sensitive publisher in Wellington voted this Taihape stretch of Highway 1 to be the most splendid drive in New Zealand. The river is banked with white-walled cliffs. You look up valleys into soft banks of green which in turn dissolve into variegated purple hues of distant mountains. In American we would call it "picture postcard" scenery. In New Zealand it is known as "chocolate-box".

When you visit the art galleries of New Zealand you may at first be unimpressed by the almost effeminate art work of New Zealand's earlier painters. Wall after wall of paintings of soft vistas. Quite unlike the vivid green on blue scenics experienced in the farmlands. Then as you tour more and more of New Zealand, you begin to see what the artists were painting. "Oh, there it is," you ultimately find yourself saying. Taihape has that kind of inspirational scenery.

Also in the district are attractive rest areas, and we pulled off into a leaf-shaded nook and had morning tea by a babbling stream.

At Bulls, on your left going through town, is a chocolate-drop Town Hall.

Among the comics the town is referred to as the only place in New Zealand where you can get milk from bulls. It is not funny locally.

Leaving Highway 1 at Sanson, we headed for Palmerston North. You note a difference in the countryside and it is because you are suddenly without surrounding mountains as is the usual case in New Zealand and you are in the fertile plain of Manawatu.

We stopped at a roadside stand and bought strawberries . . . one of many "strawberry stops" . . . and halted again further down the road and bought a head of lettuce which the lady picked fresh out of the field for us. Eighteen cents.

Palmerston North, with a population of almost 60,000, is an orderly, pleasantly laid-out city. The name has an English country-town flavor and the physical appeal of the city with its generous seventeen-acre town square vivid with spring pansies and roses, matches the name.

There is a famous rose garden in Palmerston North and a university that includes a famous agricultural college.

An enjoyable introduction to the city is to enter the Centennial Drive at the Manawatu Golf Club, skirt the golf club fairways on the left and the Centennial Lagoon on the right. Very pretty.

The new Teachers' College comes up on the left and you are on Highway 57. You cross the bridge and following the highway for a mile you come upon Massey University, a handsome plant, its agricultural element befitting an agricultural country.

Going back across the bridge you take the first turn on the left to Victoria Drive to reach the botanical garden. Further on is the Dugald McKenzie Rose Garden.

We found the botanical garden first rate. In less than an hour of strolling we were presented with the flora of New Zealand. A printed pamphlet guides you through the walk. The trees and shrubs are well marked. Even though we were not the thorough students we should have been, the short hour in this garden increased our appreciation of the New Zealand "bush" country we were to see later.

A bonus was having our first fantail birds flutter around us during the stroll.

The Dugald McKenzie Rose Garden was in full bloom and in full sunshine. Symetrically laid out with a fountain in the center . . . and a viewing stand which gives you an elevated platform to look out over the entire garden . . . it was vibrant with every imaginable color, both bold and delicate.

The city has adopted the caption *City of Roses* and here is the reason why it has gained the reputation as the rose center of New Zealand: in addition to the thousands of roses cultivated in the formal garden, Palmerston North has the only Rose Trial Ground in the Southern Hemisphere. Growers throughout the world send un-named roses to be grown throughout all seasons and judged annually for their health and color at the Trial Ground Awards Presentation.

To a rosarian it is all pretty heady stuff. To a non-gardener visitor the variety of rose shapes and sizes and the subtle varieties of colors is a lesson in horticulture.

The Esplanade complex also includes the Lido Swimming Center (three pools), the rugby-cricket-football fields, bowling and croquet grounds and the Manawatu Tennis Club with eleven grass courts.

A short distance from the Manawatu Golf Club is the Palmerston North Golf Club. A signboard beside the club house describes the days and hours of "equal rights" which means that when the ladies aren't playing (Tuesdays) and the men aren't playing (Saturdays) you can play.

After the city was laid out around the pleasant town square, the railroad came to town, split the city down the center and built the railroad station smack dab in the middle. Fitzherbert, whose name you'll find everywhere, was a director of the railroad.

In 1963 however the railway line was pulled out of town center and shifted north and so was the railroad station. The town square returned to its planned glory.

The square is dominated by a clock tower and to one side is a statue of Te Awe Awe (1820–1882), a warrior chief loyal to the Government forces. Donated by his sister Erene, it is a monument poignant in thought and grotesque in execution. You think of a suede-shoe memorial park salesman saying, "Look, Lady, here is the idea we have in mind for your illustrious, beloved brother. . ." It is terrible.

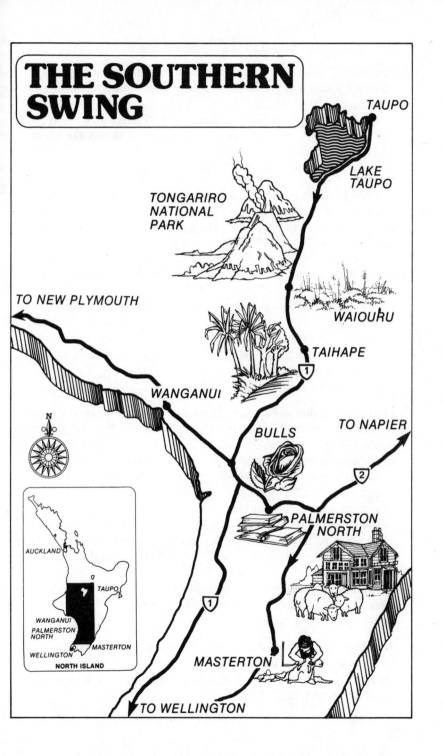

THE SOUTHERN SWING

TAUPO

LAKE TAUPO

TONGARIRO NATIONAL PARK

TO NEW PLYMOUTH

WAIOURU

TAIHAPE

WANGANUI

BULLS

TO NAPIER

N

PALMERSTON NORTH

AUCKLAND

TAUPO

WANGANUI
PALMERSTON NORTH

MASTERTON

WELLINGTON

NORTH ISLAND

MASTERTON

TO WELLINGTON

In roaming the streets on foot I scored a three-star travelling tourist victory. I found a petrol station, next to an antique shop, next to a tearoom.

The Lady Navigator disallowed the score. "First of all we aren't in the car. Secondly the antique store has moved across the street. Thirdly the tearoom has closed."

Well, it was very close.

Friends had recommended a motel in Palmerston North and we phoned from Taupo but there was nothing available. The motel made a recommendation for another motel and a phone call confirmed our "booking". When you make a reservation or "booking", you are confirmed when the operator says to you: "Good as gold". You are in the street when the operator says they are - "chock-a-block".

Our confirmed booking turned out to be in a motor lodge which meant a hotel-type unit. No kitchen. No separate bedroom. Neat. Bath. TV. But we needed at least one separate bedroom and preferably two ... the extra room takes the luggage. We stayed but avoided "lodges" thereafter.

Naturally we went out to dinner.

During our earlier city stroll we passed an attractive little restaurant to which we returned for our evening meal. At the door a charming young lady greeted us as the hostess. She seated us. She also took our order. She disappeared then for a fairly long period of time.

I tried a pâté which was borderline-rancid. When the hostess-waitress appeared, I sent it back. She whisked it away immediately, muttering something about the cook.

I ordered a very rare steak and repeated the request for the steak to be *very* rare. It was well done. Again the dish went back. Again the lady complained about the cook. She served a second steak, perfectly broiled.

After paying the bill, the hostess-waitress again having disappeared, I looked around the corner into the kitchen.

She was also the cook.

It should be noted that Palmerston North is proud of its art gallery, its rugby museum, its historical museum. And if you really run out of things to do you can visit a major company's dried milk factory in nearby Bunnythorpe.

Masterton

To reach Masterton from Palmerston North you cross the mountain ranges that form the tail-bone of the North Island.

Highway 3 follows the Manawatu River from Palmerston North into the Manawatu Gorge where the road is carved out of the cliff face on one side of the river and the railroad is sliced out of the rocks on the other side. During the road's construction in 1871 workmen were sometimes suspended from ropes hanging down from the clifftops.

It is a heavily trafficked road and you'll probably end up behind a house trailer or a horse trailer or a truck, which is just fine. It will force you to inch along enjoying magnificent river scenery.

Our timing was lucky. We had been in Palmerston North in late spring and enjoyed the seasonal pansies and first roses. Now we were going through the Gorge in early autumn to attend the international "Golden Shears" in Masterton and we were blessed by having the trees touched with the first yellow-red color of the season.

After the Gorge you reach Woodville and Highway 2 and follow it south through Pahiatua, a town planned for a railroad through the middle of the city, a plan which never materialized. In place of a railroad track, Pahiatua has a wide, green belt through the middle of the city sprinkled with playgrounds and picnic facilities.

Further south is the Mount Bruce Native Bird Reserve operated by the Government to protect endangered wildlife and to provide a place for wildlife study and for public education. Except for the breeding season from late September to mid-December the Reserve is open to the public on weekends from 10 a.m. to 4 p.m.

Masterton with a population over 20,000 is the center of the fertile Wairarapa area. It is a peaceful place untouched in its history by wars or goldrush panics and the wide, tree-lined streets and parks and adjacent river are tranquil amenities of the township.

Once a year, in the first week of March, the peace and quiet is disrupted with the explosion of the "Golden Shears", attracting hundreds of boisterous, muscled, thirsty shearers who come to try for the glory and the prizes. Shearers are the aristocrats of New Zealand labor and this is their Olympic event.

All of the 60 million sheep in New Zealand plus their 40 million lambs are sheared between October and the end of January . . . over 100 million sheep!

Millions of these sheep are sheared twice a year. The labor force is paid by the number of sheep sheared and therefore is highly skilled in the swiftness and the quality with which the job is done. A shearer no matter how fast he is will not hold down a job for long if, in his speed, he either leaves too much wool on the sheep or trims too close and nicks the sheep needlessly.

There are more than 8,000 fulltime professional shearers who earn the bulk of their income from shearing. Thousands of others, the farmers themselves, their sons . . . and sometimes their daughters . . . and weekend, free-lance shearers combine to accomplish the year-round wool-gathering.

To qualify for entry to the Golden Shears contest a shearer has to have a recorded shed tally for a certain number of sheep sheared according to his category in a nine-hour day. There are four principal categories for competitors in the Golden Shears based on their nine-hour shed tallies: juniors with shed tallies up to 200 sheep; intermediates 201-260 sheep; seniors 261-330 sheep; and the "Open" for shearers exceeding 331 sheep in a single day. That is better than a sheep every two minutes.

Look at their back-breaking day. It goes like this:

5 a.m. to 7 – shearing
7 to 8 – breakfast
8 to 9:45 – shearing
9:45 to 10:15 – "smoko" (cigarette, tea, a bite to eat, grind the shears)
10:15 to 12:00 – shearing
12:00 to 1 – lunch
1 to 2:45 – shearing
2:45 to 3:15 – "smoko"
3:15 to 5 – shearing

Why the rigidity of the hours?

The sheep shearing shed is a scene of feverish activity. Besides the shearers there are women or boys sweeping the floor of the odds and ends of wool, men are sorting the wool on tables and feeding the proper wool into proper bales, others are keeping the sheep flowing into and out of the pens. The woolshed is a synchronized operation and everyone stops and starts together.

The Golden Shears program starts on a Wednesday morning with elimination heats . . . over 500 shearers will be vying for the six final places in each of the four categories . . . nearly 5,000 sheep will be sheared in the total program. For four days the eliminations continue and the finals take place on Friday and Saturday.

Interspersed in the four-day event is a beauty contest, a wool clothing design contest, spinning, weaving and craft demonstrations, imported musical entertainment – which doesn't match the performances of the genuinely talented pre-teenage Masterton Intermediate School singing group – and various other shearing competitions including a competition between an Australian team and a New Zealand team. The event builds in dramatic attention as each day passes.

The crowd becomes thicker, the smell of sheep more dominant, the odor of beer more prevalent. The excitement reaches its climax on Saturday night when every seat is filled and the finals of the Golden Shears "Open" is about to start.

The venue for the championship is in the War Memorial Stadium, an auditorium holding around 2,500 people. On stage are six shearing stands. Each stand is powered with an electric motor to which the shearer attaches his own shearing head. (A steady shearer will own $1,000 worth of shearing tools.) Behind each stand is a pen holding that stand's allotment of sheep for the competition event.

White-gowned judges stand at each stand to attest the quality of the shearing. After each sheep is sheared the judge moves on to the next stand passing over his chart to a following judge assuring every shearer of a balanced opinion from several judges.

After the sheep are sheared, they are kept separated by stand and the judges once again inspect each sheep individually for the quality of the shearing. One nick can cost a competitor a precious quarter of a point.

From an overhead balcony time-keeping judges look straight down on each stand.

Fifty per cent of the points are alloted for time and 50 per cent for quality.

It is a highly organized competition.

On the final night of the 1976 Golden Shears the strain of the moment produced one of the few times we were to witness a break in the usual New Zealand gentle manner of courtesy.

The announcer came on the public address system: "A car with the license plate of EF 7114 is blocking the sheep trucks' entrance to the pens. *Move it or we'll flatten it.*"

At 8:00 p.m. the test between Australia and New Zealand international teams began. New Zealand won handily. Hearty cheers from the crowd.

Then the final of the Golden Shears Open Championship . . . the six best qualifiers from over 100 entries took the stage. Each had one trial sheep to shear to test equipment and to warm up. In the competition each finalist would have twenty sheep to shear.

Shouts of individual names came from the crowd. Loud. Boisterous. Happy. Beery.

"Time-keepers ready. Judges ready. Shearers ready. Get set. Go!"

Each shearer leaped through his gate, getting a quick hammerhold on the sheep and dragged it butt down to his station and with well-memorized moves he smoothly, never ceasingly moved his shear-head back and forth over the sheep's body, legs, head, rotating the sheep in a non-stop motion. A marvel to watch.

The announcer sounded like a racetrack caller with a steady stream of monologue names, placing, past histories, shearing positions now held on the sheep.

The crowd, sophisticated to the rhythm and the techniques of shearing, shouted increasingly loud words of encouragement.

The time clicked off. The shearers were now glistening with sweat, still moving gracefully, almost effortlessly. There were three early leaders . . . almost in tandem. But at the halfway point, ten sheep gone, a new leader emerged. He continued to improve with each sheep and finished well ahead of the second man.

He sheared twenty sheep in 23 minutes, 28 seconds.

Huge cheers from the crowd.

The favorite of the crowd, a thirty-five-year-old sheep and cattle farmer, who had come in second in the Golden Shears four times, finished 24 seconds later. More cheers from the crowd. This farmer had been a shearer for twenty years and he used to shear about 65,000 sheep in a season. Now his farming reduced his shearing to only about 25,000 sheep a year. He was considered a parttimer.

Finally the judges came back from their lengthy pen inspection. The experience of the farmer paid off. He was announced as the winner. The crowd was ecstatic. The newspaper later described the win as the most popular in the history of the Golden Shears.

The margin of victory was less than a third of a point.

A shy twenty-one-year-old girl made history by qualifying for the junior finals. Never before had a woman reached a championship finals in any category.

It was a new victory for emancipated women. She placed third in the final and was awarded a prize for the best turned out sheep in the juniors. The last night of the Golden Shears she was awarded as the top quality shearer of the whole contest. Another victory!

Here she was . . . a symbol of woman's liberation. A speech! A speech!

She was asked why she entered. Now was the time to speak on equal employment rights . . . an opportunity for the Gloria Steinem of the woolsheds. She flapped her arms and said, "I dunno."

Charming.

In sixteen years the Golden Shears has given focus and publicity and deserved status to a professional occupation demanding the strength of the longshoreman, the endurance of the marathon runner and the skill of the surgeon.

It is a first class New Zealand event.

The Farm
We were fortunate in having our "friendly farmer" come to our front door in Taupo. We learned much about the country and its farming lifestyles from our farmer and his family. An overseas visitor, even with limited time, can have the same privilege and enjoy the true flavor and the tempo of the country by taking what is known as a "farm holiday".

Many dairy farms, sheep stations, horse-training farms open their doors to their New Zealand city colleagues and overseas visitors. *These are not dude ranches.* They are working agricultural, pastoral farms. The owners share their everyday lives with a small number of guests each year, adding to their own enjoyment of living by becoming involved with others and slightly augmenting their farm incomes.

It is a superb way to learn about New Zealand.

Booking information about independent farms taking in visitors is available from the New Zealand Accommodations Guide or Government Tourist Bureaus or travel agents. There is also a loosely organized group called *Farm Holidays, Ltd.* comprising over 200 farms on both islands with central information and reservations in Wellington. The address is PO Box 11-137, Wellington.

A visitor can choose a farm according to the location, amenities . . . fishing, hunting, riding . . . or the occupation of the farm itself.

There are two basic types of accommodations: live-in where you stay at the farmhouse and become a member of the family, or a cottage where you live apart from the family and supply your own linen and food. Cottages range from "A4" which is little more than a sheep shearers' bunkhouse to "A1", a miniature motel. The overseas visitor should choose the "live-in" accommodations because that is what it is all about.

Prices average between $19 and $25 including six meals a day. You can't live on the road for less than that.

We wanted to combine the farm experience with the Golden Shears event and telephoned a farm listed in a Government publication from Taupo. The farm was called Linden Downs. Yes, the farm could take us and they would send a map detailing the route to the farm on the outskirts of Masterton.

It was mid-afternoon, Wednesday, the day of the start of the Golden Shears, when we pulled off Highway 2 towards the foothills, crossed two rivers and, following the instruction map, found ourselves at the gateless, white-picketed entry to the farm.

A shady drive through a small forest of trees took us to the side of a duck pond and on the other side of the bank was a rowboat and standing behind a terraced spread of generous green lawn was a 100-year-old two-story, white-painted farmhouse.

We drove through wrought-iron white gates and on a gravel drive encircling a garden filled with bright flowers and stopped in front of the steps. The front door was open.

We were at Linden Downs.

The entry hall was wood panelled. A staircase with dark, wooden hand-turned banisters led up on the left. On the stanchion at the foot of the staircase was an iron statue of a boy sheepherder. On the far wall were two crossed daggers and in the corner a World War I sword, mementoes 'of another war in another place. To the right behind glassed doors was the family parlour now curtain-shaded from the afternoon sun.

The only sound was that of a fly buzzing softly in the warm air.

Hazy curtains parted in my memory and I was back in my child-hood in Colorado Springs, Colorado. It was the way the world used to be. I wanted to go into the parlor and turn on the Atwater Kent radio.

"I'm sorry, I didn't hear you drive in!" and a twinkling, smiling, friendly woman burst on us and introduced herself as the hostess, Fay Evans. Her husband Phillip would join us after he finished the day's work.

Linden Downs is a 555-acre farm that handles 2,000 sheep and 200 head of cattle. In the terminology of farming it is known as a fattening farm. The couple works the farm alone. An eighteen-year-old son, one of three children, is at agricultural school and will join them in another four months.

There are four year-around activities on the farm. One, the breeding, the fattening, the shearing of sheep being the most time-consuming. Two, the caring of the cattle. Three, the planting, growing and reaping of fodder. Four, the year-around maintenance.

"We like farming," said Fay. "I like getting in the field and helping my husband. We enjoy the life."

Farming is hard work but farming to those who enjoy it is obviously fulfilling.

Every night we had an early dinner – Grace was said before dinner – so that we could drive a quarter of an hour into Masterton for the Golden Shears. Fay enjoyed her kitchen as much as she enjoyed her farming. Good food, well prepared, hearty, not fancy, not thinning. Farm food by a fine cook.

When we came back from Masterton at night, the lights would still be on in the parlor and our host and hostess would be waiting up for us like dutiful parents with a warm cup of tea, cold milk and cookies and cake.

Breakfast was just what you expected it to be. Fruit, cereal, bacon, eggs, grilled tomatoes, piles of toast, tea and coffee. Can't start the day feeling peckish!

The fifteen-room farmhouse will accommodate six guests but the Evans prefer to take one couple at a time, giving themselves the leisure of sharing their lives with the guests in a relaxed atmosphere.

One morning we charged off to play the Masterton Golf Course at Lansdowne. Par 72. A seventy-six-year-old course situated on top of the hill overlooking Masterton. One of the prettiest courses we were to play in New Zealand.

When we came back, Fay, little mother, had done our laundry.

Linden Downs has a privately stocked trout stream and I tried to dry-fly the waters one afternoon but didn't see a fish. There is a swimming pool on the 30-acre home ground and there are walks in the area and there is the rowboat in the front yard duck pond if you want to paddle around.

The farm holiday however is really enjoyed most by just settling down and taking part in the farm life around you. A guest wrote in the Linden Downs book, "What a perfect way to get rid of the jet-lag." Oh, yes! Can you imagine anything better than coming off a terribly long international flight and getting to a farm like this and let your body and mind come back to you? Super suggestion.

"Phillip, what do your guests do most of the time?"

"Well, they seem to sleep a lot."

Phillip was mustering sheep from the hills to the woolshed for shearing and he put Rosie, his three-year-old header, through the paces. A single dog taking 200 head of sheep through a series of gates. The New Zealand sheep dogs love their work. They look so intelligent, so happy with what they are doing. I wanted to ask Rosie for her autograph.

And there was Smokey, the cat, grey-black with unsmiling green, green eyes.

"Smokey, I have to tell you that I don't like you. It isn't your green eyes. They are lovely. It isn't your rich coat. A handsome coat. I just don't like cats."

Smokey responded like all such cats so treated. She curled around my legs and purred.

Early in the cold black of the night, deep in the double bed under the feather quilt, in our big bedroom with the 12-foot ceilings, there was the sound of nearby purring. Smokey!

I turned on the light and there she was in the middle of the floor walking in small proud circles. She had come through the bedroom window. I bounced out of bed, opened the bedroom door and hissed, "Out. Out." She stalked out with obvious reluctance.

The next morning the Lady Navigator was up first. She stopped and burst out laughing.

"What's so funny so early in the morning, Lady Navigator?"

She reached over to the middle of the bedroom rug and pulled up by its tail a very dead little mouse. Smokey had brought us a love present! Cats!

The Evans bought the farmhouse which in the past had belonged to Phillip's uncle from a trust and had re-made it into a warm home. It is a picturesque, handsome estate and they now get regular offers of $100,000 for the house alone. A visitor can have it for $20 a night with all that food!

Linden Downs station can be reached by writing to Rangitumau, Masterton.

We both kissed Fay goodbye. Went to the woolshed to take the shearers their morning tea and said goodbye to Phillip hard at work among the shearers.

A farmhouse stay? You really should.

In Masterton I found the natural grey-beige lambswool sweater favored by New Zealand men. Perfect color. Perfect fit, or so it first seemed.

"There's a dressing room in back where you can see yourself on three sides," said the Sales Lady. In the mirror the color was right but there was something wrong with the fit.

Back to the Sales Lady. "It's fine but it's sprung in the middle."

The Sales Lady looked at me in silence.

"You see, down here, where it kind of pooches out. There's something wrong."

The Sales Lady looked at the Lady Navigator. The Lady Navigator looked back at the Sales Lady. They seemed to exchange a conversation but no words were spoken.

They both looked at me rather sorrowfully.

Five months in New Zealand. Slowly there arose before my eyes a stream of dishes filled with peaches and globby cream. Piles of Vogel's toast with butter oozing down into the rich crust. Barbecues with each plate piled high with a steak, a lamb chop and two sausages. Chocolate Wheaten biscuits, Toffee Pops, washed down with cold, thick milk. Filet mignons with Béarnaise sauce. Large bottles of frosty beer. Cabernet Sauvignon. Hock from Napier. Dry White from Lincoln Road. Pavlovas with fresh strawberries. Ice cream covered with whipped cream. *Blackout.*

I sucked in my stomach as far as it would go.

"On the other hand I think it fits splendidly."

I paid for the sweater and the Lady Navigator and I went down the street in silence. I had the uneasy feeling that any word from me would have triggered a session of laughing hysterics. And we wouldn't want that, would we?

South to Wellington from Palmerston North takes you through the farm center of Levin and the fruit-and-vegetable basket area of Otaki and then to Paraparaumu, a beach resort town, where the notorious Paraparaumu Golf Club eats visitors as a hobby. It has to be the most difficult course in New Zealand. Tight. Windy. Sand-trapped. Two par-4 holes are 450 yards long. Try one of those in a good headwind.

From Paraparaumu it is a forty-five minute drive into Wellington.

South to Wellington from Masterton you go through the little town of Greytown where the environmentalists have succeeded in preserving the colonial buildings and persuading new builders to keep new construction in the style of the old. The fertile farm land sells for $1,000 an acre.

Over a mountain range and you are in Upper Hutt where there is the Wellington Golf Club (Heretaunga). A huge park. Two courses. A short 64-par course. A new 72-par course. We were there at eight o'clock in the morning and the club captain graciously opened the pro shop and set us out on our way properly.

Less than half an hour's drive from the golf course takes you into Wellington through Lower Hutt.

9. Windy, Wonderful Wellington

Capital City ... Lunchtime Symphony, Hot Pies and Mozart ... Cable Cars ... A Good Day for Antiques ... A Terrible Day for Motels

Wellington is a distinctively individualistic city.

It is the capital of the country. As such it enjoys a sophisticated diplomatic corps. It has attracted several important financial institutions. It is the headquarters for bureaucracies, associations and Influential People.

Outside of Wellington it is known as "Windy Wellington" and outside of Wellington there is a tendency to speak disparagingly of the city. In Auckland they hardly speak of it at all.

The motto of Wellington is *"Suprema a Situ"* which figuratively can be translated to "We have a much better location than Auckland".

In 1865 the commissioners – all from Australia, the citizens of Auckland are quick to point out – ruled that the Capital of the country should be moved from Auckland to Wellington thus confirming more than two decades later the hopes of the founders of the New Zealand Company that a community with the central location of Wellington would one day be the capital of the country.

The motivating visionary of the New Zealand Company was a fascinating character, Edward Gibbon Wakefield (1796–1862), who was responsible for much of the early settlement of New Zealand. He was an Englishman who eloped with a schoolgirl, caused a scandal, spent three years in an English prison where he wrote a book on Australian colonization out of which grew his "Wakefield Scheme" of planned settlement.

In the end Wakefield's theory, endorsed by the Duke of Wellington, collapsed and so did the New Zealand Company but not before it had in two years' time established colonies in Wellington and up the west coast at New Plymouth and Wanganui and across the Cook Strait in Nelson on the South Island. The "Wakefield-type" colony

139

also served as a basis for the foundation of Christchurch and Dunedin in which Wakefield was involved although through different companies. As a result of his initial efforts, New Zealand between May, 1839 and January, 1843 was to receive 19,000 immigrants, the backbone population for the new country.

Mt Victoria is a splendid place to start your visit to Wellington. Easily accessible around the harbor from downtown Wellington by taxi, bus or car, you can stand on the mountain top and look across the port to the mouth of the Hutt River where, in 1840, the first immigrants of the New Zealand Company established their colony modestly naming it *Britannia*.

However the flooding of the Hutt proved too damp for the new community and you can see from Mt Victoria why they moved into the cozy corner of the harbor at your feet where the colony was renamed after the noble believer of Wakefield's theory.

You look back to Hutt Valley, which became in time a bedroom and golf community for Wellington, but now is an industrial center of its own. Behind you is the airport, almost downtown, settled between Evans Bay and Lyall Bay, with a one-direction run-way too short to handle the jumbo jets, an embarrassment to the city fathers.

Wellington spills out over the hills in almost all directions and with impressive high-rise buildings in the center, the metropolitan city looks much larger than its 350,000 people.

Despite its touristic attractions and despite an obvious need of convention facilities, it would almost seem that Wellington doesn't want outside visitors. The number of tourist-visitor accommodations is miserly.

Again we had called ahead for accommodations, received the "chock-a-block" reply and referral to another motel and got a "good-as-gold" confirmation. The price was substantially higher than the going rate we had become accustomed to but we were satisfied that we had secured good quarters.

The place we drove up to was dismal. It was dirty on the outside and dirty on the inside. The Lady Navigator gave it one fast sweeping inspection and told the cleaning lady that it wouldn't do and we drove off in proper indignation.

The Lady Navigator disappeared into the Automobile Associ-

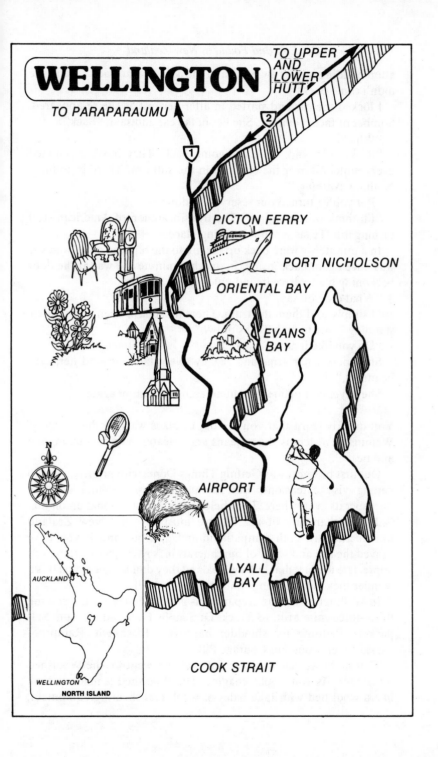

ation building not far away . . . and she didn't come back . . . and she didn't come back.

I locked the car and started in after her just as she re-appeared. Somber of face. *Unfunny.* She got in the car and said, "Back."

"What?"

"Back," she said. "We are going back. They have telephoned every motel all over the city and in the suburbs. There is nothing. Nothing. *Nothing.* "

"But you've turned our reservation down."

"I'll think of something." The transformation of American steel turning into Texas syrup was taking place.

In a minute we were back up the hill to the rejected motel and she was once again back inside. In another minute she was at the door beckoning me to drive in and unload.

"What did you say?"

"I simply told them the truth. There must have been a misunderstanding – due to mah Texas drawl."

"Do you like it now?" I asked.

She opened her arms and regally swept them around her, "It's beautiful."

She never complained about an accommodation again.

You quickly learn that you are out of place walking the streets of Wellington in tennis shoes, jeans and sweater. You belong in coat and tie.

Our first business was Getting Things Done, with priority given to getting visa extensions. Bureaucrats in New Zealand are like bureaucrats everywhere. They belong to an international union that is bigger than any of us. But we must say that New Zealand bureaucrats are both sympathetic and gracious and if you have braved the fire and scorn of bureaucrats in, say, France or Italy, you appreciate the fact that in New Zealand they don't sneer at you. It's a wonder they made the international union at all.

In Wellington serious preparations got underway for the coming thirty-three-mile Milford Track. Dr Scholls Foot Pads, Epsom Salt packets. Padding for shoulder harnesses. Flashlight. Rainproof parkas. Everything but Courage Pills.

That night we celebrated our arrival and went to The Woolshed for dinner. As you would imagine, The Woolshed is made to look like a woolshed with fake bales of wool, real shearing equipment, lambskins on the seats, rams' heads on the walls. The dance band is made up of human beings.

In New Zealand we liked to become friends with the waitresses. We learned their names, complimented them on their hair or eyes or whatever. They were fast to respond always and it was much easier to be waited on by a friend than a stranger.

Our Woolshed waitress was Polish. I said she had dimples. She laughed. I said she had a lovely laugh. She blushed. I was going to say she had a hell of a figure when I got kicked under the table.

"I was just trying to be friendly."

American Steel, the eyes told me, was back again.

"Like to dance?" I asked the Lady Navigator.

We danced for almost ten minutes and ambiance was all around us again. The band was good. The music was right.

There was a tap on my shoulder as if someone were cutting in. I looked around – and down – and there was our Polish waitress. "I've overdone it," I thought. "She's going to ask me for a dance."

"Sir," she said. "Your scallops are ready."

There are several good ways to discover Wellington.

The place to start, after the Mt Victoria visit, is the Wellington Public Relations Office in the Town Hall near the waterfront where you can pick up a current, monthly *"Wellington Guide"* plus other informative literature.

There are three scenic drives in Wellington, the Blue Route, the Orange Route and the Green Route, all appropriately marked with the proper colored discs.

You can step across the street from the PR office at two o'clock and take a city bus on a two-and-a-half hour city and marine drive tour for $2. It's not a greatly informative tour but you can inexpensively learn where everything is.

One of the best parts about Wellington is that walking tours reach the most interesting places.

The Public Relations office puts out a brochure, thoughtfully funded by the Challenge Corporation, called *"Wellington City Walks and Tours"*, which describes many areas and buildings which we thought to be the highlights of Wellington.

Top of the list: the Town Hall, freshly painted, is a handsome, vintage building which houses the town mayor and council and also a large auditorium, a town hall of the type which once we had in

America and have now lost.

We were in luck in timing because the New Zealand Symphony Orchestra was performing one of its lunchtime concerts at the Town Hall. Outstanding idea . . . Mozart and hot pies . . . and we eagerly lined up with people with little brown bags . . . "Two dollars upstairs, one dollar down, sit anywhere" . . . and listened to a fine symphony orchestra in shirt sleeves play to an enthusiastic audience who had to put down sandwiches to applaud. The acoustics were excellent, the rapport between the conductor, John Hopkins, the orchestra and the audience was immediate and obvious. The small one-sheet program, illustrated with an apple and half a sandwich, thoughtfully reported the playing time of each musical selection so members of the audience with appointments could pre-determine how long they could stay. It was one of the most enjoyable symphonies we've ever attended.

With the lunchtime concert as a start Wellington could do no wrong.

The two-tone painting of Town Hall gives the building a sparkle which can't be duplicated today. Other stately buildings along the waterfront are being repainted and they spring to life. (Said the bus driver about a building in front of us: "I didn't know it was there until now!")

There is much about Wellington to remind a visitor of San Francisco. Hills. Winds. Wooden buildings.

In San Francisco there is almost a city industry of restoring and repainting industrial buildings and one hopes that Wellington will soon do the same and at once save a precious heritage and for a small price gain a charm which modern architecture lacks.

For example the *"Wellington Walking Tour"* brochure describes Glenbervie Terrace off of Tinakori Road. Glenbervie is a short loop road up and around a hill with quaint wooden houses, untouched, that cry out for someone to buy them, polish them, show them off. You'd like to buy and restore the whole street.

In the same vein the growth of Wellington in the center of the city threatens many handsome, historical buildings. There is new building everywhere.

Shopping in Wellington goes along what the merchants describe as the "Golden Mile". As you go along from department store to sheepskin shop to tearoom, it is hard to remember that this used to be the waterfront. All the property to the present harbor edge has been reclaimed.

While shopping look up now and then and take in the buildings. All of the buildings have overhangs to protect the pedestrians against the rain. It creates a tendency to keep the eyes down.

Cuba Street . . . where does a name like Cuba come from? . . . It was the name of one of the first immigrant ships . . . Cuba Street has a pedestrian mall and features a water-bucket sculpture that has to be seen . . . it also has the *Normandie Restaurant,* one of the city's leading restaurants which we tried to "book" unsuccessfully two nights in a row.

The DIC department store carries a theater booking office. You can reserve seats for theatrical and cinema attractions. You can also pay your electric bills and buy milk tokens.

What are milk tokens? They are metal or plastic tokens you put into your empty milk bottle for the milkman to replace with full bottles and the tokens prevent a crime wave of children pinching the cash and buying lollipops.

You'll see signs in motels that say, "Please put empty bottles with milk tokens in appropriate box." It pays to buy a handful. You can always use them as golf markers.

Wellington turns out to be informative for shopping. New Zealand with all of that home-grown wool is a good place to shop for sweaters. Only they aren't usually called sweaters in New Zealand. They are known as jerseys. Unless they are crew-necked sweaters. These are not sweaters. These are not jerseys. These are jumpers.

Another step forward: "Devonshire Teas" the teashop advertises on the outside.

We stop for tea.

"I'd like a Devonshire Tea, please."

Out comes a hot pot of tea, a scone covered with strawberry jam which is covered with whipped cream.

It's enough to tide you over until breakfast.

Is Wellington windy?

The first time I visited Wellington there were gusts of winds up to eighty-five miles an hour. It was unnoted in the newspaper.

The most noted wind storm in the district was in April 1968 when winds reached a velocity of about 140 miles an hour.

The auto-passenger ferry ship *"Wahine"* trying to negotiate the harbor during the storm was pushed on to rocks in the harbor entrance and capsized with a tragic loss of life.

A friend of ours in Auckland had an uncle on the ferry. He was thrown into the water. He made it to a liferaft. The waves washed him off of the liferaft.

He was in the water again and trying to swim towards shore but with great difficulty because he was arthritic and while in the water guarded his cane because if he lost it, he would be unable to walk and he knew he couldn't survive even if he reached shore.

But the waves pounded on him and in keeping afloat he lost his grip on the cane. It was gone.

A short while later a wave washed him up on the rocks. "I'm saved . . . but I'm lost," he thought.

The second wave washed his cane up beside him.

We enjoyed Wellington fully. There is good shopping. There are excellent restaurants. There are parks, parliament buildings – one old, one new – historical buildings and, of course, the Dominion Museum.

One day we decided should be "sports day" and we scheduled a return to the resort town of Paraparaumu, thirty-five miles north of Wellington which we had come through and was fond to the memory of the Lady Navigator. (Two cut-glass shot glasses, six forks, one piece of silver plate.)

In New Zealand there is a habit of shortening all Maori place-names but curiously for some reason the bastardization of Paraparaumu to "Paraparam" revolts everybody including the people using it.

Our weather in windy Wellington had been splendid and we scheduled a dawn take-off without a qualm to play the Paraparaumu Golf Course in the early morning.

At six o'clock in the morning it was black and raining. Having had a full evening the night before, we thanked the weatherman, turned off the alarm clock and went back to sleep.

A rainy morning is a good morning to visit the Dominion Museum and National Art Gallery. The Museum is a grim-looking, fortress-like structure but there are worthwhile exhibits inside.

As is appropriate there is considerable space given to the Maori culture and to Captain Cook. Particularly appealing is the figurehead of Cook's ship *Resolution,* used on his second and third voyages. It is a comparatively small carving of a wolf's head but this carving overlooked the beach in Hawaii where Captain Cook was struck down by the natives, ending his astounding career. (If you enjoy adventure-history, read *"The Life of Captain James Cook"* by J. C. Beaglehole, 1974, Adam & Charles Black, London.)

Included among the other Cook exhibits are a model of the *Endeavour,* a lifesized model of Captain Cook's cabin and a replica of the ship's deck. Interesting reading is a list of the *Endeavour's* supply of food and drink. Provisioning the *Endeavour* in London took from May 27 to July 29 1768. Here is the beverage portion of the provisions:

    Beer 19 tons
    Wine 3,032 gallons
    Malt 80 bushels
    Inspissated juice of beer 19½ gallons
    Spirits 1,397 gallons

They might go hungry but they weren't going to go thirsty.

In the Hawaii section of the museum are two excellent feather capes which came from Cook's voyage and a curious feather hat which must have come from a later period. Also contained in the museum is the skeleton of probably the most famous racehorse to come out of the Pacific, the legendary Phar Lap. He was bred in Timaru on the South Island. His name at that time was Lightning. At the Wellington Yearling Sales he was bought by a New Zealand trainer on behalf of an Australian businessman for only 160 guineas ... less than $1,000 ... and he was shipped to Sydney.

Unfortunately the horse had a miserable crossing and he came off of the ship *Wanganella* in a sick, droopy condition. The Australian businessman took one look at the young horse and refused to accept him. He later relented and shared ownership with the New Zealand trainer.

Lightning whose racing name in Siralese was Phar Lap didn't take much time to get into form. His giant-like 25-foot stride left field after field behind and he went on to win a fortune in the late 1920s and early 1930s. He was shipped to California where he ate poisoned grass and died. It was an international shock in racing circles and there are still Australian racing fans who look at America with suspicion.

The skeleton of the horse is here in Wellington. His stuffed hide is on display in Melbourne. His outsized heart in Canberra.

The museum is well-known for its Maori collection of Maori life, hunting, clothing, tribal lineage, burial customs, village construction and war implements. The carved meeting house, Te Hau-ki-Turanga, which came from Gisborne, is a famous example of Maori carving. If an overseas visitor wants to appreciate the meaning of the carvings, he needs a program and there is one available for a few cents. Some details are explained on signs opposite the entrance to the meeting house, including an explanation of the curved design one sees on the roof beams and the rectilinear designs seen on the wall paneling.

One interesting exhibit in the museum is devoted to the eruption of Tarawera in 1886.

The upstairs of the museum is the National Art Gallery devoted to European and Pacific artists. The collection includes many examples of that "soft" art typical of New Zealand, reflecting the vistas seen on the highway between Bulls and Taihape.
    There are also superb antiques in the collection.

In Wellington we knocked over four antique stores in one day. We learned that there is a New Zealand Antique Dealers' Association and it would be a wise move for a visitor to obtain a list.
    The Lady Navigator picked up an early 19th century game table, a mother-of-pearl etched Chinese brush case and a brooch. Funds low but morale very high. Repeat: There are no bargains in antiques.
    We went to dinner at the *Plimmer House* . . . a piece of Victorian fruitcake over 100 years old settled down among the skyscrapers like a quaint grandmother in a rocking chair among chrome and concrete neighbors. It is a gabled cottage with a miniature spired tower . . . and it is now . . . and we hope forever . . . a licensed restaurant.
    The Plimmer House is known for its mussel soup. Excellent wine list. Service. Ambiance. First rate. On a subsequent trip to Wellington we also enjoyed the cuisine of the *Normandie,* also *Orsini's.* Orsini's had the most ambience with a nice upstairs bar. Normandie had the better kitchen. Two other restaurants recommended by

Wellingtonians were *The Coachman,* licensed, and *Bacchus,* unlicensed.

Wellington has a cable car which, like San Francisco's, serves the residents as a functional commuter system and not as a tourist attraction.

However if you avoid the business rushhours, it is a visitor "must". And an easy means of access to the Botanic Gardens.

A sign at the top reads:

> *Cable Car 10c on Monday – Friday*
> *10c on Saturday*
> *10c on Sunday*

It starts at the bottom from the "Golden Mile" and climbs, with several stops along the way, up 400 feet to Kelburn, a suburb whose developers put in the cable car. There is a beaten-up restaurant at the top, Greek-run, which offers so-so food with a first rate view.

If the day is right, you should take the easy walk down through the Botanic Gardens, a 62-acre domain. Near the bottom are the Lady Norwood Rose Gardens and the begonia House. The begonias were not yet in bloom but the roses were lovely when we were there.

You come out on Tinakori Road. "What do you know," said the Lady Navigator innocently. "We are back among the antique shops."

On Tinakori Road, besides antique shops, is the girlhood home of "Katherine Mansfield" (Katherine Beauchamp), (1888–1923), New Zealand's most important story-writer.

If you are strong of foot you can pick up several more architectural gems within walking distance. Old St Paul's in Mulgrave Street is a quiet, charming, church visually satisfying on the outside covered with white paint and sunshine and, inside, warm and intimate and friendly with polished native woods everywhere. You can't believe that this aesthetic, Gothic structure, finished in 1866, could be so beautiful and its replacement a modern Moorish(!)-styled cathedral could be so ugly.

There is a saving grace next to the new cathedral, across the street from Parliament, and that is a coffee shop and lunch room operated by three separate church denominations who have forgotten their theological differences to run the little restaurant. It is called *The Loaves and Fishes.*

Immediately across the street is the General Assembly Library with a superb neo-Gothic facade and porch which you can admire from the exterior. You can't go in the Library rooms but you can step inside the lobby and admire the deeply carved woodwork and the stained glass.

Next door to the Library is the Parliament House. It is a ponderous looking thing and we tried three times to get inside and always failed the open-hours test. Inside, we've read, are relics of the nation's past.

Still under construction . . . along with much other new Government building construction in the neighborhood . . . is a new Parliament building known locally as "the Beehive". It looks like one.

You are now almost at the head of Lambton Quay and here is the old Government Building which was built in 1877. It is the largest wooden structure in the world except for the Japanese temple Todaiji. When first completed it contained 143 rooms, 22 chimneys, 64 "conveniences" and 18 flights of stairs. Although it is a wooden structure, the exterior was designed to resemble traditional stone architecture, which it does.

In a suburban post office I went up to the man at the toll call desk and said, "I would like to call Auckland."

The man said, "Yes. Name and number?"

"Mr Bookman at 33199."

"Pay and pay?" asked the young man.

It was immediately apparent that there was an international communications misunderstanding.

I leaned closer to understand better. "I beg your pardon?"

He leaned closer and spoke louder so I would understand better. "Pay and pay?"

Pause. I leaned closer. "I'll pay any way you like as long as I get Mr Bookman person to person."

"That's what I asked," he said gently.

"Oh," I said.

To call Auckland, pay and pay, or person to person, costs 35c extra.

We spent an evening in the Wellington home of a successful city executive. (Lost on the way we ducked into a small grocery store where a customer took us outside and pointed out the correct route inquiring anxiously, "You're sure you don't want me to lead the way?")

The sixteen-year-old daughter of the family was off to attend a graduation party. She was dressed in jeans, no shoes, a satin-quilted bed jacket adorned with her father's wartime naval aviator wings. In other words she was dressed according to the international code of sixteen-year-olds.

We remarked how charming it was to see the older ladies of New Zealand and their careful ritual of dress: Queen Mary hats, gloves, neat handbags. In a sloppy world they represent lost tidiness and self respect.

Was this going to be lost in future generations in New Zealand? The sixteen-year-old was shocked by the idea. Immediately, "Of course not. It will come back. We like to dress up."

It was a reassuring moment in a very nice evening.

At the time of our visit the national elections were under way, building momentum daily.

The principal part of the radio industry and all of the television industry is controlled by the Government and we remarked how we kept watching for some "tilting" of the media in favor of the Government in power to our host, who is in the communications industry.

"Oh, no," he said. "It wouldn't be a fair go – it isn't the New Zealand way. All of the people would become very upset."

Later we were to read a public chastisement of a few radio commentators who had strayed off the un-biased line.

Even the newspapers which would be expected to lean heavily to the right or left were quite fair in space and treatment to both parties.

"Which way is the election going to go?" It was to become one of our stock questions for two months. "Oh," said our host with the easy authority that comes from all people who live in a nation's capital, "the political professionals say it is going to go –."

His professionals proved to be about 100 per cent wrong.

We learned that St Mary's of the Angels has the finest organ in Wellington and a fine choir.

We learned there was a street carnival in a suburb the next morning.

Saturday in a sunny Wellington the whole city turns outdoors washing cars, clipping hedges, going on picnics and jumping into every type of sports uniform.

We went to the street carnival and ate Samoan doughnuts and chocolate sundaes and watched all of the do-it-yourself money-making booths in action.

We went to the Wellington Lawn Tennis courts which are public courts but filled on weekends with inter-club tournament play. There are fifteen grass courts and three hard courts.

We found our way to the Wellington Zoo, the oldest in New Zealand, where we awarded an "A" to the brown bear, a "B+" to the elephant and an "A+" to the kiwi house. There are lots of kiwi exhibit houses in New Zealand, you'll find, and the Wellington Zoo kiwi house is excellent.

As kiwis are nocturnal, the houses are kept dark, barely lit inside by a dull red lamp. You go through a darkroom to let your eyes get accustomed to the lack of light before stepping into the kiwi room where behind glass you can barely discern the little featherly, flightless birds scampering about.

In another glassed area are the live opossums that you see dead on the road throughout New Zealand.

We then had a picnic on a mountain top and went to the beach and then to a big public park. Cricket on the left. Softball on the right. Lots of softball in New Zealand.

Further on, in Evans Bay, we stopped to watch a yacht race in progress. You can't be a second-class sailor and race in Windy Wellington.

We went through Oriental Bay. Sunbathers were everywhere. Visited the Harbor Board Museum, the railroad station and finally, from the outside, Hannah House which is on Boulcott Street, not far from the Plimmer House. They both belong to the same era. While the Plimmer House is a cottage and the Hannah House is a mansion, they both exude the handsome charm typical of the style of the early century.

Sunday morning we packed for the Picton ferry.

I ducked down the hill to St Mary's of the Angels. Too early for the organ. Could hear choir practising in back. Angelic.

Rare sight. A Maori priest, one of only five in the country, gave the sermon. He wore a Maori feathered cloak and carried a taiaha, the symbol of the orator and of rank.

He spoke in that gentle voice that is directly related to my

Hawaiian friends and I could almost see Diamond Head listening to his words.

The ferries from Wellington to the South Island take passengers, automobiles, house trailers (caravans), motorcycles and railroad cars.

The ferries go to Picton several times a day. The transportation costs are modest.

It is well to have advance reservations coming and going, *and absolutely essential if you are travelling in the summer season.* You can make ferry reservations at the Government Tourist Bureau (GTB).

Note: the tourist industry is extensively controlled by the Government. As noted, many hotels are owned and managed by the Tourist Hotel Corporation (THC). The international and domestic airline, Air New Zealand, the railroad and the national bus service and a tour company (Tiki Tours) are all Government owned.

Mount Cook Airlines is a private corporation but 20 per cent of the stock is owned by Air New Zealand.

The Government Tourist Bureau is not just an information office but functions as a competitive, commercial travel agency as well. We used GTB constantly to make (and change) reservations for us all over the country.

10. The Northern Part of the South Island

A Watery Highway . . . The Real Rai Bread . . . Pretty Nelson . . . A Comic Opera Character . . . A Three-Star Picnic . . . No Bed at the Springs

When we went to New Zealand and started travelling around the North Island, people would ask us three questions:
1. How long have you been here?
2. How do you like it?
3. Have you been to the South Island yet?

We finally asked a fishing guide friend, "We think the North Island is absolutely stunning. Why is it then that North Islanders always ask if you have been to the South Island yet?"

He looked at the ground and thought for a long minute and then said carefully, "Because on the South Island, you can go for miles and never see anyone."

You line up for the Picton Ferry to take you to the South Island one hour before departure time. A checker takes your ticket, marks your name off of his list and traffic men direct you into the proper boarding lane. There is a stand-by lane for cars without reservations and their passengers can be observed in attitudes of prayer.

The ferry is divided into an upper deck which takes a limited number of passengers' cars and a lower deck, a vast cavern which takes the bulk of the automobiles, trailers, caravans and railroad cars. Loading the ferry is executed professionally and efficiently. Both going to and from Picton we were moved into the upper deck where, one at a time, cars drive on board to a hand-operated turntable, you set your brake, a deck-hand swings the car around to the proper direction for backing and then you are hand-signaled into the smallest space possible and the car is roped down and secured.

A sign reads: "Double check lights and radios, lock car and proceed immediately to the passenger decks."

There is plenty of passenger space. A lounge-bar. (Contrary to

154

New Zealand custom, if you don't tip the waiter, don't expect a refill.) Fore and aft observation lounges. Deck seating. Game rooms. A functional café not on any "best restaurant" list. We learned by watching other passengers with brown-bag snacks, and four weeks later on the return trip we were prepared with our own hamper-carried picnic.

Wellington was finally windy but gloriously sunny for our Sunday crossing and the ferry gave us an excellent sea-gull's view of the city.

The trip to Picton through the Cook Strait was relatively calm. It can be tough. An occasional porpoise brought passengers to the rail.

You can be sure on the Picton Ferry that there will be at least one group of school children on a school exercise. They will be playing tag.

Ferry time from Wellington to Picton is under three and a half hours. Clearing the Wellington harbor takes over a half hour, slightly over an hour gets you safely through the strait and you slip between the narrow gap of the Tory Channel entrance to the South Island and you are on glory road. For over an hour you glide down Tory Channel and then into Queen Charlotte Sound, the hills close on both sides, stations and vacation houses clearly visible from the deck.

The approach to Picton on the watery highway is scenic and serene. Unique.

Picton itself is a vacation port town. Water activities everywhere. Outbound ferries, fishing boats, water taxis, yachts. Hotels and motels and boarding houses and camping grounds on shore. It all looks a gay, holiday painting.

Clearing the ferry happens quickly, *zip,* it's done and you are on the road out of town.

By this time it was getting late and we were heading for bedding at Nelson ... without a reservation ... and with an estimated driving time ahead of us of about two hours. A new game had started with our New Zealand friends called: "What Is Your Favorite Drive in New Zealand?" The longer, Picton-Havelock-Nelson route via the Queen Charlotte Drive had won many votes. Magnificent views, we were told, and after all, isn't this why we came to New Zealand in the first place? The Queen Charlotte Drive begins almost immediately in Picton, turning right off the highway and up the hill to a twisting, *dirt* road but with those views ...

In our uncertainty of accommodations and driving time we

plowed ahead on Highway 1 ignoring the scenic road turn-off and in not too long a time we were already in Havelock.

It was a mistake.

("What's time, Mate?")

A sign on the side of the road reads: "Game. Wild Pig. Goat. Deer. Highest Prices. Cash."

It is hunting country.

Havelock wears such a peaceful air. Sitting on the head of Pelorus Sound, it is a most attractive setting.

And listen to this: you can get permission from the Department of Lands and Survey in Blenheim to camp on one of the reserves in the Marlborough Sounds. You can make arrangements in Havelock for a launch to take you in, bring you provisions during your stay and later come back and take you out. Doesn't that sound like a super holiday?

On the road to Nelson from Havelock we passed the old goldtown of Canvastown and through Rai. Signboard: "Wholesome cheese and wholesale prices". We didn't know that Rai is also known widely throughout the South Island for its small-bakery bread.

Coming out of the mountains we were at Tasman Bay and shortly into Nelson. Attractive motels are everywhere in Nelson, mostly south of the city near beaches and after doing a "drive-by" noting the "vacancy" signs we settled on a motel without difficulty.

It was eight o'clock in the evening and time for another New Zealand travel lesson. Being Sunday the shops were closed and there was no way to buy food . . . not that we had seen any shops along the way. We decided we would dine out on arriving in Nelson.

Not after eight o'clock in Nelson on Sunday night were we going to dine out. Everything was locked up. Our proprietor sold us half a dozen eggs and said that his daughter had passed through Rai and bought "hot bread" at the bakery, a Sunday speciality. He gave us half a loaf. We had cheese omelettes and the famous Rai bread toasted for dinner.

The entire northern coast of the South Island is a vacation ground. There is swimming, golf, boating, fishing, tennis.

From Nelson to the west is rich agricultural land.

Monday was a rainy morning but we headed anyway up the coast towards Tasman National Park, passed through orchards where

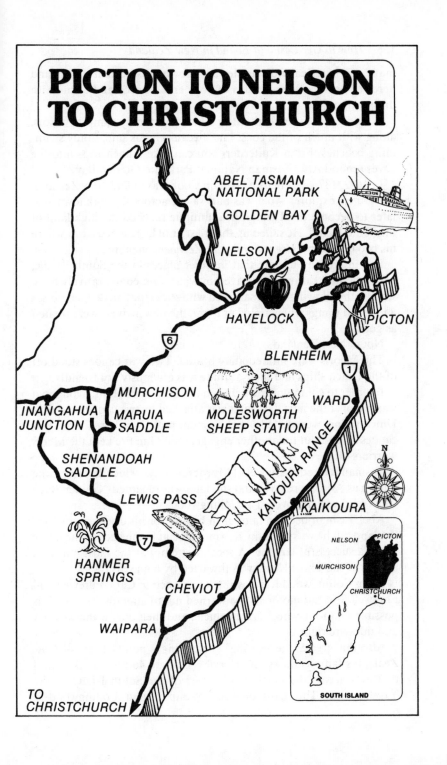

PICTON TO NELSON TO CHRISTCHURCH

ABEL TASMAN
NATIONAL PARK

GOLDEN BAY

NELSON

HAVELOCK

PICTON

BLENHEIM

MURCHISON

WARD

INANGAHUA
JUNCTION

MARUIA
SADDLE

MOLESWORTH
SHEEP STATION

KAIKOURA RANGE

SHENANDOAH
SADDLE

LEWIS PASS

KAIKOURA

HANMER
SPRINGS

CHEVIOT

WAIPARA

TO
CHRISTCHURCH

NELSON

PICTON

MURCHISON

CHRISTCHURCH

SOUTH ISLAND

many of New Zealand's apples are grown, passed dairyfarms and herds of beef cattle and fields of hops and tobacco and farms with drying kilns.

We drove as far as Kaiteriteri which is a family camping resort, along with much of the coast line, because it has safe, sandy swimming beaches. From Kaiteriteri you can take launch trips into the coves around Abel Tasman National Park into Golden Bay.

In 1642, 137 years before Captain Cook was to find New Zealand, the Dutch explorer Abel Tasman sailed across the unknown sea, later to become the Tasman Sea, until he reached the high land of the South Island. He sailed up the coast until he reached a bay where his two tiny ships, *Heemskerck* and *Zeehaen,* anchored.

It is interesting to note that in other places in the South Pacific, when the first Europeans arrived in what were comparatively huge ships with billowing white sails and with sticks that made loud noises and killed things when aimed at them, the new arrivals were treated as gods.

Not in New Zealand.

The Maoris were immediately hostile. Two war canoes stood off of the Dutch ships and their attitude was obviously not friendly.

In order to communicate between the two Dutch ships, a longboat was put over the next day but it was attacked by two canoes and four Dutch sailors were killed. Abel Tasman pulled anchor. Eleven war canoes started out for another engagement. Gun fire kept the Maori warriors off.

Tasman named the waters "Murderers Bay" which later became known as "Massacre Bay" and still later was renamed "Golden Bay" when gold was discovered at Collingwood.

Abel Tasman became famous in history for his discovery of New Zealand but he was officially reprimanded at home because he never made a successful landing. A second attempt at the most northern islands of the Three Kings was thwarted by high seas.

From Collingwood it is possible to proceed to Cape Farewell and Farewell Spit but motorists are warned not to attempt the Spit. It is possible in a four-wheel drive vehicle, and then only if the weather and tides are right.

Also this area is the starting – or ending – point of one of New Zealand's famous walks, the Heaphy Track, a 46-mile marked trail that cuts across the north-west corner of the South Island to the Tasman Sea. This land between Westport and Collingwood is known as "the back of beyond". The country is glorious. There are huts along the way and the walk takes four to six days depending upon the hiker's pace and the weather which can be treacherous. The best months of the year for the Heaphy walk are February and March, but it should not be attempted unless you are relatively young and fit . . . it is far tougher than the Milford Track.

There is talk of building a road from Collingwood to the west coast and, as you would expect, all the hikers are vehemently against the idea.

Retracing the coast road we stopped for morning tea at Motueka. A line at the bottom of the menu reads: "Don't knock the menu off! We will be happy to sell you one." (Menu sample: bacon and eggs $1.15. All meals served with chips, mixed veges, coleslaw, tea or coffee.) We bought two menus.

We stopped at a vegetable stand and bought an armload of fresh vegetables and stopped again at a butcher shop next to a freezing works and bought an entire fillet of beef for $2. Back in Nelson we got a dozen fresh scallops next to the fishery . . . Nelson scallops are known to be made in heaven.

That night we had scallops delicately done in butter and sherry. Thick sliced filet mignon. Fresh garden vegetables. And good dry, white wine. (McWilliams Cresta Doré).

You just can't eat better than that.

Typical of New Zealand weather, the sun was edging out the rain by the time we got back to Nelson, the self-acclaimed *Sunshine Belt*.

There is much to see in Nelson. There is a city tour that takes you through residential areas, scenic spots and places of pride to the 40,000 residents. Pick up a brochure titled *"Nelson Historical Gems and Museums"* and the seventeen-mile drive pamphlet from the Nelson Public Relations office.

You learn to watch for opening hours information because unless you visit in high season many places have restricted hours and many closed days.

The Isel House Museum and, behind it, the Provincial Museum were closed but we tippy-toed in behind a touring class of school tots. The china from Dresden in the Isel House was easily matched by the Dresden complexion of the children.

Of interest in the Provincial Museum were reminders of Baron Rutherford (1871–1937), born in the area and educated at Nelson College. He became "the father of nuclear physics" and first succeeded in splitting the atom for which he won the Nobel Prize in Chemistry in 1908 and was elevated to the peerage in 1931. He lies buried in Westminster Abbey. (Question: is he the only New Zealander buried in Westminster Abbey?)

The Cawthron Museum, next to the Cawthron Institute, is one of the main agricultural museums in the country. It serves as a showcase to relate science to agriculture. "An exquisite museum," says the brochure, "in an exquisite setting." It was closed.

Christ Church Cathedral dominates downtown Trafalgar Street and is a natural city-wide landmark. It is the fifth church to be built on the site.

Broadgreen was our favorite Nelson historic building. A two-story cob (dirt) house completed about 1855, it is a magnificent example of country-Victorian style, gracious and warm, particularly set off in an expanse of green lawns and fronted by rambling rose gardens. The Lady Navigator talked to a lady gardener whose only job was to snip off the wilted roses. Daily.

"How long do you do this each season?"

"From October through June," was the reply. Nine months!

We went away with a handfull of "wilted" roses that would turn most florists green with envy.

Had we stayed in Nelson another day we would have thrown a party, because you can rent Broadgreen for parties of six or more through the Public Relations office and wouldn't that be fun?

The Suter Art Gallery is adjacent to the small but watery-woodsy Queen's Park. The Gallery was erected in 1898 to house the collection of Bishop Suter. Featured among other New Zealand artists is John Gully whose paintings are excellent examples of the "soft" landscapes.

Our first South Island golf tournament was launched at 4:30 in the afternoon at the Nelson Golf Club, at the end of the Nelson Airport runway where your golf is frequently punctuated by overflying airplanes. Par 72.

In the fading light I hit a perfectly placed wedge shot to the white pin. The white pin turned out to be a light marker leading to the airport runway.

I protested vigorously to the Lady Navigator pointing out that directional problems were her responsibility. She never heard a word. Lost $3.

Highway 6 from Nelson to Murchison goes through Brightwater where Rutherford was born and where there is a memorial erected in his memory and through Wakefield, named after Arthur Wakefield, one of Edward Wakefield's brothers who was killed in an early Maori confrontation.

You pass through farmland that also offers roadside garden produce. Stop and shop before you reach the mountains, and fill up with gasoline.

From Wakefield you enter the Spooners Range and when you reach the summit you have views over the vast Golden Downs Forestry plantations. On a clear day you can look to the north and see the Tasman Sea and D'Urville Island. There is a section of the forest here known as Coronation Forest which is planted and cared for by school children.

You drop down the range to Motupiko Junction and proceed to Korere. The AA strip map offers a detour which will take you through Golden Downs and beech-covered country and eventually bring you back to Kawatiri Junction.

Staying on Highway 6 you follow the Buller River down to Murchison. Try to arrive in time for morning tea. About eleven, not earlier we learned. You might luck out at the Collins Tearoom and have Mrs Collins' hot scones. (She adds an egg to fluff them lighter.)

Murchison, population 580, stands in a lonely little green plain, surrounded by mountains and forests that tower over it and junctioned by the fish-filled Buller and Matakitaki rivers.

Born in the goldrush and later a farming community, the town was nearly exploded off the map by an earthquake in 1929 whose epicenter was near Murchison. The earthquake was of a size that rocked the entire country and evidence of earth that dropped and earth that was lifted and twisted is still visible on the Buller River below Murchison.

Murchison was also the center stage of Captain George Fairweather Moonlight. Books could be filled with stories of early New Zealand characters. Every book would have to include this perfect comic opera figure.

An American gold prospector in California and Australia, he

made successful findings in the goldfields of New Zealand, leaving the claims for others to mine. In Murchison he became a hotel keeper and also a keeper of the law, self-appointed. He was handy with his fists and was called "Yank" with respect.

Picture him in Wellington boots, jodhpurs, maroon sash and crimson shirt. And when he travelled, legend says, he only travelled at night.

Unfortunately, his end was tragic. His wife died. His business failed. Returning to prospecting, Captain George Fairweather Moonlight died alone in the bush.

There was talk of putting a large sawmill into Murchison. A local leader was indignant about the idea of such expansion and was quoted as saying, "Why, that could mean that some day we'd have stop lights in Murchison! As it is the policeman only comes by on Fridays."

Leaving Murchison towards Hanmer Springs and/or Christchurch you have three roads from which to choose.

Going straight ahead out of Murchison will take you over the Maruia Saddle Road which is probably all right if your teeth are firmly glued in place.

The easier and recommended route turns right out of Murchison, crosses the bridge to join Highway 65. It is not the easiest drive in the world either, even though it carries the name of the Shenandoah Route. Later you cross the Rappahannock River. Where did such American Indian names come from? They came from Captain George Fairweather Moonlight.

The third route is Highway 6 to Inangahua Junction, then Highway 69 to Reefton and then Highway 7 which goes across country joining Highway 1 on the east coast.

Following the Shenandoah Route you join Highway 7 at Springs Junction and head over Lewis Pass to the Hope River.

The summit of the Lewis Pass is 2,968 feet.

The Maoris used this mountain pass among others to reach the west coast, home of greenstone (nephrite) which was used as a cutting stone in peace and war and for decorations. It was much prized.

The journey by foot from one coast to another and back again was hard and long and food was a problem although slaves carried provisions for the party and fresh food, such as eels and birds, was found along the way. Part of the problem was solved on the return trip when the slaves, now carrying greenstone, having reached the summit and only downhill track in front of the party remained, were slain and eaten.

A place near the summit was known to the natives as "Good Eating of Human Flesh". It is now known as *Cannibal Gorge*.

We stopped after crossing the Hope Bridge at an ideal picnic spot tucked out of the wind beside Horseshoe Lake ... in the hills of the Glyn Wye homestead. The Lady Navigator covered a picnic table with a red checkered table cloth. Poured a medicinal portion of sherry into a tin cup. Served salad. Cold beer. Sandwiches of tender steak left-over from the feast of the night before.

One of our several three-star picnics.

Down the Hope River and the Waiau River, the banks on either side of the valley were blanketed with yellow *broom,* a noxious but beautiful plant in bloom. The scene looked like a float in the Rose Bowl Parade.

Hanmer Springs – 'n' *before* the 'm' – is the principal hot water spa of the South Island. Set in tall trees it has a 68-par golf course, tennis courts and good fishing in nearby rivers. Thermal pools are open to the public. There is horseback riding available, walks in the woods and, in the winter, skiing at the Amuri Ski Club on Mt St Patrick.

The Queen Mary Hospital specializes in the treatment of alcoholics.

Accommodations, despite the accolades of guidebooks, are thin. We didn't have a booking and after inspecting the available grim accommodations decided to push on to Christchurch.

The size and the amount of our luggage discouraged us from checking availability at The Lodge, which has fifty bedrooms and looks like a gracious hostel.

When we checked into Christchurch that evening the proprietor said, "I went to Hanmer Springs on my honeymoon and it wasn't any good then!"

Due north of Hanmer Springs is the giant Molesworth sheep station, its half-a-million acres comprising the largest single holding in New Zealand.

In its earliest days Molesworth produced fortunes but the rabbit pest put the bankrupted holding into Government hands in 1938. With modern control measures it now operates at profit to the taxpayer.

At Waipara Highway 7 joins Highway 1 which comes down from Blenheim.

Our route through Nelson to see the northern part of the South Island precluded taking this coastal road, but in our "what's-your-favorite-drive" game with New Zealand friends, several picked it as their favorite, referring to it as the "Kaikoura Drive". (When we reviewed the final results of our little game, all of the New Zealanders, with one exception, picked coastal roads.)

The Kaikoura Drive after leaving Blenheim first passes over easy, open grades through Seddon, named after a prime minister, and then skirts Lake Grassmere where the only solar salt works in New Zealand is located.

At Ward the first major South Island sheep station, Flaxbourne, was established in 1847. It reached a peak run of 60,000 sheep in 1879.

The drive then follows the coast, crossing the Ure and the Clarence rivers where a shipwreck in 1876 cost all but fifteen of forty-eight passengers' lives. Another shipwreck in 1924 didn't result in any loss of life but the remains of the wreck can still be seen from the road.

At the town of Kaikoura, visitors are recommended to drive out on to a peninsula and look back at the Seaward Kaikoura Range, particularly if it is covered with snow.

Beyond Kaikoura through Goose Bay and Oaro the road turns inland after crossing the Conway River and runs through Parnassus and Cheviot, where there is a pleasant picnic spot.

Shortly after leaving Cheviot it passes Nonoti which looks like another Maori name to overseas visitors but actually came from an incident dating back to the establishing of a railroad station there. An original settler, asked to name the station, replied: "No, not I." And Nonoti, one word, became the name of the siding.

The remainder of the drive is comparatively easy into Waipara Junction where Highway 1 joins the road coming from Hanmer

Springs. From Hanmer Springs to Christchurch is a straight, flat, easy drive after the winding mountain roads.

We were in Christchurch in time to shop and get ensconced into a spacious two-bedroom motel. $18 a night with newspaper and milk.

In Christchurch we learned that in a two-story motel it is better to take the upper story because it is better to have a party going on below you than above you.

Christchurch is a favorite city for many people in New Zealand and it is easy to understand.

When we first started to drive in New Zealand, we went 80 kilometers an hour. That is the national speed limit. We passed, in the first week, two house trailers, (caravans) and one broken down truck.

In the next week we boosted our speed to 90 kilometers an hour, and we passed three house trailers, two horse trailers and the same broken down truck that had driven straight through without stopping for tea.

Gradually we kept boosting our speed until we were passing policecars, ambulances and low-flying airplanes. In other words we were driving just like all the other New Zealanders. Then we realized we weren't seeing New Zealand at all. Those little white lambs out in the pasture had become a vast white carpet. The trees in the forests had become a wooden wall panel.

We slowed down to where we started and enjoyed the scenery ever after.

The advice of the Automobile Association is that tourist drivers shouldn't expect to make more than thirty-five to forty miles an hour on an average trip.

"Right on," as they say in New Zealand.

11. Christchurch ... More English Than The English

School Children in Uniforms ... Splendid Gothic Buildings ... A Quiet River ... Gardens and Gorges and Antique Shops

Christchurch is a city of 300,000 people yet it maintains the serenity of a quiet village town.

Backed by vast, verdant Canterbury Plains, the income for Christchurch is mainly agricultural.

A gentle little river, the Avon, willow-lined and oak-lined flows, wandering and carefree, through the city. Students in boats paddle on the river.

The number of pleasing Gothic buildings, the Canterbury Museum, Christ's College boys' school, the old Canterbury University, the Provincial Government buildings lend the city the proper solidly-English air.

School children in uniforms including some in straw boaters, and professors on bicycles with beards flowing and coats flying and satchels swinging on handlebars are a part of the everyday city scene.

So too are the matrons in their gloves and handbags, tailored pumps and Queen Mary hats, numbering more in Christchurch than in other New Zealand cities.

The city takes great pride in its gardens and the first thing a tour driver will want to do is to take you through a residential area to enjoy the multi-colored, obviously loved gardens. Christchurch calls itself the *Garden City*. Outside of Christchurch it is known as being "more English than the English".

It is not a surprise to read in the history of Christchurch that among the assignments of the first surveyor was to include space for the city's Botanical Garden and the Government Domain, a common early New Zealand practice.

Today the Botanical Garden in Christchurch covers 75 acres and

166

is worth as much time as you want to give it. If you don't want to stroll, there is an electrical tram called the Toast Rack which covers all of the walking paths seven days a week from September through April.

In back of the Botanical Gardens are the vast North Hagley and South Hagley Parks which contain sports fields including a golf course and a tennis club with over twenty-five grass courts.

Christchurch is a fine city for a walking tour. A good place to start a tour would be in the Canterbury Public Relations office which is housed in a Chamber of Commerce building. In 1887 the building served as council chambers for the city. The building carries the right flavor of the city including the motto "Britons Hold Your Own" on heraldic shields at the entrance. Here you can pick up current literature including the invaluable monthly guide.

Across the road from the Chamber of Commerce building are the Canterbury Provincial Government Buildings, a complex of buildings dating from 1859 which are considered the finest examples of Gothic architecture in New Zealand.

You can visit the stone Council Chamber built in 1865 which is the gem of the complex with much stone carving, stained glass windows, press and public galleries, and a barrel ceiling extensively decorated. Equally intriguing are the older vertically-timbered sections surrounding the courtyard which were part of the buildings completed in 1859.

Provincial Government was abolished in 1876, and the original Council Chamber is now sometimes used for court hearings. We weren't able to look inside but walking through the constricted, narrow, dark-timbered hallways filled with attorneys and their clients was sensation enough. Oliver Twist had to be around the next corner.

Along the riverbank from the 19th century Provincial Buildings is the modern Town Hall, the first real town hall for Christchurch, built at a cost of $5 million and completed in 1972. It boasts a large auditorium, a theater, conference facilities and a restaurant. Fronting the Town Hall is the spectacular Ferrier water fountain which, especially at night, looks like it is made out of fine lace.

You'll notice walking about Christchurch an abundance of statues.

At Cathedral Square you are in the spiritual and physical heart of the city. The spire of the Cathedral dominates the Square. You can climb to the top of the spire for views of the city; however when you learn that it has been damaged three times by earthquakes you might want to stay closer to the ground, as we did.

Even though Christchurch had been started with much Church of England backing, the lack of capital and a succession of economic problems held Christchurch back from erecting the places of worship and schooling originally envisaged for the new community. As a result the Cathedral was not completed until 1904.

Nearby the Square is New Regent Street with Spanish architecture – very different from what your eye has become accustomed to seeing in New Zealand. Most of the buildings on the street had been newly painted, and they sparkled.

From the Cathedral you walk west on Worcester Street, over the bridge, past the Chamber of Commerce building on your right and then the Canterbury Club on your left until you reach the old buildings of the University of Canterbury. They now house the art centre of Christchurch. (A vast, modern university has been built on the outskirts of the city and is included on daily conducted tours).

You are now facing the Canterbury Museum, a most enjoyable institution. Behind the Museum is the McDougall Art Gallery.

As you would expect the Museum has artifacts of Maori and other Polynesian cultures. There is a stagecoach and a hansom cab. Upstairs are the remains of an original snow tractor used by the Antarctic explorer Ernest Shackleton in 1907. (It was a failure.) The Museum also has a planetarium and a good exhibit summarizing the early exploration of New Zealand.

A great deal of space is devoted to recreating the past. Pioneer bedrooms and living rooms with mannequins dressed in the costumes of the era. There is a reconstructed shopping street of the 1860s, almost lifesize. It is well done. You wish the shops were still real and you could go inside and buy things.

Shopping in modern Christchurch is not bad.

We bought as presents sheepskin boots, sheepskin gloves and laminated placemats of New Zealand scenery. In one shop we bought soft lambswool sweaters to send to Italy. Yes, they would airmail. But the lady didn't have a weighing machine. She went next door. The proprietor next door was busy so she scooted down to the post office and came panting back with the correct postage. Beneath the English reserve the people in New Zealand are like that.

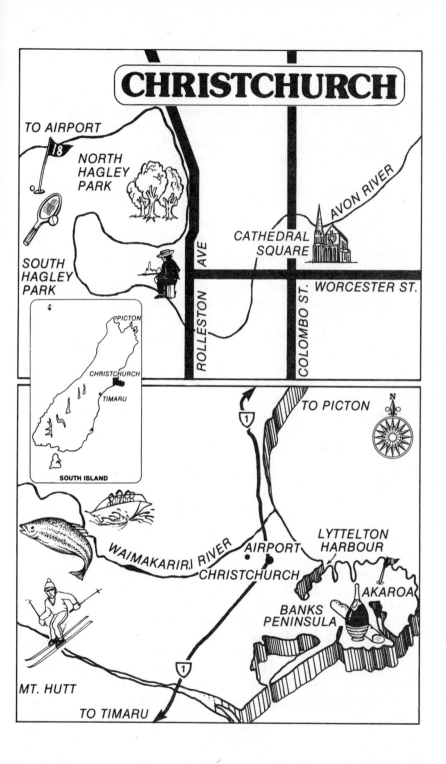

In one day we rummaged through four antique shops.

Also the first full day we were in Christchurch was the final of an auction of the large Gough estate and, fortunately, they were down to the kitchenware and linens. One antique dealer we visited had spent $7,000 during previous auction days which made the Lady Navigator faint with envy. Thank heavens we arrived so late.

There are many things to see and do outside of the walking distances in the city.

You can at least look at the exterior of Mona Vale, once the home of one of New Zealand's wealthiest women, the daughter of the owner of one of the great Canterbury sheep stations of long ago. The house with available picnic grounds was built in 1905 and is now used for receptions and exhibitions. You might luck out and find it open. It has a kauri staircase that is noble. The house and grounds are now owned by the Riccarton and Christchurch City Councils.

Ferrymead Museum, a technological museum, is still in the process of development.

You can go to the races.

Christchurch is known for its horse racing, particularly trotting. There are two official racetracks and seemingly hundreds of training tracks which you can spot from the air when you fly in. During November is "Race Week" when there are flat races one day alternating with trotting races the next day.

We made three trips to the city's environs. One to play golf, one to visit the little town of Akaroa, which still has traces of its French origins, and a third to go fishing in the Waimakariri Gorge, celebrated for its wild beauty.

Golf courses are everywhere in and around Christchurch.

Attracted by the description in a Government-published pamphlet on New Zealand golf, we went to Waitikiri, "a championship course, one of the most picturesque in New Zealand". It was indeed pleasant. The pro, who had worked in Oklahoma City, furnished us with free trundlers. The secretary gave us a pen.

The Lady Navigator gave me the usual beating.

Waitikiri is three and a half miles northwest of the center of the city. Par 72 over a 6,600 yard course. Greens fees are $3.00.

A golf course we wanted to play and didn't was Russley which you pass on the way into Christchurch from the airport. Russley has hosted many national and international golf tournaments.

Our second mission outside of the city was to spend a full day on Banks Peninsula visiting Akaroa, the once-French village forty-seven miles southeast of Christchurch, and to explore Lyttelton, the port town, and to poke around other bays on the peninsula.

Banks Peninsula was originally named Banks's Island after Sir Joseph Banks, the botanist who accompanied Cook on the first voyage. Later when the "island" was found to be a peninsula the name was changed.

Before the arrival of the Europeans, Banks Peninsula was heavily populated with Maoris but a violent fratricide conflict known as the "Eat-Your-Relations War" all but decimated the tribe and what their own intra-tribe conflict didn't destroy was later finished off by a mighty northern Maori warrior.

In 1840 a band of sixty-three French immigrants landed on Banks Peninsula, a portion of which had been bought by a French sea captain for 6,000 francs.

By itself the establishment of the French colony could have posed a threat to Britain's claim to sovereignty. However after the French had set sail from Europe, but before they landed, the Treaty of Waitangi had been signed and to make sure that there was no mistake about who had arrived first, a British ship was sent to the Peninsula to establish the flag which it did five days before the French arrived.

Akaroa is today a pleasant Victorian village with half of the street names being in French, the other half being English.

One street is named after the French Catholic Bishop, Pompallier, another is named after the Anglican Bishop, Selwyn.

One of the early cottages constitutes a museum. It is furnished in the style of the period. When it is closed, you can peek in the rear windows and see most of it. The age of the cottage is not certain but it may be the oldest remaining structure in Canterbury, having been evidently prefabricated in France.

Up the street from the cottage-museum is *L'Auberge Suzette,* a cottage-restaurant with an excellent reputation for its table. Seating is limited and you should have reservations if you are going to enjoy a French meal in what was once the only French colony in New Zealand.

Returning to Christchurch, we left the direct route of Highway 75 and cut north to Teddington which put us at the base of Lyttelton Harbor and then we leisurely drove around an inter-harbor coastal road until we reached the port town of Lyttelton.

Lyttelton is built on the side of a hill and it looks like any minute its population of just over 3,000 is going to slide down to the wharfs which supply its livelihood. It is small wonder that the town was passed over by the original settlers, who crossed the hills and established Christchurch.

A road tunnel, completed in 1964, now connects Lyttelton with Christchurch. It is the longest road tunnel in New Zealand and one of only two toll roads in the country. (Cost: 20c.) The other toll charge is for the Harbor Bridge in Auckland.

We had given top priority to fishing the Waimakariri River.

Rained out of going to the "Waimak" Gorge one day, we nevertheless took off on the trip the following day, despite warnings that the river was "milky" and fishing could be unrewarding.

We left the city on a sunny morning and followed the Waimakariri on the south bank and crossed it above Fairview and continued west until we reached the sheep station of Woodstock, a distance of fifty miles. (After crossing the river, as we turned to the west, we saw a little two-tennis court club, stuck out in the middle of nowhere, a sight we were to see many times in New Zealand.)

Following the disc markers of the Alpine River Jet Tours, we descended until we reached the river where our guide signaled us, told us where to park the car in the bush, led us to the cabin and poured morning tea. Our jet-boat was still in its cradle half in the water, attached to a tractor which could negotiate the river rocks without problems.

The guide backed the boat out of its cradle into the swift-flowing river and then pulled the craft around to the river bank and we clambered in and roared away.

The Hamilton jet-boat was invented and perfected in New Zealand by a station-owner-cum-inventor for just such rivers as the Waimak which flows through deep, comfortable stretches of water and then changes to shallow rapids with a minimum of water. Without using a propellor but by using water as a jet propellant, the Hamilton jet can safely negotiate four inches of water at high speeds.

Winding up the Gorge is an exhilarating experience because you are in virgin country and the birds and the scenery and, hopefully, the fish are not disturbed by great numbers of people. The fish were not disturbed by us either.

The sun turned to wind and then to rain and there were a few sprinkles of snow. We would stop and cast and then move on again.

The wind blew my hat into a shallow in the river. The guide with waders said, "I'll get it." He stepped over the side of the boat into quicksand. There was a moment of panic but he managed to pull himself back into the boat and the hat sank slowly into the river and away.

The Lady Navigator hooked a trout. It turned out to be eight inches, well below the allowable minimum. It went back. Later I caught a fairly good fish but that was released too.

We had lunch on the riverbank. The sun returned and the hot coffee and the sandwiches made a pleasant noon-time break. We didn't see any more fish except in another jet boat returning from further up the Gorge. Two sizeable rainbows.

The rainbow run in the Waimak from October 1 until January 1. Salmon run in the river from January 31 until April 1.

We followed the other boat in a spray of water back to the landing site at Woodstock and the boats were driven into the cradles and then, with the passengers still in the boat, were tractored over rocks and to dry land . . . in time for afternoon tea.

You can take an all-day river cruise by jet including transport to the river from Christchurch for $24 each. Jet charter for fishing is $120 a day including transport from Christchurch.

A raft trip costs $23 for one day and $60 for a two-day trip.

Signs in front of pubs: "Wednesday night housie: 7:30."
    What kind of hanky-panky is "housie"? Group sex?
    "Housie" is bingo.

We had dinner at an exclusive restaurant. Roast venison. The restaurant was so exclusive there was no one in it. Perfect. The dance floor was ours. We bought a drink for the two-man orchestra. The English waitress . . . always be kind to waitresses . . . said in a low tone: "Don't try the pavlova."

If you are in New Zealand for any length of time, you should have a checking account on a New Zealand bank along with a bank identification card.

There had been a two-day bank strike . . . the first in eighty years

. . . and we returned from the Waimak on a Friday night. We were fundless and heading for Mount Cook the next morning. We survived from Friday in Christchurch until Monday afternoon in Dunedin without any cash. You can cash New Zealand checks anywhere in New Zealand.

"The Yellow Rose" is a light car and, unlike heavier cars, tends to skip and jump about, particularly on dirt (metal) roads.

When the Lady Navigator was driving, she was urged not to point out the scenery with either hand thereby coming off the wheel but simply describe with a "left" or "right".

"But you know I don't know my left from my right."

"How about 'gee' and 'haw'?"

"I can never remember which one is which."

"How about port and starboard?"

"I don't know the bow from the stern. Go back to sleep."

We asked directions in a department store in Christchurch of a young saleslady.

She answered: "You go upstairs and it is to your left."

"Which way is to your left?" I asked.

She looked at her wrist and triumphantly said, "It is *that* way." We laughed and she added, "I never know until I look at my watch."

12. Christchurch to Dunedin via Mount Cook: The Alpine Route

The Chicken War ... New Zealand's Newest Thirstiest Town ... A Ski Plane to Tasman Glacier ... Man-made lakes ... Cave drawings ... Salmon fishing ... Giant bowling balls ... Serve-yourself vegetable stands.

Leaving Christchurch and heading south on Highway 1 just inside the coastline, the roads are bullet-shot straight across multiple rivers.

After crossing the Rakaia River you can turn to the west and reach the ski fields of Mt Hutt, a ski area fast growing in reputation particularly among the students in Christchurch.

Two and a half hours of easy driving and you are entering Timaru.

Chicken is a popular, fast-food item in New Zealand drive-in-take-away stands. Competition is heavy. Entering Timaru there is a drive-in stand on one side of the road that advertises: "CALIFORNIA CHICKEN". On the other side is a second drive-in. Not to be outdone it advertises: "INTERNATIONAL SOUTHERN FRIED CHICKEN".

Timaru is a solid port town with spruced up Victorian hotels. You'd like to wrap them in a package and send them home.

Overlooking Caroline Bay, it wears the prosperous air of a town that does well in commerce and with tourism. A three-week carnival at Christmastime fills the town from border to border.

There is a handsome church, St Mary's Anglican Church, with a crenelated stone tower, and beside it the Pioneer Museum which is in a modern building. It is one of the few modern-building museums we were to see in New Zealand, but it was closed, as was the highly recommended art gallery with the impossible name, Aigantighe.

Timaru is remembered as a birthplace of leading sport figures. Phar Lap ... or Lightning ... was born here. Bob Fitzsimmons built his physique in his father's Timaru blacksmith shop and went on to

175

win the world middleweight, light-heavyweight and heavyweight titles.

He had 354 fights of which 350 were in the boxing ring and four were in the matrimonial ring. Won first. Lost second.

Another sports figure was John Lovelock, a progenitor of New Zealand's successful distance runners, who set the world record for the mile and for the 1,500 meter in the 1936 Olympics held in Germany. He was presented with an oak tree by Adolf Hitler which is still growing at his alma mater, the Timaru Boys High School.

Turning back north out of Timaru we picked up Highway 8 to Mount Cook.

Highway 8 goes through villages with pleasant names like Pleasant Point, Cave – I always think of wine cellars – and Fairlie. There's a transport museum at Fairlie. (New Zealand must import old railroad cars to stock all of the transport museums.)

Soon we were at Lake Tekapo and shortly thereafter at Lake Pukaki. It was a sunny day and Mt Cook with its diadem of snow-covered peaks was regal, the perfect mountain across a perfect lake.

The Government Tourist Bureau in Wellington couldn't find space for us at any of the accommodations at Mount Cook, all operated by the Government-owned THC, but they did find us space at the construction town of Twizel, a few miles south of Lake Pukaki.

We had been in Russell in the Bay of Islands, the oldest town in New Zealand, and now we drove into Twizel, the youngest town in New Zealand.

Twizel – as in *twilight* and not as in *twiddle* – was started in 1971 by the Ministry of Works for the labor force required by the vast Upper Waitaki Power Development. Dam builders. Canal builders. Construction men. Thirsty men.

There are 6,000 people now in Twizel and we had a room in the only hotel in town. It also housed the only public bar. It was late Saturday afternoon when we rolled in and you could say the party in the public bar was going pretty good.

The Lady Navigator wanted to go have a look.

"Not with me, you don't," she was firmly told.

Later I asked a man from Twizel what was the record for drinking at the public bar at Twizel Inn in a day.

He knew. "It was 160 dozen bottles of beer." (That's close to 2,000 bottles.)

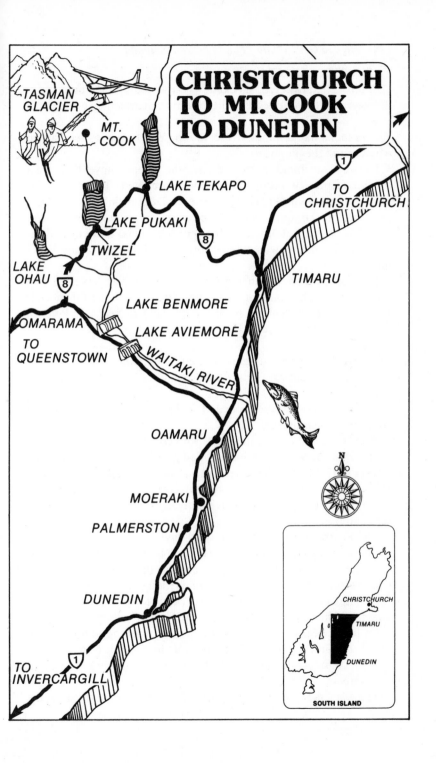

"Pints?" he was asked.

"Pints?" he answered, shocked. "You wouldn't have time to get the tops off the wee ones. Oh, no, 26-ounce quarts, they were."

Twizel looks like a military reservation. You expect to see barbed wire around the perimeter.

Isolated, surrounded by rawness, the people have that great human faculty of keeping themselves occupied. There are over ninety different kinds of clubs. Sewing clubs, gun clubs, flying clubs, on and on. To quote the Government's brochure on Twizel: "...active organizations cater for sporting, social and cultural interests as diverse as winemaking, breast feeding and square dancing".

We took advantage of there being a golfers' club and, blessed with the long daylight hours of early summer, went to the Ohau Golf Club – a member lent me his trundler – and played nine holes to finish off the day's drive.

The next day we were up early to make reservations for a Tasman Glacier flight from Mt Cook which we hadn't been able to book in Wellington.

We could have stayed in bed. The Twizel hotel operator didn't come on duty until eight.

After the hotel chef, a nice lady who couldn't be disguised from being what she was, a camp cook, had given us a light construction worker's breakfast – juice, cereal, eggs, bacon, sausage and racks and racks of hot toast together with tea and coffee – we grunted our way towards Mt Cook, an hour's drive away, with phone "good as gold" reservations assured.

The weather held up beautifully all day.

There are New Zealanders who tell you that they have been to Mt Cook several times and have never seen the top of the mountain. We had the sun and the peaks with us all day long.

Mount Cook is a national park. It is known for its alpine peaks – among the highest in the Southern Alps – and for its glaciers.

Of its 27 peaks, Mt Cook is the highest reaching almost 13,000 feet. It was first climbed in 1894. The more formidable Caroline Face was not conquered until 1970. Naturally the whole park is a delight for climbers.

The glaciers are to many people the first attraction of the park, the

Tasman Glacier being the best known. (I had tried to ski here in July and was rained out. Now it was early summer and the snow looked gorgeous.)

Hunting is permitted in the park, which is not surprising when you learn of the destructive nature of the Himalayan *thar* and the European *chamois* to the vegetation. Shooting is therefore encouraged. Shooting permits must be obtained from the Chief Ranger.

There are many good walks in the area although, after becoming accustomed to the greenery and lushness of the New Zealand bush, the bleakness of hiking through the grey-rock shingle left by the glaciers is a different experience.

We checked into the park's information center where there were early climbing pictures, examples of flora and fauna, maps and brochures to pick up.

If you are interested in a hike, you can ask at the counter for a recommendation and they will plot out a hike for you from a half a dozen routes. We opted for a walk up the Hooker Valley after inspecting the accommodations of the Hermitage Hotel and the Tasman Lodge and the Glencoe Lodge and the Mount Cook Motel. The Hooker Valley walk starts at a picnic spot and goes by the original site of the first Hermitage. There is a dramatic swing bridge, one of two, before reaching the Sefton Stream and then to the face of the Hooker Glacier.

Any walk in the Mount Cook Park on a fine day is one of awe. The surrounding peaks, the fields of snow, the overhang of glaciers are simply awesome sights.

We lunched in the picnic area, surrounded by the tall mountains and fell asleep in the sun, tired from our walk and then, refreshed, drove to the airport and signed on for our flight to the Tasman Glacier.

Flying up the Tasman Glacier and landing on the snow is a mass operation.

Six planes, each carrying five passengers plus the pilot, take off in tandem, fly up the valley, and land on the glacier. The pilot volunteers to take your picture with a Polaroid camera and mount it in a "certificate" for $2.50, and you fly out again.

When the weather is brilliant in a mountain area where the weather is so often unpredictable, the flying tour goes on all day long. While we were waiting for our plane, a flight came in bringing four skiers.

"How was the snow?"

The tanned, happy skier just beamed, "Real beaut! You could do anything on it. We were just going good when they came to take us out."

The ski plane takes skiers to the top of one plateau and then flies down and picks them up again. What a great way to ski.

Lots of little old ladies were also waiting for the Tasman flight.

Overheard. First lady to third lady: "I still have the West to do and Japan and Europe."

Second lady to third lady: "Isn't she brave? And she only lost him last Autumn."

Despite the mass operation of the Tasman flight, it is still a thrill. Wing-tip to jowl with the mountain peaks is sensational. Landing and taking off on the snow is fun.

We turned down the $2.50 opportunity for a "certificate" which smacked of hustle . . . one of the rare times in New Zealand we were to encounter it . . . and took our own pictures.

The cost of the flight was $26 for forty minutes or $37 for sixty minutes.

We returned to Twizel, driving down the length of Lake Pukaki, which being a glacier-fed lake and without any nutrients doesn't hold the trout of the usual New Zealand lake.

At the dam site we detoured to visit the observation point and overlooked the massive construction elements. The earth-moving statistics were staggering. For example the concrete required by the dam amounted to 194,000 square yards.

The information office for the project was still open and we found it to be both interesting and educational.

Isolated as New Zealand is and without any oil deposits to speak of, the country is saved by its rushing waters which are converted, although at huge initial costs, into hydro-electric projects.

In New Zealand it is best just to listen and not comment about hydro-electric projects because the amount of money being spent, how and where the electricity is being used and the environmental aspects of raising the levels of lakes and controlling the flow of water in rivers is more than a little controversial. Especially in the South Island.

However, the point is a visitor to New Zealand will often see as part of touring suggestions, a visit to a hydro-electric project. To us, it would be one of the last things on our list of desired tours. Twizel taught us that it was a visit not to miss.

Twizel also brought us a realization of a characteristic of the New Zealand people we hadn't appreciated before ... and that is their reserve, their reticence.

The average New Zealander is extremely friendly, hospitable and polite. Once you are picked up by a New Zealander, you enter a roaring relationship and, having great New Zealand friends, we were somewhat apprehensive that we wouldn't be left alone. Not at all. Until you cross a delicate line, your life is your private affair.

We were brought to face with this characteristic not by New Zealanders but, being in a Government hotel and back in the middle of the tourist circuit, by Americans. Six out of the twelve hotel guests were Americans and two out of the six Americans were drunk.

There is nothing worse than a drunken American out of his own country.

He is loud, conceited, obnoxious and, the drunker he is, the more provincial he is.

"I was the Golden Boy of Florida real estate!"

Oh, save us, God.

As the camp cook gently said, "Some Americans are more American than other Americans." And she added the usual non-didactic question: "You know what I mean?"

Twizel to Dunedin

From Twizel to the coast city of Oamaru the man-made lakes and power stations of Benmore, Aviemore and Waitaki can be seen and visited and bring the hydro-electric scheme of New Zealand into better focus.

The promotional information at Twizel emphasizes the positive recreational aspects of the hydro-electric system pointing out, with added colored pictures, that damming the Waitaki not only pro-duced needed power but also created boating, water skiing, swim-ming and fishing where there had been comparatively none before.

The lakes are well stocked with rainbow and brown trout and land-locked salmon.

Lake Benmore is mammoth and is the largest man-made lake in

the country holding one and a half as much water as Wellington Harbor. You can turn off Highway 83 at Otematata and visit the observation point or arrange for fishing trips.

After Kurow you follow the Waitaki River to Duntroon. Before reaching Duntroon . . . a Brigadoon-type name . . . you will see a cliff of white rock known to the Maoris as Takiroa ("rock-cry" or "echo rock").

According to the AA guide the peculiar hollowed formation results in an original sound being eliminated and only the echo being audible. It didn't echo for us.

Within the hollow of the walls are ancient Maori paintings, many of them vandalized.

At Duntroon there is a Scottish church that looks like it belongs in a little village called Duntroon. Picture-taking time.

From here to the mouth of the river, the Waitaki is famous for its salmon fishing, which starts in January.

Oamaru with a population of 14,000 is a port town, a stone town, and birthplace of the modern meat-export market.

Many of the buildings in Oamaru are made of the creamy Oamaru stone which can be cut in a quarry with a hand saw. The stone hardens and endures with weather and time. Many of the classical buildings in New Zealand have used the stone from Oamaru.

Naturally its own buildings favor the local stone to the city's advantage because the white facing has a pleasant air.

The early beginning of Oamaru's port was disastrous as the attempt of establishing a successful harbor was marked by ship-wreck after shipwreck. Finally a huge breakwater and a protective wharf were constructed, the bottom of the harbor proved dredgable and Oamaru at last had its own port where surrounding livestock could be exported and goods imported.

However the fame of the area is not in the town itself but in the successful efforts by executives of the giant New Zealand & Australian Land Company to export frozen meat in the 1880s.

Sheep up until this time were grown for wool and once beyond that use the sheep were destroyed, driven over cliffs in some cases.

On the nearby holding of the company, the first attempt was made in 1882 to export refrigerated meat. The first load of 130 tons was shipped from Dunedin to England and arrived in good condition after being more than three months en route. This was the break-through that led to the giant frozen meat industry which, today, is such a vital part of New Zealand's economy.

South of the city, on the road to Dunedin, is a monument to Thomas Brydone who was the colonial manager for the company and who, with the general manager of the company, William Davidson, was responsible for the frozen meat experiment.

Further along Highway 1 you come to Moeraki, the site of one of nature's curios, the Moeraki Boulders which are giant-sized, per-fectly rounded boulders formed with a core of carbonate of lime and surrounded by layers of silica, aluminum and peroxide of iron. Early sailors called them The Ninepins.

Many of them have been removed but many others, too heavy to remove, still dot the beach.

There is a Moeraki Boulder outside of the Otago Museum in Dunedin.

Continuing south from Palmerston (you want to stop at many of the colorful picnic areas) you pass through farm country and, of course, vegetable stands. We stopped at the first one.

There was a young man there who we thought was the proprietor but who was waiting for the proprietor.

There wasn't meant to be a proprietor.

We finally made the right deduction by looking at the signs with prices on the vegetables . . . an open cigar box to receive money and make change . . . . There was no proprietor.

You made your own selection, weighed what needed to be weighed, wrapped your own vegetables in newspaper, added up your own bill, made your own change if necessary and were on your way.

Later we found out in Dunedin that this is a common practice in Otago. The owner might lose a little to the dishonest but he certainly saves on labor.

It marked the kind of independence that we were to find in Dunedin and all of Otago.

13. Dunedin: Edinburgh Of The South

Chocolates and Whiskey and a Gingerbread Railroad Station ... A Mansion and a Castle ... Early Settlers ... A Wandering Whare

Dunedin is a candy kiss.

Founded by rebel Scots, funded by miner's gold, decorated with noble buildings, Dunedin is the *Edinburgh of the South.*

They make chocolates and whiskey in Dunedin. The streets smell of chocolate. They say that when coffee is being roasted in the Gregg's plant and is mixed with the odor of chocolate being made in the Cadbury plant, it will make you walk on tiptoes.

If this doesn't please you, look at the railroad station. Gad, what a grand building! Gingerbread in stone. Turrets and battlements, stained glass and mosaics, ceramic figures, decorated ceilings. Look at the station master's office door with its beautiful wood and brass fittings and etched glass.

The railroad station is symbolic of Dunedin and of all of the pride of yesteryear.

Once the most populated city in New Zealand and with the money from the Otago goldfields skillfully employed by Scottish bankers, 19th century Dunedin rode a wave of booming prosperity it was not to see again.

Today city fathers decry the growth rate of only three per cent a year. Secretly they seem pleased about it.

Dunedin is still economically healthy. There are woolen mills and foodstuff manufacturers and the construction of railroad rolling stock and a prosperous port and a university with 6,000 students, and a growing tourist industry.

In tourist terms of bed-nights sold, Dunedin has a growth-rate second only to Auckland.

Fortunately we had friends in Dunedin who made reservations for us. A large convention had taken all rooms as far away as Oamaru and our local friends were busy for a week finding us a place to stay. It turned out to be quite luxurious in a new hotel-motel which was dedicated the same day we moved in. On a fourth floor we had a bedroom, bath, sitting room with pullman kitchen and a huge balcony. The milk was in the refrigerator down the hall. Newspaper, of course, at the door every morning. Color television and maid service. $26 a day.

There is a nice rebel air about the people in Dunedin we noticed immediately. They park their cars where they like. They ignore seat belts. They jaywalk. They don't put coins in meters. They more or less do what they like, when they like and as they like. It's their nature.

However Dunedin is thriftily organized and prides itself as being the cheapest city in New Zealand for retail goods. Its new building costs are 20 per cent below those of the North Island.

Besides serving as a gateway to the many scenic offerings of Otago, Dunedin has in itself a basketfull of goodies to see and do.

A visit to the Otago Public Relations office produces a mass of what-to-do literature. Besides the standard monthly visitors' guide, there is a "Know the City Walk", "Know the Region Drive" and "Dunedin's Golden Arrow Scenic Drive".

But walk Dunedin first. Start at the Octagon which was planned to be the center of the city two years before Otago was first settled in 1848. Befitting the Scottish heritage there is a statue to Robert Burns.

In the center of Octagon is the Star Fountain, donated by the local evening newspaper, which gives a display every evening of water and lights and music.

Facing the Octagon are St Paul's Cathedral and the Municipal Chambers, both worth visiting. When we went into the Municipal Building a lady asked us if we would like to see the upstairs Council Chambers and another lady met us at the second floor and took us into the Chambers, a dark room with curved desks and walls filled with paintings of former city fathers looking sternly down on us . . . like city fathers are supposed to look.

Walking down Stuart Street you pass the *Evening Star* building on the left and the Law Courts on the right. The Law Courts, built at the turn of the century, are of Leith stone and complete with battlements. A worthy building.

At the end of Stuart Street you are facing Anzac Avenue and the marvelous Railway Station. Across the street and down a block is the Police Station which was built in 1895 on the site of the old jail in a style taken from New Scotland Yard in London.

The Law Courts, the Railway Station, the Police Station, all within a block of each other, make a happy trinity.

The Lady Navigator, who is forever rearranging things, wanted to move the functions of these buildings into the nearby Cadbury chocolate plant and move the making of chocolate bars into the Railway Station, bonbons into the Law Courts and chocolate-covered cookies into the Police Station.

And at holiday time, she went on, they should make chocolate replicas of all the buildings to hang on Christmas trees. She was promised a chocolate milk shake for good thinking and was led happily down the road to the Early Settlers' Museum.

When you walk into the Early Settlers' Museum you are overwhelmed by the walls covered with hundreds of early photographs and paintings of the men and women who first settled in Otago. There is a nearby office which will help you trace your ancestry if you think one of your forebears was one of the pioneers.

Suddenly the country's string of pioneer museums and the re-creating of early settlers' villages and the preservation of names of ships come into focus.

The European immigrants take great pride in their inheritance. The pride manifests itself in the re-staging of the pioneer life including the preservation, almost idolization, of the ships that brought the first settlers.

In America the custom of heritage is as deeply established. If one's forefather "came over on the *Mayflower*" which goes back to the first Pilgrims in 1620, the inheritor has established territorial one-upmanship for all who came after.

In Hawaii there is a Cousin's Society which hands down the early settler-missionary inheritance with the same pride.

Pre-dating them all was the Maori. As we have learned, he continues to trace his ancestors back to the original canoe that came from *Hawaiki* and often the tribe was named after the canoe.

Looking at the walls heavy with the stoic, formal pictures of the Early Settlers, you suddenly see them in a new context.

The Early Settlers' Museum has the last of the kerosene lamps that used to light the city streets, a locomotive in a glassed-in windowcase and an old cable car. Cable cars used to sprinkle the hills of Dunedin, copied and improved upon from those of San Francisco.

There are original town-plan drawings and rare furniture, for example a steamer trunk that converts into a desk and a barrel organ

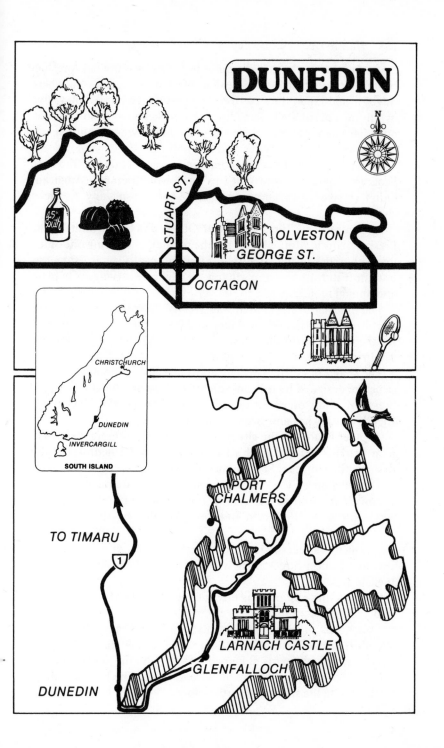

that came over on the ship *Dominion* in 1851. It was used in Anglican church services which were held in the old jail (gaol) and where waves would lap at the steps during high tide. The organ plays five hymns on a perforated metal disc and we listened to its surprisingly fine tone when a curator played it for a band of school children.

Why were church services held in a jail?

You are reminded that the community was founded by the Free Scots (Presbyterian) and that the English immigrants (Anglican) didn't receive much encouragement. There wasn't any Anglican church.

By contrast, the First Church of Otago which was built by the Presbyterians in Moray Place, has the reputation of being one of the finest churches in the country. Of unreinforced Oamaru stone, its interior features a fine rose window and delicate carvings with plant and animal motifs.

The minister of the church was Thomas Burns, a nephew of the poet Robert Burns, and the young architect who won a competition for the design of the church was R. A. Lawson whose imaginative stamp is seen on other buildings in Dunedin.

The Otago Boys' High School, above the city, is another beautiful structure designed by the same architect. You are appalled to learn that there is talk of tearing down the old school (1885) but Dunedin friends say this has now been dismissed.

Another church in the city by the famous English architect, William Petre, is the St Joseph's Roman Catholic Cathedral. He also designed the adjacent St Dominic's Priory.

The religion of the city, not surprisingly, is dominated by the Presbyterians with 40 per cent of the population, followed by the Anglicans with 20 per cent and Roman Catholics with 15 per cent.

The principal street of Dunedin is George Street. At the Octagon, it becomes Princes Street along which are several classic buildings of the late 1800s.

Opposite the post office is the Australia New Zealand Bank, now undergoing restoration.

Two hotels on Princes Street that are rich in nostalgia are the Wain's Hotel, 1878, done by Mason & Wales, an architectural partnership which still exists in Dunedin today, and the Southern Cross Hotel which incorporates the old Grand Hotel. The bank buildings further along the street are worth noting.

Also on Princes Street is the Government Tourist Bureau. Snappy-eyed Scottish lasses. Lovely. They booked an airline to Stewart Island, changed motel reservations, made new ones, hunted down information on the Golden Shears event in Masterton in March.

We went to a small "buffet" given by friends at their home in Dunedin.

There was salad, rainbow trout in egg batter, steak casserole, Jewish meat balls, Thai chicken, smoked salmon, eggs, potatoes, tomatoes, red wine, white wine. For dessert there was pavlova, fudge cake and cookies.

Said the Dunedin friend, "We" – chomp, chomp, chomp, – "in New Zealand" – chomp, chomp, chomp – "eat" – chomp, chomp, chomp – "too much!" And he roared with Falstaffian good humour.

Early the next morning a member of the party took us to his country club, the Otago Golf Club. In Dunedin it is called Balmacewan because that is the club's location. It is the oldest club in New Zealand, founded in 1871.

It was Tuesday morning and, as every golfer knows, Tuesday is usually ladies' day, which is a pit of potential horrors in which you do not want to drop. However our friends got us on the back nine which we were able to complete, speedily, before catching up the women who were still teeing off the first tee. We retreated to the car and quietly, unobtrusively, carefully, drove away. Fees: $6 including trundler.

The Otago Golf Club has an absolutely unique feature. After finishing the *tough* par-five 11th hole – the Lady Navigator made a par – you come to an invention you've never seen on a golf course. A rope tow! You press a button, grab the moving rope which helps pull you and your trundler up the hill.

"Oh, yes," said a member. "We used to have a tractor and cart down there to take you up the hill – but with the price of help these days –."

The canny Scots.

Another outstanding golf course is the St Clair Golf Club which was holding a professional tournament when we were there. It is a hill-top, scenic course with undulating fairways, heavy on trees. It is open to visitors on Mondays, Wednesdays and Fridays only.

Logan Park, one of the many parks in the city, is a playing field for the Otago University and also has a tennis club with twenty-five hard courts and twelve grass courts.

In the afternoon the Lady Navigator went antique hunting with a Dunedin friend. She reported that the claim of good pricing in Dunedin carries over into antiques. Great things to be had at great prices.

That night we dined sumptuously at *La Scala,* a highly successful Italian restaurant which is a Dunedin favorite for banquets, wedding receptions, and private dinner parties.

In a morning you can visit two unique homes, one in Dunedin, one outside of Dunedin, and then have lunch in a gracious country garden.

The home in Dunedin is "Olveston", a Jacobean-style mansion of thirty-five rooms built between 1904 and 1906 for a wealthy, much-travelled Dunedin businessman and his wife and bequeathed to the city by the daughter of the family, along with a trust fund for its maintenance. The city debated almost a year before accepting the offer.

Olveston is now a living museum of the "upstairs-downstairs" life of yesterday, a cache of tasteful antiques, art works, curios. Everything is left as it used to be.

The mansion is a bit unnerving in a way because you feel the clock has stopped. The calendar on the wall will read "1910", and a door will open and the master of the house will step through and ask imperialistically, "What are you doing here?"

The whole thing is a treasure. The men will be particularly attracted to the billiard room and the women to the progressive kitchen – progressive at least for that time.

Wandering from room to room you can feel the depth of personality and sensitiveness of the owners. They took understanding care of their help. They collected *avant-garde* paintings. They incorporated innovative ideas into the design of their home. They had creative, interesting friends.

For example the formal dining table is set with actual placecards found in a drawer for a select dinner party believed to have been held on the night that Sir Truby King introduced the idea for the founding of the future Plunket Society, the phenomenally successful mother-and-child care system.

Now you wish the master and his mistress would step through the door because you're dying to meet them.

Fortunately the guides conduct the tours with obvious love and enthusiasm for *their* mansion.

To see Olveston make a booking and you'll take precedence over visitors without reservations. You can only see the house on a guided tour. The first tour starts at 9:30.

The home outside of the city is Larnach Castle which is reached on a scenic drive out the Otago Peninsula.

Before taking the Peninsula Drive, you can incorporate the Golden Arrow Scenic Drive into the outing.

The Automobile Association of Otago has published a pamphlet on the drive which is available at the Public Relations office or at the AA office. With the brochure's map laid out before you, you can quickly understand the pride the city holds in the green network of continuing parks which surround the city.

The Town Belt, as it is called, was part of the original plan of the city . . . the city planners were a hundred years ahead of their time . . . and today the 500-acre Town Belt provides a green visual pleasure as it winds through the hills above the city. Don't miss it.

To drive out the peninsula you can take the Highcliff Road out and the Harborside Drive back.

Larnach Castle is a curio.

Built in 1871 by William Larnach, an Australian-born Dunedin banker, entrepreneur and politician, for his French wife of royal blood, no money was spared in its construction. Craftsmen were imported from England and Italy. Two hundred workmen were employed at one time constructing the shell. Tiles, glass, woods, bricks and marble were imported from Europe. The bricks in the stables were imported from Marseilles at a cost of sixpence each and you can't miss the upstairs Italian marble bathtub that weighs a ton.

Much of Larnach, compared to the quiet exquisiteness of Olveston, is in a shambly state but the climb to the rooftop battlements through a stone spiral staircase is worth the visit alone. Magnificent views from Dunedin to Port Chalmers to the beaches on the Pacific Ocean.

Again, like Olveston, you find the character of the owner in this extravagant relic. The promoters call it a castle. With its forty-five rooms you would at least class it as a mansion. Larnach, in a reverse of character, called it *The Camp*.

You have to remember that the building was started when Dunedin was still only twenty years old and its location thirty miles from town posed an awesome commute for the banker. But he had matched teams of blood horses ... six greys and six blacks ... and you can imagine his carriage leaving the estate in a thundering clatter of hoofs. Marvelous!

Larnach's ending was similarly exhibitionistic. Whether triggered by financial collapses all around him or a personal scandal which was hinted at, he committed suicide in Wellington's Parliament Building, shocking the country.

Our Dunedin friends, Tom and Phyllis Cole, stopped the car for morning tea. Because of the high wind, no table cloth was spread and tea was served out of the trunk (boot). However Tom provided a dampened cloth for refreshing the hands and another cloth for drying them, a nicety we had been lacking in our car teas which was brought to the attention of the Lady Navigator. Worthy observation. Chilly reception.

Almost all museums in New Zealand have bird exhibits of one sort or another. You should remember to look for a Royal Albatross, a huge bird, because at the end of the peninsula, at Taiaroa Head, is a world rarity, a breeding colony of the Royal Albatross. With a wing span of over three yards, the birds can sometimes be seen airborne from the road.

The colony is severely protected. A full-time officer is on duty and you have to obtain permission for a visit from the Government Tourist Bureau. The colony was closed when we were in Dunedin because an albatross had made a nest across an incoming path.

Returning from Larnach via the Harbourside Drive brings you by Glenfalloch Woodland Gardens, originally a homestead built more than a hundred years ago by a Dunedin businessman. The gracious, white homestead today caters private parties.

The property is now owned by the Otago Peninsula Trust and is known for its collection of azaleas and rhododendrons and fuchsias.

It is a pretty spot. In addition to the homestead, morning and afternoon teas are offered in a new Swiss-styled building called the *Chalet* and there is dining and dancing in another facility, the *Log Cabin*.

Curious why all signposting in New Zealand is done by the Automobile Association instead of the government, we called on the AA in Otago.

The Automobile Association grew out of individual regional motor clubs which, probably for their own safety, took on the responsibility of road signs.

Today the Automobile Associations are still independent organizations, there are fifteen of them in the country, but they all belong to a central council located in Wellington.

The job of signposting is subsidized by the Government, which covers 75 per cent of the cost. The Otago AA Official said that his council is known for the best signposting in the country.

In Otago there are 30,000 members of the AA. There are over one-half million in New Zealand.

Throughout New Zealand you will find commercial tours as part of the attractions offered to visitors. Cigarette works, automobile plants, woolen mills, slaughterhouses, etc.

As part of our research we were determined to sacrifice ourselves and take part in whatever New Zealand had to offer, including commercial tours. We signed up for the tour of the chocolate factory and the whiskey distillery.

The Cadbury-Fry-Hudson plant is a major operation. In one four-story building over 900 employees are engaged in making dark chocolate, light chocolate, bitter chocolate, sweet chocolate and turning the chocolate into every conceivable form of candy and cookie. The Lady Navigator who whimpers like a puppy at the mere sight of a chocolate bar was in heaven.

There was chocolate being swirled slowly in huge vats, there was chocolate being dripped on to candy cubes, there was chocolate being mixed with roasted nuts, there was chocolate covering biscuits and chocolate being wrapped in foil and chocolate being decorated ... and on and on.

Offered samples, like greedy little children wide-eyed, we refused nothing. I thought when we returned to the hotel the Lady Navigator would ask to lick my shoes. We were even given a box of chocolates on departure.

One of our Dunedin friends said that from time to time the factory offers a surplus of coconut husks for sale which make ideal garden mulch. He uses the husks with the result that his garden smells faintly but distinctly of chocolate.

The making of whiskey is a Scottish inheritance and to the first Scottish farmers the family whiskey-still was as much a part of the family furniture as the family bed.

The Hokonui Hills near Gore are synonymous with the making of illicit whiskey which went beyond family consumption and spread to a fairly sizeable public market. Like the Blue Mountains of Virginia in America, the Hokonui Hills contained a high number of bootleggers and there was an almost comic duplication of "moonshiners" and "revenooers" in Hokonui. Although there are rumours that whiskey is still being made in the hills, the lack of any arrests seem to deny the rumours.

It is astonishing to learn that only one whiskey distillery exists in New Zealand and that its whiskies didn't go on the market until 1974.

Whiskey was produced successfully in Dunedin from 1869 to 1875, when the Government imposed crippling duties on New Zealand-produced spirits. The distilling of New Zealand whiskey was banned from that time until 1964, when approval was given to Wilson, a maker of malt extracts, to distill spirits.

With the backing of the giant food firm, Gregg's, Wilson Malt Extract Company Ltd. was changed to Wilson Distillers Ltd. and now produces 200,000 gallons of malt and grain whiskey annually.

45 South is a light whiskey and *Wilson's,* a second brand, is darker and fuller.

In the name of research we tried both brands and found them remarkably mature and smooth. The more we sampled them, the smoother they became.

In order to promote a New Zealand drink, the marketing men have come up with "45 & Paeroa" which calls for two ounces of 45 South over ice and filled with Lemon & Paeroa. It will never replace a good dry Martini.

In the same area of town as the distillery are a group of visitor "must-dos": Dunedin Public Art Gallery, the University of Otago, Otago Museum, the Botanic Gardens.

The Dunedin Public Art Gallery, while functional in name, is imaginative in its collection. Disappointingly, its collection of Frances Hodgkins, one of the largest in the country, was displaced by a showing of costumes from a period motion picture.

The visitor to New Zealand will come across the name of Frances Hodgkins (1870–1947) many times. She was considered to be the nation's finest painter. Although only "discovered" internationally in her later years, which were spent in Europe, she displayed the vigor and dash of a much younger person in her paintings. Looking at her paintings, you would not attribute them to a girl born and raised in a genteel fashion in far-off Dunedin.

At the Public Art Gallery we picked up a booklet, *"Face Value"* for an exhibit devoted to paintings of the Maori, an excellent educational book. In it you learn the value of the *moko* (personal tattoo design) and you become acquainted with Charles Frederick Goldie (1870–1947) – if you own a Goldie in New Zealand you are *rich* – and the modern, contemporary Colin McCahon.

The University of Otago was the first university in New Zealand and is particularly known for its medical-dental school. The old buildings on the campus of bluestone off-set with Oamaru white stone with Gothic windows and turrets and spires look like what you would want a university in Dunedin to look like, resting beside the Leith Stream.

Expansion of the university, however, has forced it into a large number of new buildings that could belong to any modern campus anywhere, monolithic and sexless by comparison to the graceful old university buildings.

Pop architecture can be seen in various forms throughout the world. But when you see the poppiest architecture in New Zealand, reserved conservative New Zealand, the spiritual home of Queen Victoria's architects, it is startling to say the least.

In Dunedin we met an estimating engineer who explained that the architecture seen at the Whakatane Airport, the Wellington Club and other places around the country is known as "Noddy" architecture. "Noddy" is a children's picturebook character. The style is attributed to a new wave of architects out of Wellington.

The Otago Museum is housed in a classical building near the university. As a sign of the city's wealth, the Museum can boast of Roman and Greek art and sculpture . . . a collection other museums could not afford.

However if the visitor has become more and more immersed in Maori culture he will find in the museum the Great Carved House, *Mataatua*, of Whakatane. Work on the house was begun in 1872 and completed in 1874. The Maoris presented the house to Queen Victoria in 1875 as a sign of goodwill. Later it was dismantled and shipped to Sydney for the Exhibition of 1880. Later still it was dismantled again and eventually reached the Victoria and Albert Museum in London, where it was stored. In 1924 it was resurrected and placed in the New Zealand pavilion of the British Empire Exhibition held in Wembley Park, London, in 1924.

The Botanic Gardens are worthwhile if you have the time. As so much of Dunedin is a botanic garden, the time-pressed visitor may not have enough hours to visit the formal Botanic Gardens. You will have missed another statue of Peter Pan and Wendy.

Port Chalmers, Dunedin's deep-water port, is an important factor in the economic health of Dunedin today with roll-on roll-off shipping and containerization facilities. During the goldrush Port Chalmers was the main port of entry for the thousands of gold diggers who came to Otago after gold was discovered in 1861. The prior year, in 1860, the harbor was entered by eighty ships. By 1863 the number had risen dramatically to 689 ships.

The first frozen meat shipment to Britain sailed from this harbor in 1882, an idea conceived in Oamaru.

Two important lookouts that give the visitor a breath-taking panorama of the city and the countryside are Mt Cargill, which carries a television antenna, and Signal Hill, which has a piece of rock from the base of Edinburgh Castle, a centennial present from Edinburgh (Scotland) to Edinburgh (Dunedin) New Zealand in 1940.

14. Dunedin to Invercargill: And Stewart Island Too

Forests and Waterfalls . . . Beaches and Birds . . . Stewart Island . . . Training for the Milford Track . . . Meet "Henry" and "Stephanie", the Friendly Little Dragons . . . Fish and Chips on The Hill . . . The Election

From Dunedin to Invercargill you have the choice of two routes.

One takes you on Highway 1 on a good road through farmland to Gore, an agricultural community of 9,000 people whose leading attraction is the country's largest cereal factory. From Gore south, still on Highway 1, you are in excellent fishing country with multiple rivers to choose from. Wyndham, just east of Edendale, is a popular headquarters for anglers.

The second choice was another strong candidate in our "favorite-drive" sweepstakes: The coast road from Balclutha to Invercargill, much slower driving on mostly dirt (metal) roads, goes through scenic reserve lands with views of the sea.

To the AA official in Dunedin there was no choice. "You have to go by the coast road. It is one of the last unspoiled scenic reserves in the country."

To do the coast road justice you should (1) get an early start – we didn't (2) not get lost in Balclutha – we did (3) not stop at an antique store – we did.

In fact if a visitor has the time, enjoys the luxury of just poking about in a beautiful, remote, scenic area – one of the last in the country – it would be worthwhile to overnight halfway at Owaka – and enjoy the region to its fullest.

Our stop in the outskirts of Dunedin was at a shop where the Lady Navigator the day before had found a full set of 18th-century ornate English cut-crystal glasses, from liqueur to water goblets, seven sizes, for a mere $2,000. Breakfast was difficult to swallow that morning. However we escaped with only porcelain and brass wall hangers and an antique beer jug, losing the road time but saving the bank account.

Thirty-seven miles south of Dunedin, after passing Lake Waihola which was a water passage for goldminers heading inland to central Otago, you come to Clarksville Junction where Highway 8 bears west to Alexandra and Queenstown and Wanaka.

Continuing south on Highway 1 for another thirteen miles you approach Balclutha. On the left side of the highway is Lovells Flat Sod Cottage, a restored colonial cottage furnished in the period of the time.

The mighty Clutha River nears its end at Balclutha. Clutha is the Gaelic name of the River Clyde in Scotland and Balclutha means the town on the River Clyde.

The town with a population of 5,000 serves the surrounding sheepfarming country. Over a million and a half sheep are processed here annually.

From Balclutha, Highway 92, the coast road, begins turning to the south. Somehow we missed the turn off and spent more time than was necessary wandering over country roads until we finally found the correct highway.

Most of the South East Otago Scenic Reserve is not on the coast and time has to be budgeted to include detours to such places as Port Molyneux, Kaka Point, Nugget Bay, Cannibal Bay, Jacks Bay and Jacks Bay Blowhole.

Even if you don't go exploring off the highway, it is still a grand trip. You never see anybody and the road through the forest reserves, filled with songbirds, is the way the world should be.

Our one exploratory trip was to Purakaunui Falls.

It was Thanksgiving Day. For our Thanksgiving Day feast we had a can of sardines, cheddar cheese and a hot pie picked up in Balclutha. We spread our repast on a bench leading to the falls . . . we had the surrounding forest all to ourselves . . . and it started to rain. We finished Thanksgiving luncheon in the car.

Then like the click of a switch everything started coming right. The sun came out. The wind died down. It was *Spring.*

We walked down a rain-scented path through a forest of silver birch and the birds resumed their singing.

At the end of the path we reached the falls, where the Forestry Service had carved out a walk to a platform at the bottom of the falls.

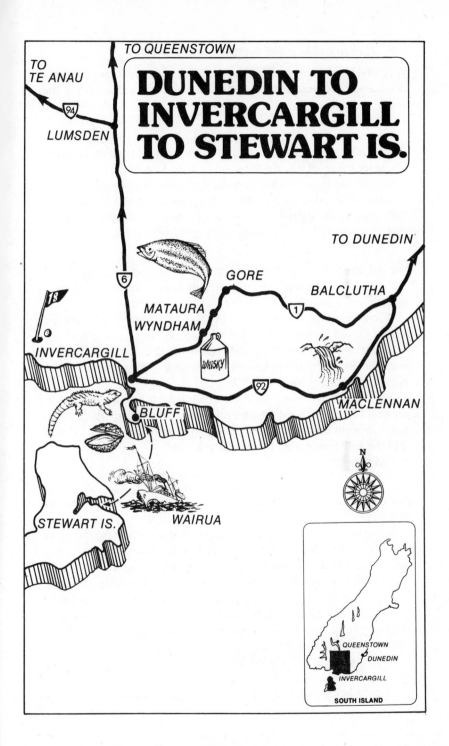

TO QUEENSTOWN

TO TE ANAU

DUNEDIN TO INVERCARGILL TO STEWART IS.

94

LUMSDEN

TO DUNEDIN

6

GORE

BALCLUTHA

MATAURA
WYNDHAM

1

INVERCARGILL

WHISKY

92

18
6

BLUFF

MACLENNAN

STEWART IS.

WAIRUA

N

QUEENSTOWN
DUNEDIN
INVERCARGILL

SOUTH ISLAND

We could almost feel the falls thundering over us. The water tumbling down a series of terraces in a stepdown waterway was superb in the sun-lit noonday.

"Thank you, God."

We returned to the car, hand in hand.

Rejoining the highway from the detour we were soon on the coast where long lines of white rolling waves surged up on golden beaches. A rugged cliff line stretched in both directions. Picture-taking time.

Two visitor attractions, Lake Wilkie and Cathedral Caves, came further along the highway and then it was a return to flat sheep country and Progress Valley on a steady drive into Invercargill.

We did one thing right and several things wrong at Invercargill.

First we had, through the Government Tourist Bureau, confirmed motel reservations. Right.

Wrong: we arrived just in time to get in food shopping before the stores closed – we were determined to improve upon our Thanksgiving sardines-and-cheese luncheon – but we were too late to visit the local Public Relations or the AA offices for any good background information.

The next day, Friday, we were scheduled for a dawn take-off to Stewart Island and we'd return again too late to find anything open. Saturdays the shops are closed, the AA and the PR offices are closed and the golf courses and tennis courts are full.

Bad planning.

We spent a day at Stewart Island which is like taking a half a spoonful of *pavlova*.

Reporting at eight o'clock at the Invercargill Airport for the flight to Oban in our hiking boots and parkas, we boarded a six-seater amphibian Grumman for the twenty-five-minute flight.

A pretty Maori mother and her two saucer-eyed children, the Lady Navigator and I made up the passenger list. The pilot was a lean-faced Scotsman with salt-and-pepper hair. (We like grey-haired pilots.) He did everything. Loaded the luggage, unchocked the wheels, took the tickets. He was a one-man airline.

The little Grumman bounced over pasture-land, ignoring the runway, and was airborne.

The sea below was white with stormy waves and we thanked our stars for not attempting the ferry which takes two hours from Bluff on a calm day – and it is almost never calm, leaving the day passenger with just enough time to recover from the ocean before getting back on the ferry again.

Landing in an amphibian is even more fun than landing in a ski plane. Halfmoon Bay lay straight ahead of us and the pilot put the plane down gently towards the water, which started coming up faster and faster.

If you've landed in a glider, you know that the closer you are to the ground, the more of a sensation you have that you are going to carve a furrow in the runway with your tailbone as opposed to the lofty, slow sensation you have in landing in a giant 747.

So it was with the amphibian. The water rushes to meet you. You crunch up in your seat. Splash! And splash again! Water comes over the windshield. You are down.

To the Lady Navigator: "That is the hottest, wettest landing I ever made!"

Pilot to passenger: "Never landed on water before?"

Meekly: "No, Sir."

The amphibian chugs up to the water's edge of Halfmoon Bay and then waddles up the beach and you are in the middle of the "city".

You disembark and look a hundred yards up one way past the general store and the dock and then look a hundred yards the other way past the post office and the one-room museum which is never open and that's it . . . that's downtown Oban.

In front of you is the South Seas Hotel. It is full of workers on an oil drilling project in the ocean to the south. The Ferngrove Lodge, the holiday headquarters for Stewart Island with thirty-six rooms, had recently burned down.

There is a motel just over the hill with three units.

That is metropolitan Oban.

There are twelve miles of negotiable road in Oban and there is a minibus tour according to the tourist literature. You ask the party who is taking over the air freight about the bus tour.

"Well, I'm not sure," he says. "Wait until the ferry gets in and we'll see if we can't jack something up."

The ferry is not due for another hour and a half.

To "jack something up" in New Zealand means that there is a good probability of getting something organized but don't count on it.

It started to rain.

There are three things you can do on Stewart Island. You can hunt, you can fish and you can walk.

We went to the forest ranger's hut to get walking data and learned that the favorite walk is the Northwest Loop which takes seven days. We crossed that out. Another favorite walk is the Mason's Bay which is a two-hour trip. There is a half-day walk to Ackers Point where there is a lighthouse and we settled for that to start with.

Part of our program in coming to Stewart Island was hiking because the scheduled Milford Walk was only a week away and so off we slogged into the rain.

Hiking to Ackers Point takes you past secluded bays and through forests and along the water's edge. In our hiking, which eventually took up the whole day, we never ran across any other hikers but we were never without birds. Singing bellbirds and tuis were everywhere.

There is a strikingly handsome bird, the native wood pigeon, which has a lovely green-blue coat and a white butcher's apron down his front. One pigeon swooped down from behind us, passed our heads and landed up in the trees in the path before us. When we would walk beyond his perch, here he would come on another "fly-by". He did that three times before disappearing into the forest.

At the end of the point, we shared a chocolate bar. On the rocks below us a giant seal was sleeping restlessly.

We walked back to the South Seas Hotel, just in time to miss the hot lunch but we had ham salad, several helpings of scones and a refreshing beer.

Our plane was not due back until 4:30 so we bundled up again and struck out in the rain in the other direction of Horseshoe Bay. The road was sloppy with mud but a mile out of town the Forest Service has established a botanical garden and a hut overlooking Butterfield Bay where you can dry out on a rainy day.

We proceeded down the road to Horseshoe Bay and then came back via the trail that takes in the lookout point. The trail is well maintained by the Forest Service but it took us the remainder of the afternoon getting back to the South Sea Hotel in time to have another beer and then get aboard the amphibian for the fly-back to Invercargill.

The water take-off in an amphibian is just as exciting as the landing except you *know* you are going to land coming down but you aren't *sure* if you are going to clear the surrounding water taking off.

Looking down on Oban and the surrounding bays from the air gives you a feeling of what you have missed. Stewart Island is an island about 40 miles by 30 miles ... about as big as Oahu in the Hawaiian chain.

We had walked all day but if we had done the same thing in Waikiki it would be like going around Diamond Head and back in one direction and downtown Honolulu and back in another. We hadn't seen any of Stewart Island.

The ideal way to do Stewart Island would be to rent a holiday house at Oban and then charter launch trips and amphibian trips to the remote parts of the island that aren't accessible any other way. That would make a four-star vacation.

Unique to the island is the muttonbird which you might see advertised in a fish store window.

The muttonbird may only be killed by the Maoris, who used to store it in seaweed kelp bags. It is boiled and boiled to take away the gamey flavor. When you ask a New Zealander friend if you should try it, you're likely to get a closed-eyes, slow, emphatical negative shake of the head.

The plane back to Invercargill passed over the huge frozen-meat works and the controversial, foreign-owned aluminum plant and then fluttered down slowly to another pasture landing, almost at the terminal door.

"Why don't you land on the runway?"

The one-man-airline pilot looked at the passenger with that you-don't-understand-anything look and replied: "Hard on the tires".

Invercargill

Invercargill will not win an award as New Zealand's most charming city. However its streets are broad and carry such names as Tay, Dee, Esk and Forth after Scottish rivers. Queen's Mary Park within the city and Anderson Park outside of the city are handsome and are worth visiting.

We spent most of a Saturday morning in Queen's Park. At the south end of the park are tennis courts and hockey and cricket fields. In the middle is the Southland Museum, which starts out to be interesting, grows to be absorbing and emerges to be fantastic.

Its ground floor is a good example of a regional museum

accomplishing its primary job of preserving for the local people their own regional heritage: displaying the natural resources, the local flora and fauna and recreating the local history. Part of the Southland Museum's history exhibit was a three dimensional, miniature reproduction of a Maori *adze factory* found near Bluff. Upstairs is early European history including a striking, busty figurehead taken from the vessel *England's Glory,* wrecked near Invercargill in 1881.

The most intriguing object is a stone found by sealhunters in 1832 at Cape Providence with discernible scratchings on it reading like the first line of a Robert Louis Stevenson book: "Beware the Natives Plentey *(sic)* at Preservation".

An equally intriguing story lies in a wooden float on exhibit. In 1866 a ship was wrecked in the Auckland Islands, far to the south of New Zealand. The wrecked sailors built this float carrying their SOS and launched it into the waters. Incredibly it found its way to Stewart Island and the sailors were rescued.

The final stage, the fantastic stage, of the Southland Museum exhibits is a visit to the Museum's *tuatarium,* a 15' x 15' enclosure duplicating nature and skylighted for sun, probably the only one of its kind. Here is where "Henry" and "Stephanie" live.

It is difficult for the mind to accept the fact that 200 million years ago in the Triassic Period there lived a reptile whose fossils have been found and whose living relation is in front of you in an enclosure in Invercargill.

The tuatara is the living descendant of that period. The fossil form of their ancestors found in the Northern Hemisphere is little different than the forms of "Henry" and "Stephanie" who make up the occupants of the tuatarium in the Southland Museum.

The tuatara which in Maori means "spined back" still lives on the islands in the Cook Strait between the North Island and the South Island and on some islands off of the east coast of the North Island.

We were fortunate because "Henry", who lives at one corner of the tuatarium, and "Stephanie", who keeps her own burrow apartment in another corner of the tuatarium, were on full view. At most they come out for an hour or two a day to take the sun, being primarily nocturnal creatures that disappear for months during the semi-hibernation period of winter.

The two tuataras are only about eighteen inches long . . . but that's because they are estimated to be only thirty-five and forty years old. By the time they reach 100 years, not uncommon for the tuatara they may be two feet long.

The reptiles are carnivorous and have powerful jaws but are easy to manage if handled gently. Their manner has earned them the name of "friendly little dragon". Despite the "his" and "hers" apartment arrangement and their slow-motion pace, officials were fairly certain that "Stephanie" was in the family way. The officials were excited and, by the time we left, so were we. Alas it was to prove a false pregnancy. No dragonette. . .

Queen's Park offers the visitor a splendid rose garden and a rhododendron walk, a deer park, duck pond and a children's playground. The tearoom is recommended.

On the west side of the park is the Queen's Park Golf Club with eighteen holes, par 71, closed to visitors on Tuesdays and Saturdays. With the surrounding trees it looked inviting but then it started to rain and we were glad that they didn't take visitors on Saturday. At the end of the park is the handsome Tudor-style Southland Boys' High School.

Bluff is only seventeen miles south of Invercargill and is the southernmost tip of the South Island. Having been to Cape Reinga, the northern tip of the North Island and having taken pictures of the directional post pointing out mileages in all directions we felt we must take the same pictures at Bluff and we did.

On the way to Bluff you pass a road to the right leading to Oreti Beach where there is safe bathing, a golf course and motor racing.

Bluff in New Zealand is synonymous with oysters, and a limited season starts in March and continues no later than August. Twenty-three boats comprise the oyster fleet. They are limited to a catch of 5,000 sacks per boat.

We went to a fish shop but of course there were no fresh Bluff oysters in December. We settled on fish and chips for lunch and took them to the top of Bluff Hill and ate in the car, which was rocked with ferocious winds. Later we read in the AA strip map: "Get advice before taking your car up the final straight to the summit of Bluff Hill." The sun came out and we could see the mountainous waves of Foveaux Strait in the sunshine.

The door of the fish shop was decorated with Christmas art. On the back of the door there was a sign which read: "The Christmas decoration is done in colored chalk and if you touch it with your hands, it will come off and we wouldn't want that, would we?"

In Brooklyn this would read: "Kids! Keep your grubby little paws off the door or else!"

The politeness in New Zealand is everywhere. Road signs say *please.* Counter girls interrupt their conversation without being asked to and say "thank you" for your purchases. Even post office clerks are courteous.

Anderson's Park, north of Invercargill, is a handsome property consisting of sixty acres of bush, manicured lawns and a stately home now used as an art gallery. It was donated to the city by the family of the late Sir Robert and Lady Anderson. There is a tearoom as part of the home. Closer to town is the Waihopai Scenic Reserve with delightful picnic sites in forest settings.

There are buildings which reflect their times: the Railway Hotel opposite the construction of the new railway station is memorable. You can't imagine staying there but in its day it must have been vibrant with action. There is the Majestic Theater and the bank corner with the four banks facing each other in Victorian opposition and the Government Insurance Building, positively dashing in a new two-tone paint job.

The two landmarks in Invercargill are two churches, one being the First Church with an Italian-square campanile rising over the trees and the other is St Mary's Basilica, done by the same architect, Petre, who did the St Joseph's Basilica in Dunedin. The interior of St Mary's shows off Oamaru stone to its best advantage, milk-white and graceful.

We wanted to be in Invercargill on Saturday because with its flat landscape and its major population of over 50,000 we knew we could be sure of good color television reception and we wanted to watch the returns of the national election.

Fascinating.

The situation was that the party-in-power, although lagging seriously behind in the earliest of polls, had made the kind of steady progress you look to see in a horse you have your money on, and the latest polls and man-in-the-street feeling was that the gap was closed, the home stretch drive was successful and party-in-power would be back in.

Political pundits held forth on the tube an hour before the first results came in explaining the situation.

If the party-out-of-power were to gain sufficient number of seats in the unicameral legislative body to give them a majority and therefore the right to take over the control of the Government, then they would have to earn a certain percentage gain of the popular vote since the last election. A graph was introduced to trace the percentage spread as the votes came in.

The stage was set.

The first results came in and the swing to the party-out-of-power was large. "An isolated example," agreed all the commentators. "Keep your eye on the chart."

The second and third results started to come in and the percentage swing was repeated. "These are results from the country seats," said the confident political analyst, "Wait until we see the results from the urban areas."

"Yes," wisely nodded all the commentators. "This is true."

But the vote percentages held and the graph chart couldn't hold the results and the commentators said, "Well. Well!" and the pre-taped skits which were meant to be entertaining were fatuous and disastrous and the whole thing threatened to turn into the kind of shambles that you wished would only happen to somebody else's network.

The producers were able to get enough political headquarter interviews in time to save the situation, but just barely.

It was over. The party-out-of-power won a smashing victory.

The surprising part about the New Zealand election was the next day. While the campaign had a hectic fever building to its election day climax, to a non-partial observer the language and manners were commendably civilized.

While most countries have tougher, dirtier, more bitter campaigning, the rule-of-thumb is that after the election everybody makes the proper polite noises and goes to his corner to privately gloat or cry.

Not in New Zealand. After the election, the gloves came off.

Racism, religious interference, bigotry, fiscal irresponsibility were all tossed off by participants and quoted in the national media.

It made you feel that the politicians hadn't read the sign behind the door of the fish and chips shop.

In Invercargill we learned something about the country's unique liquor laws.

Licences are granted to outlets by local authorities according to local option. There are some areas in New Zealand which until recently have been "dry" . . . the prohibition of liquor having been the preference of the local population.

Invercargill was a dry municipality for thirty-seven years and only changed in 1943. During the war everybody needs a drink.

The city fathers however took a new direction. They said, "Why do we give out licences to hotels to sell liquor when we could keep the licences and the profits to ourselves?" They did. Today the Invercargill Trust has assets over $7,000,000 and distributes over $450,000 in after-tax profits to local organizations. The success of the local-ownership format has spread to some other parts of the country.

15. Te Anau and Fiordland National Park

Teddy Roosevelt's Elk . . . The "Lost Tribe" . . . The Rediscovered Bird . . . The First Trout On A Fly

Sunday is a good day to travel in New Zealand for a visitor.

All the shops are closed. Golf courses and tennis courts are full. No horse racing. Limited spectator sports.

So we felt we were making best use of our time by driving from Invercargill to Te Anau on a sunny Sunday.

The first leg of the drive to Lumsden was less than fifty miles through agreeable countryside. Coming over a pass on Highway 6 at Caroline, we looked down on Lumsden sleeping in the sun, a picture of pastoral tranquility.

After Lumsden, following the Oreti River on Highway 94, the country becomes barren, although there are posted access roads to the river for fishermen which make the heart jump a bit.

The barren drive doesn't last too long. The distance from Lumsden to Te Anau is another fifty miles and one of nature's most exciting canvases is about to unfold in front of you.

You come over a rise and slide down into the town of Te Anau.

In 1972 a hydro-electric project on Lake Te Anau and Lake Manapouri was proposed. It became a highly emotional issue and was a factor in a national election defeat of the political party in power. While the debate was going on the future of the area was in doubt.

Saved by the election and with a more secure future in its favor, Te Anau has been rejuvenated and is now sprinkled with new motels, shops, residences, post office. The township has grown to a permanent population of around 2,000.

The townside of Lake Te Anau is comparatively flat and dry but the visitor looks across the waters of the lake to the thickly forested mountains and their wild, deep green, untouched beauty.

This is Fiordland National Park.

Fiordland National Park with over 3,000,000 acres is the largest national park in New Zealand. It is, in fact, one of the largest in the world.

The Park's reputation is not because of its size but because of the grandeur of its scenery. Magnificent deep-blue fiords. Majestic peaks. Superlative waterfalls. Hanging glaciers. Mossy rain forests.

Captain Cook, who originally sighted the Fiordland country in 1770 and returned to Dusky Sound in 1773, speculated that "beyond the mountains could well lie lakes, ponds and rivers". As usual he was right.

Lake Te Anau is the largest lake in the South Island, covering 130 square miles and stretching thirty-eight miles in a north-south direction. Other large lakes in the Park are Manapouri, Hauroko, Monowai and Poteriteri. A myriad of smaller lakes, like the larger lakes, are filled with rainbow and brown trout.

Many varieties of wild flowers and native birds fill the rain forests. The rarest bird is the *takahe*, at one time thought to be extinct. A colony of takahe was found in recent times in a pocket of the Park. It is now a sanctuary and cannot be visited without a permit.

A romantic title for the Park is *"the Country of the Lost Tribe"*. The Lost Tribe, unlike the takahe, has never been found. In the fierce tribal warfares that marked the history of early New Zealand, a strong tribe chased a weaker tribe across the lower end of New Zealand, gradually reducing them in number until the last remnants of the tribe escaped into these mountains.

Later the early Europeans reported seeing smoke from campfires in the mountains suggesting a locale of Maoris, and the legend of the Lost Tribe was born.

Wild life in the park includes red deer, elk (called *wapiti* in New Zealand), wild pigs, goats and some chamois.

In 1905 President Roosevelt gave eighteen elk to the people of New Zealand as a present from the people of the United States. The elk proliferated to the point of endangering the Park's vegetation and there is now open season on both the deer and the elk which are hunted commercially by helicopter.

Hunting is but one of many activities drawing New Zealand vacationers and overseas sportsmen and sightseers to Te Anau and the Fiordland National Park. There is outstanding fishing, sailing, picture-taking, popular sightseeing tours and hiking.

The most popular hikes near Te Anau are the Milford Track, the

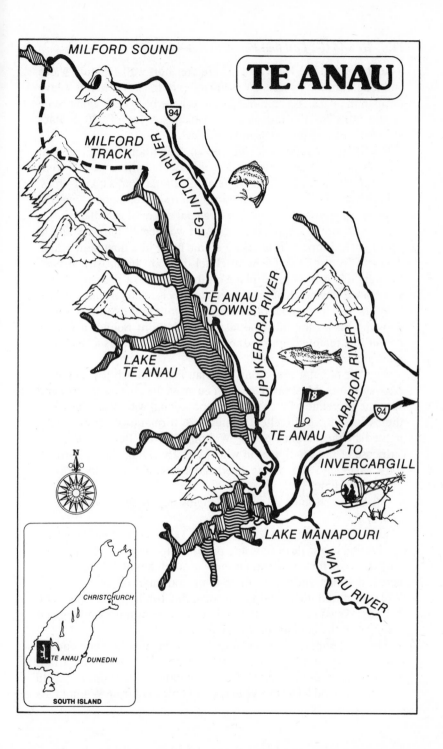

Routeburn and the Hollyford. There are short walks, nature walks and long, tramping walks. Over 300 miles of tracks for hikers weave through the Park. Accommodation huts have been built along some of the trails for the independent walkers. A fee of $30 enables independent walkers to use huts and fuel.

Hikers are requested to fill out an "intentions book" so that rangers have needed information in case of emergency, a common-sense practice in all New Zealand National Parks hiking areas.

Park headquarters is also an information source. A good, low-cost souvenir suggestion is to buy the large park map of Fiordland.

A quick way to sample the variety of wonders of the park and to get oriented properly is to take a scenic flight in a floatplane which docks in front of the Te Anau Hotel or from the nearby airport. Looking down from an airplane on the vastness of the park makes you realize why much of the rugged country is relatively unexplored.

Of the scenic trips out of Te Anau, the tour to the Milford Sound is, with reason, the most popular. The Milford Sound, a remote corner in a remote country, draws over 300,000 visitors a year. You must go.

Another popular tour from Te Anau is the launch trip to the Te Ana-au Caves. Most satisfactory. You cross the lake on the trip and skirt the shoreline where you see an occasional wild deer. The caves themselves have excellent limestone formations, dramatically lighted in the manner of the Waitomo Caves. Best of all is the suspense of the small boat in which you are riding gliding through dark caves and the ceiling overhead becoming a Milky Way of glow-worm lights.

Other launch tours of varying lengths depart from the Te Anau docks.

Lake Manapouri, just south of Lake Te Anau, also has lake trips graduating in a scale of time and prices. You can go to the little store and rent oars for a rowboat and row around the inlet. You can row across the inlet and take a three-hour, trail-marked hike. You can hire a boat and guide and get in some fine fishing or you can get a boat to take you to a remote beach for private fishing or hiking and arrange for the boat to come back for you later.

The most popular tour is a launch trip to Manapouri Dam and the hydro-electric station. An extension of this trip, an all-day affair, takes in the hydro-station and then continues over Wilmot Pass to Doubtful Sound. (The twelve and a half mile road from Wilmot Pass

Doubtful Sound. (The twelve and a half mile road from Wilmot Pass to Doubtful Sound was built at a cost of $5 an inch and is the most expensive road in New Zealand.) Another launch meets your bus and you glide through the waters of the spectacular Doubtful Sound as far as Hall Arm.

Manapouri is a soft, gentle lake known for its feminine beauty, surrounded by towering forest-clad mountains. The ride to the West Arm of the lake, location of the power station, takes over an hour and it is a relaxing, gentle trip in keeping with the lake's character.

From the launch you board a bus which takes you to the power station and you drive down a granite tunnel in a 360-degree circle over 800 feet below the level of the lake to the immensely vaulted chambers housing seven giant turbines. The incredible access tunnel is wide enough to accommodate two buses side by side.

The Manapouri project was an international accomplishment. Initiated by Australians, it was designed and supervised in construction by Bechtel of California. Part of the major tug hauling was done by Dillingham of Honolulu. The turbines came from Scotland and the generators from West Germany.

Recommendation: there is a small restaurant called Pearl Harbor at the Lake Manapouri launch site where you are better off taking a small snack or buying a box lunch rather than buying the package trip which includes luncheon on board.

Our first desire upon reaching Te Anau was to repeat a successful fishing trip.

Three years before on the Waiau River which winds between Te Anau and Lake Manapouri we had hired a jet-boat and went bouncing down the river with our guide, a long-haired jet-jockey.

We'd stop and cast and, unsuccessful, speed off again.

Finally I hooked my first river trout. The distance between the trout that jumped far down the river and my reel looked like a distance of a hundred miles. The drag on the line produced by a heavy fighting fish aided by the rush of water made it feel like a whale. When this gorgeous silver creature was finally beached at my feet later – ten minutes? – two hours? – I was trembling from the miracle of it all.

The jet-jockey, with his hands in his pockets, said, "You get excited real easy, don't you?"

He was the only guide I ever had in New Zealand I didn't care for.

Heck Thompson was, on the other hand, a guide who couldn't have an enemy.

He had been a fishing guide around Te Anau for fifty out of his sixty-eight years. Grey-haired and diminutive, he could cover more rocky ground in thigh-high waders than a jolly green giant. Remember his helping me cross a small rapids holding my elbow and thinking: "This is ridiculous. Which one of us is sixty-eight?"

Heck came over to our lake-front motel the evening before to survey the clients. Part of his routine. The Lady Navigator wanted to catch anything that was edible. I wanted to catch my first fish with a fly rod.

Heck's Land Rover was at the motel at 8.15 the next morning loaded with rods, reels and waders. After going about five miles east of Te Anau we went bouncing through pastureland, unlocking and relocking gates and fished the Mararoa River. No luck.

We went back to the other side of the highway, through all of the gates again, to the Upukerora River in country where only a four-wheel drive vehicle could go.

Heck was a lodemine of information. Passing the Government-owned sheep stations, he explained how the Government has taken over run-down lands in the area and, through judicious use of the scientific knowledge developed in the agricultural universities and by using public funds to take out scrub, to furrow and fertilize, has successfully been revitalizing the country. It is becoming more economically valuable, and, more beautiful.

He cited as example the country we were in. Previously it ran 15,000 sheep and 2,500 bullocks but the land was steadily deteriorating and becoming unprofitable. The Government took the leased land back and put a restoration program into effect. The same land now runs 125,000 sheep and 10,000 bullocks.

Later the land will be subdivided into units small enough to be economically run and will then be auctioned off to young farmers. The plan brings young people back to the land and returns the Government investment back to the public coffers.

By the time we reached the Upukeroa River it was time for lunch. Heck parked the Land Rover in a field of lupin, vividly colored wild flowers. Cardtable. Chairs. Tablecloth. Canned salmon and mayonnaise and salad greens and crackers and sandwiches and mayonnaise and salad greens and crackers and sandwiches and candy and hot tea.

That afternoon was spent on my education. How to sidecast with the wind. How to fish a "pool". How to inspect a fly.

Later his efforts paid off when at the bottom of a favorite pool a rainbow hit the line, jumped out of the water and started to fight for its life. Heck, the instructor was at my side with a constant patter of advice. "Keep the rod up. Never let the line slack. Let the fish run if it wants to but always keep the pressure on."

Catching a good fish on a fly rod is a thrill that doesn't let you go back to any other kind of fishing with the same amount of pleasure. It would be like riding a tricycle after being on an English racer.

When the fish was successfully beached without using a net, Heck was properly congratulatory and the pictures were snapped while the trout was held tenderly and then Heck suggested that it was a little thin and didn't I want to turn it back? On agreement the fish was released and quickly flashed away.

The Lady Navigator said to friends later that this was a trained fish which was taught to take the line of a beginner when all of the guide's other favorite pools were exhausted. The understanding of course between the guide and the fish was that the fish was not to be kept out of the water for more than two minutes. Unfair!

As a long-experienced guide, what did he think of women anglers?

He was full of praise. Women, he said, are easier to instruct. They are more sensitive to the lighter touches required for trout fishing. Men tend to try too hard to improve too fast.

Heck charges $70 a day for two plus 20c a mile. Which for us was an extra $10. Not inexpensive by New Zealand standards but well worth the price.

There are good fishing holes on the Waiau River which you can get close to by car and reach by walking. Balloon Bend. Horseshoe Bend. We didn't catch any fish but the walks through the lovely forest glades surrounded by singing birds and then fishing in quiet pools along the beautiful winding Waiau was an experience to remember.

Te Anau has an eighteen-hole golf course run by the Tourist Hotel Corporation which is unique in having its greens fenced off with two-foot wire fences to keep out sheep grazing on the fairways. Thrifty mowing – but watch your step.

There is a new club house at the golf course although the honor system of paying for greens fees ($1.50) still prevails. Put your money into an envelope into a wooden box at the first tee.

The Te Anau course was a nice easy walk and a good way to unlimber for the coming Milford Track. The only disconcerting thing about it is the nearby helicopter pad. Frequently helicopters will skim over the course with carcasses of deer and elk dangling from the undercarriage. If you are weak of stomach and have a shakey three-foot-putt reputation anyway, it doesn't do anything for your game.

Note: a rule-of-thumb in rating a motel: if you see the owners constantly buzzing around doing duties, you can be sure that you are in a motel that is cleaner, neater and better run than the one down the block where the owner or manager is never seen.

At a pre-Milford Track feast at the Te Anau Hotel to celebrate the coming event, a loud little grey-haired lady orders hot water and toast for dinner and then changes her mind and loudly orders a portion of mashed potatoes. Where do they come from?

A giant truck loaded with sheep going to market passes in front of the window. Shortly thereafter it is followed by a giant bus full of tourists. The mind plays a fantasy and sees the sheep all going to the Auckland Airport and all the tourists, including the mashed potato lady, going to the freezing works!

16. The Milford Track: The Glory Road

"The Finest Walk in the World" ... The Nervous Challenge ... The Preparation ... The Green River ... Sandflies ... Trout ... and Birds ... The toughest day ... Arthur's Walk ... A day of rest? ... A mighty waterfall ... A day in the rain ... Waterfalls on waterfalls ... Sandfly Point ... A damn good party

The day before our Milford Track exercise was to begin we picked up a young German couple on our way to Manapouri.

They had just completed the Routeburn Track as "freedom walkers" i.e. they weren't part of an organized group. The couple was now going to explore other parts of the Park and New Zealand before pushing on to Australia for more of the same before returning home to Germany.

Like all of the other hikers we saw around Te Anau with their large, lightweight packs, they slept in what they carried, they ate what they carried and they wore for the length of their entire trip what they carried.

It was just the dash of humility we needed. We had begun to cast ourselves in the role of rugged explorers, intrepid climbers, wilderness adventurers.

But our meals would be prepared for us. The most we would have to carry were our clothes, a sandwich and a sheet. There would be bunks with blankets. We would only need one change of clothing before rejoining our pile of luggage. The Milford Track is a comparatively manicured hike.

The comparison didn't hold down our mounting nervousness or excitement.

By arriving in Te Anau early we were able to check into the Milford Track office well before the required time. The office, connected to the Te Anau Hotel, confirms reservations, has storage space for excess luggage, will forward luggage to either the Milford Sound Hotel or the Johnston Hostel for 80c a bag and sell you plastic bags to wrap your belongings in for 10c each. The office issues without charge specially designed rucksacks and large, ankle-length capes with hoods. These are turned in on arrival at Milford Sound.

The office also issues a *"Milford Track Adventure Pack"*, information we should have received at the time our reservations were confirmed but didn't.

Part of the pack includes a "getting in trim" leaflet describing exercises worked out by the Department of Education. "Every year, the hundreds who walk the Milford Track with a fine sense of achievement range in age from teenagers to quite elderly adults," says the leaflet. "The adventure is well within the capacity of anyone who is normally active and reasonably fit. Nevertheless, the situation of being in the open air all day 'miles from anywhere' by a town-dweller's standards, and the need to use unaccustomed muscles makes a certain amount of both physical and mental preparation desirable."

Extracts from a second leaflet, *"Briefing for Milford Track Walkers"*:

FOOTWEAR: Boots or shoes, it is important that they are well broken in – by *you.* If you have to buy footwear, consider basketball boots.

CLOTHING: It's better to be too warm than too cold ... there is nothing to beat wool.

PACKS AND PACKING: So far, no one has invented a self-carrying pack – the power beneath the poundage will be *you!*

PROVIDED... all food, blankets, envelope-type sheets, which you carry from hut to hut, pillows, mattresses, towels, soap, etc. The huts have electric light and hot showers. Power is 230v a/c suited to most electric razors.

RETURN TRAVEL: Because the Milford Track season coincides with the peak tourist season, it is essential that you make reservations for your return home from Milford Sound before you leave home.

CHANGING: There are changing rooms with toilets adjacent to the Milford Track Office at Te Anau Hotel.

MILFORD TRACK

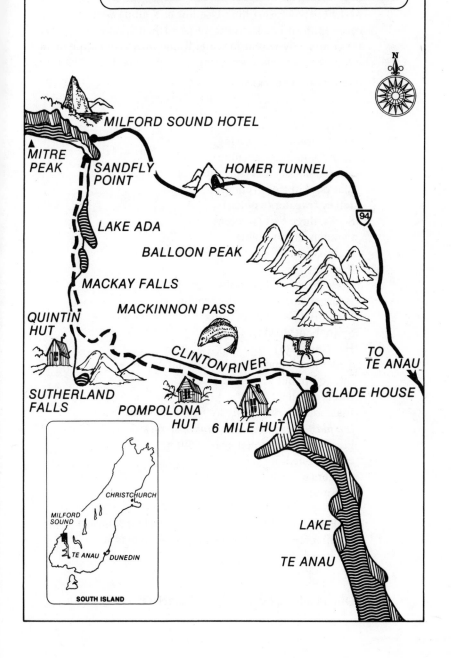

BOARDING: Coach leaves Te Anau Hotel at 3 p.m. Please check in no later than 2:45 p.m.

MILFORD TREKLIST: Use this as a guide when packing for your Milford Track adventure. (And then the checklist prints a not-completely-reassuring line: Remember: your enjoyment could depend on what you bring – or what you leave behind.)

There follows a checklist:

    Underwear, two sets
    Shirt/blouse (for walking)
    Shirt/blouse (for evening)
    Shorts/slacks/skirt (for walking)
    Slacks, skirt (for evening)
    Jersey/sweater (woolen)
    Socks, three pair (woolen)
    Pyjamas (lightweight)
    Handkerchiefs, etc.
*Pack
*Waterproof cape/windbreaker/parka
    Boots or strong shoes (for walking)
    Light footwear (for evening)
    Spare boot shoelaces
    Hat (rain/sun)
    Toilet needs and items of personal nature
    (make-up, but very little!)
    Insect repellent
    Elastoplast – *(on asking we found that elastoplast is a plastic bandage – good for blisters!)*
    Plastic bags (for toilet gear, clothing, camera, etc.)
    Camera
    Close-up lens (for alpine flowers)
    Film
    Ticket (you need it for boarding launch at Milford)
    Small torch (useful for nocturnal excursions to the loo)

*Obtainable on loan at Milford Track Office, Te Anau.

Guests staying at Milford Hotel have pre-paid for
breakfast only – luncheon and dinner and
à la carte meals are available at reasonable
prices.
For added comfort:
Two pieces of foam rubber for placing under straps
of pack *and hopefully – (my italics . . . the significance*
of this little plea-phrase didn't become apparent
until later). . . sun glasses and suntan lotion

From the beginning there was confusion in our minds about the
length of the walk. In some literature it was described as a three-day
walk. In other literature it was described as a seven-day walk. Other
references made it six days. The actual walking time of the thirty-three
mile Milford Track is three days . . . one day from Glade House to
Pompolona Hut, one day from Pompolona Hut to Quintin Hut, one
day from Quintin Hut to Milford Sound.

Our package included two nights at Quintin Hut and two nights at
Milford Sound. The second night at Milford Sound is necessary to fit
in the launch trip on the Sound the day after completing the Track.

The costs of the Milford Track vary according to the time of the
season.

When the Track becomes operational in mid-November, parties
take off every other day, Monday, Wednesday and Friday. This
schedule allows the hikers the luxury of spending two nights at
Quintin Hut and two nights at the Milford Sound Hotel or the less
expensive Milford Hostel.

During the peak of the vacation season, in order to take care of as
many people as possible, the parties take off on the Track daily,
meaning that only one night can be spent at Quintin and one at
Milford Sound.

The highest priced package at $200 per person includes two nights
at Quintin, two nights and breakfast at the Milford Sound Hotel, a
launch trip on the Milford Sound. Bus transport back to Te Anau is an
extra.

The lowest end of the cost scale is during the high season when the
one night at Quintin Hut and one night at the Milford Hostel come to
about $150. Later I looked at the Milford Hostel facilities, which are
quite adequate with a large recreation room and a family-style dining
room. However the rooms are small bunkrooms and there are

common bathroom facilities. We were happy we opted for the comfort of the Milford Sound Hotel.

We had other pre-Track niggling questions. What were the sleeping arrangements like? Did "hot showers" imply running water and flush toilets? How many people make up a party?

When we learned that *forty* people were the standard number for a group, we were dismayed. That was an *army*. It was going to be an organized military operation . . . an apprehensiveness which was to be proved needless.

It was December 5. We were to be the sixth group to take the trail in the new season which would end in mid-March.

At 2.30 in the afternoon "The Sixth Party" began to form.

If there was a military aspect to the group, it was in resembling the first gathering of a bunch of new recruits. Some too hearty. Some too shy. All nervously looking each other over.

There were men and women ranging from sixteen years old to sixty years old. There were tennis shoes and walking pumps and "basketball boots" and hiking boots. Dress varied from tweed skirts to walking shorts and jeans and corduroy trousers. Tennis sweaters and ski parkas. Everybody had read: "Your enjoyment could depend on what you bring – or what you leave behind!" and applied his and her personal needs to the warning.

At three o'clock, under overcast skies, we were loaded on buses and taken twenty miles to Te Anau Downs where we boarded a launch and set out for the head of the lake. The launch trip took an hour and a half. As the waters grew more narrow, they seemed to push the surrounding mountains up more precipitously and soon we were almost at hand-touching distance from the rocks while looking straight up 5,000 feet to mountain peaks.

All was wooded and at close hand you could see how greenery had somehow found a foothold in the craggy rocks and flourished.

It started to drizzle.

Of all the elements of the Milford Walk, the most uncertain and joy-controlling is the weather. In recent weeks the weather in Fiordland had varied from bad to terrible with just enough sunny days to give hope. It was what New Zealanders call patchy.

We landed at the mouth of the Clinton River and shouldering our packs for the first time set off on the first small stage of the track. "What is a 'track'?" we had wondered. In this case it was a tree-lined road, leaves underfoot, silver beech and fern trees on every side.

Hey, we said to ourselves, this is *good.*

In a half a mile we came out of the woods into a small glade. We were at our first destination: Glade House. Easy!

Glade House is the headquarters for the Milford Walk itself. The main house contained a double-tiered bunkroom for sixteen men and a double-tiered bunkroom for sixteen women and a nearby "cottage" with the same bunk arrangement for six men and eight women. There are traditionally more women than men on the walk.

Folded neatly on each bunk was a pile of wool blankets and a bath towel.

Taking your "sheet shroud" out of your rucksack, you make up your bed. There is an envelope at the head of the shroud which takes a pillow. In the morning you fold your linen and put it back in the rucksack. Fold up the blankets and leave them with the towel. You'll get a fresh towel at each hut.

The cottage had the advantage of having a little living room of its own and a fireplace.

There were separate facilities, as there were to be all along the hike, for men and women. Hot showers, wash basins . . . and flush toilets.

The main house also contained the kitchen and the dining room and shortly after arrival, dinner was served.

It was obvious from the beginning that dinners were to be early and they would be hearty and they would be fast. Soup, main dish, dessert, tea or coffee. Twenty-six minutes.

When the dining room was cleared, it became the meeting-recreation room.

Each stopping place also had very limited "canteen" items: postcards, cigarettes, candybars, souvenir books, etc.

After dinner we were advised to relax or take a nearby walk and reassemble at nine o'clock. We elected to stretch our legs and like most of the members took the short hike up to a mountain stream called Glade Burn. The forest was a motion picture stage set with trees covered with moss of a vivid green. Bellbirds serenaded us. At the clear, fast-running Glade Burn we dipped our noses into the brook and took an after-dinner drink. Delicious.

"Why hadn't the checklist included a water canteen?" we had wondered. Here was the answer. For the next three days, whenever we were thirsty, there was always a nearby, clean stretch of water to quench our thirst.

On the way back to the cabin we saw fantails, little birds that flew around us with their tails in a blurred flutter and then we saw a rare black fantail.

We'd had our first real taste of "the finest walk in the world".

At nine o'clock the "Sixth Party" assembled and the manager of the Glade House, Phil Turnbull, who was also responsible for all of the huts along the Milford Walk, introduced himself and his hard-working wife, Betty, who ran the kitchen, and his son Ian, who was to be our supervising guide for the next day. Every day we would have a new guide.

Then each guest did his own introduction and, if not already "pinned", went to a world map and put a pin in the city of his origin. Before the end of the season, Mr Turnbull said, pins representing every country of the world would blanket the map.

There are 2,700 hikers a year who do the guided Milford Track, the maximum which can be accommodated with the present limitation of facilities and the limitation of the season.

Of these 2,700 about 1,800 are New Zealanders and 900 are overseas visitors. Australians comprise the majority of foreigners. Canadian and United States citizens make up about 5 per cent and the rest are scattered from over the globe.

Another 1500 independent "freedom" walkers take the Milford Track annually, staying in three National Park huts and packing their food and sleeping bags. A small fee for the track and for the accommodations is charged. Freedom walker applications have to be made at the Fiordland Park Headquarters in Te Anau.

In our group the cast of characters of the play *"The Sixth Party"* began to appear.

The established percentages somewhat tilted to North America. There was a Canadian professor and his bright-eyed family of wife and three sons. Two college-aged girls from California, an American couple from a giant international company, and The Lady Navigator and I completed the American contingent.

There were two slender, grey-haired lovelies from Salisbury, England, who couldn't have been under sixty, who looked like they were made of doily lace and who proved they were made of English leather.

A roaming Dutchman, giant-sized, who roamed among the ladies.

There was a strong representation from Australia and, as usual,

There was a strong representation from Australia and, as usual, the majority of New Zealanders. Farmers, executives, car salesmen, engineers, scientists. All were here.

"A few words of advice," said Mr Turnbull. "Weigh your pack. If you are over twelve pounds, you are better off lightening your load. Anything feels all right the first couple of miles. After that it is another story . . . We have scales outside in the hall and anything you want to leave behind, we will send back to Te Anau Hotel and you can pick it up on your return.

"You can't take everything. In Te Anau there was a little boy whose father was going to take him on the Track. I don't think the boy was very keen about it. 'Can I take my pony?' he asked me.

" 'No, I'm afraid not. Animals aren't allowed, you see,' I had to tell him.

" 'Can't I even take my dog?'

" 'No, it is absolutely against regulations. I'm truly sorry.'

"There was a pause and the little boy looked very sad. Then he looked up and asked, plaintively, 'But who do you tell your secrets to?' "

"Another piece of advice, take your time. The longer you take, the more you'll enjoy it . . . There is no group walking. You set your own pace. And you have plenty of time to get to each hut on each leg of the walk."

There was an audible sigh of relief. The military march was not going to happen after all.

"One last word. It is the tradition that those in the top bunks serve tea to those in the bottom bunks." (The "tradition" also proved a useful traffic device for cutting down the rush to the bathroom.)

"Breakfast will be served at seven in the morning and you'll be off at nine. Lights go out at quarter of eleven . . . Good night."

Later Mr Turnbull came over the cottage and chatted in front of the fireplace.

The pass that made the walk possible was discovered in 1888 by a Scottish Highlander, Quintin McPherson McKinnon, who in 1892 signed a contract to guide visitors over the track and to also carry mail. The same year he was assumed drowned on Lake Te Anau. Four years later his sailboat was found, still with sails set, in six feet of water at the bottom of the lake. The pass which he discovered is spelled Mackinnon.

In 1908 the Health Department was in charge of the Track. The Tourist Hotel Corporation assumed its responsibility in 1955 and refurbished the accommodations and re-established the Walk's popularity.

Between three and six hikers a year don't complete the journey.

A couple of times a year there is snow. Last year it snowed for five days continuously but, we were assured, this was very unusual.

The lights went out but we chatted for a few minutes more by firelight. "The Milford Walk is famous as 'the finest walk in the world' but I've never read in a simple word or phrase *why* it is 'the finest walk in the world'. What's your reason?" we asked Mr Turnbull.

"It's the variety," replied Mr Turnbull. "You walk up this magnificent river. Then you come out to an alpine glacier plain. Then you climb the Mackinnon Pass with beautiful views and descend to the other side and see Sutherland Falls, one of the highest falls in the world. Then you follow the Arthur River with spectacular waterfalls along the way and then come to the incomparable Milford Sound. It's variety of the highest order."

There was another addition to the variety which he didn't name which we were to find for ourselves later.

The night was almost over.

When was the last time you went to bed by candlelight?

When was the last time you undressed in the dark in an upper bunk?

There were four wool blankets on the bed and they weren't enough. I shivered all night.

Light pyjamas, indeed.

"I'd like to take the Milford Walk," said a shipping executive in Auckland, "but four or five nights without my wife? Forget it."

Lady Navigator, where are you?

Glade House to Pompolona ... Ten Miles
The morning dawned cloudless.

A fire was lighted in the fireplace at five.

A pot of tea and hot water for instant coffee and tea biscuits were put out at seven. Breakfast at eight of hot porridge and scrambled eggs and toast and marmalade and honey, more coffee. *Note:* the

Australians and the New Zealanders eat their toast with marmalade and honey *after* the scrambled eggs and not *with* the scrambled eggs.

The tempo of excitement was now building up. There was a last minute weighing of shoulder packs. And exchange of sandfly lotion. (Several of us were already welted from the little beasts and although diethylmetatoluamide was supposed to keep them off, it was less than perfect.)

The sun had now slipped down the mountain sides and was filling the valley. Hikers were beginning to pull out in groups of twos and fours and sixes.

At the beginning there was a long "swing" bridge which is a wooden pathway suspended from cables. It bounces when you walk. The swing bridge across the placid Clinton River was the longest bridge of the many we were to cross. In earlier days all of these crossings had to be made by fording the rivers on foot or by ferry boat.

At the end of the swing bridge was a sign: "33 Miles To Go. Good Luck!"

It was an absolutely perfect day.

The morning sun slanted through the trees dappling the track in front of us. The track itself was a well graded road . . . the Pompolona Hut, our destination, is supplied by vehicle . . . and the grade to Pompolona only rises 165 yards over a ten-mile stretch. It was a picnic.

Everything visually was chocolate sampler box.

The Clinton River was clear green. According to Mr Turnbull, it is the best fishing river in New Zealand. Brown trout are in the waters up to three miles from the mouth and rainbow trout go up ten miles.

Occasionally in the shadow of a larger rock we would see a fat trout swimming lazily in the current. (No one said anything about bringing a telescoped rod but you could and there is lots of time. But if you catch a trout and keep it, you're going to have to carry it.)

We were always surrounded by the forest. The trees were covered with green moss and hanging from the branches were long vines known as "creepers" and strangling pieces of green lichen known as "old man's beard".

The river was constantly beside us curtained by a few trees. In the openings there were vistas of snow-covered peaks. Coming off the mountains was a succession of constant little streams, forming little waterfalls, gurgling alongside the path.

Each mile was marked with a wooden plaque hanging alongside the path with a native bird pictured and labeled for your education:

Mile 1 . . . Tui
Mile 2 . . . Rifleman
Mile 3 . . . Fantail
Mile 4 . . . Bellbird
Mile 5 . . . Kea
Mile 6 . . . Wood Pigeon
Mile 7 . . . Kingfisher
Mile 8 . . . Tomtit
Mile 9 . . . Kiwi
Mile 10 . . . Rock Wren

At the end of six miles was the Six Mile Hut where a track employee served a cold gelatin drink called a "cordial" and luncheon sandwiches of corn beef and egg and fruit and hot tea and coffee. A parrot-like kea bird which is known for its brassiness came down and ate lunch with the hikers.

The Lady Navigator had brought along her mini Mark Cross opera glasses which served as excellent, lightweight field glasses. Scanning the surrounding mountains at Six Mile Hut and passing the glasses among the rest of the hikers made us appreciate the value in bringing them.

The time from the Glade House to Six Mile Hut, strolling, had taken three hours. Two miles an hour was, if anything, too fast.

From Six Mile Hut to Pompolona was more of the same enchanting environment, except just short of the Pompolona Hut there was a river crossing which had been wiped out the week before by a sudden flash flood, typical of this mountain region. It was awesome: the power of the water to move giant boulders was evident everywhere. A previous party of walkers had to be roped across the torrent.

We were more and more thankful for our fine day.

Because we had deliberately slowed our pace . . . the last shall be first and the first shall be last . . . we were sure we would be the last to arrive. We were the first.

The only advantage of arriving first is that you get a pick of the bunks and the first shower. That's not all bad. The purpose of the walk, however, is to enjoy nature at its best and when you don't take full advantage of the opportunity that *is* bad.

At Pompolona Hut there was tea and scones and cakes at four o'clock.

The name Pompolona. Where did it come from with everything else being so Gaelic?

It seemed like McKinnon, the track discoverer and the first guide, made a batter of sorts which he fried in the fat of mutton candles! A guest said it reminded him of an Italian pancake called "pompolona" and from that time on the rest area was called Pompolona Hut.

Some hikers took a swim in the snow-fed river. Others fed the kea birds which now numbered a half dozen and kept shrieking *"kay-ah – kay-ah"*. (They also had the reputation of sliding down the roof at night, terrorizing the guests.)

Others cleaned up and took naps.

Each stopping place had a large efficient drying room and the importance of it was brought into focus by reading the visitors' book. Almost all of the comments had to do with water: *"Rain, rain, go away, please come back some other day."*

"Raindrops keep falling on my head."

"Glug, glug, it's the finest, wettest walk in the world."

The most succinct comment was in two words: *"Up periscope!"*

After dinner at 6:30 we were shown slides of the river in torrent pushing six-ton boulders around like rubber balls and pictures of the Pompolona Hut covered with snow: "It always snows the day after Christmas on Boxing Day," said the manager. There were slides of the peaks and valleys and paths we would take the next day and the next day's guide gave us a briefing: tomorrow's hike would be the toughest of the three hiking days going up the zig-zag trail to the top of Mackinnon Pass and then a less arduous but leg-straining walk down to Quintin Hut. He warned us that we couldn't inspect the caves near the track because of two snow overhangs which momentarily could trigger an avalanche.

Everybody listened in silence.

Supper was served at nine. Tea, coffee, cakes, biscuits.

Lights were out at eleven.

Despite the fact that the Milford Walk is a tailored hike, the weather is that of the mountains: never completely predictable. It can turn from sun to rain and sleet and snow in a matter of a few hours, and calm rivers and streams can be changed just as fast into uncrossable stretches of rising waters. As the Pope books say: RISK OF EX-

POSURE IS GREAT. Independent hikers are warned to have the proper experience and the proper equipment before taking the Milford Track. And the proper respect.

Pompolona to Quintin . . . Nine Miles

The hike the next morning started at eight, again across a swinging bridge which we were asked to take one at a time.

Again the sun was with us and we were most grateful. (For the rest of our stay in New Zealand we were to listen carefully to the weather forecast for Fiordland and shudder when, as it frequently did, it predicted clouds and showers.)

Soon the mountains opened out and we were in the alpine meadow. The double track had disappeared and we were not to see a double track again until we were on the final miles towards Sandfly Point.

A wingless weka bird came out of the bush, like a tame chicken, and looked us over at close range and even followed us a way down the path.

Leaving the track we diverted to the nearby Hidden Lake which was fed by a sheer cliff waterfall. Here most of the Sixth Party shed their packs and bathed in the sun but not in the snowy waters.

Back on the track and skirting Lake Mintaro, the climb began to steepen and soon we were on the zig-zag trail. Mountain flowers were on every side. Poppies, buttercups, mountain lilies. There is even edelweiss but we weren't to see any. We didn't see an avalanche either but we did hear one, a thundering rumble that reverberated through the valley. Frightening.

Before noon we had reached the summit at 3,850 feet, slightly sweaty but triumphant.

The views were magnificent. To the southeast we looked down the valley of the Clinton River from which we had come and felt superior for having done it. On the northwest side you can go to the edge of the cliff, have your picture taken on an overhanging rock, and look almost straight down on Quintin Hut and the airstrip.

There's an endearing line written by an eleven-year old girl, the first female to have made the pass, in one of the earliest parties: "The only way I could look was to lie down flat and pull myself to the edge of the cliff, and get my father to hold my ankles!" The little alpine pool at the summit is named, Lake Ella, after the girl.

The Lady Navigator, of course, went out on the ledge of rock and

I did the only noble thing and stayed back and took her picture.

Also on the summit is a rock cairn built as a memorial to Quintin Mackinnon ... "erected by the Gaelic Society of New Zealand and the Otago Rugby Football Union assisted by the Government".

At the pass hut, hot tea was being served and we pulled out our sandwiches and, huddled on benches, munched happily. I reached into my rucksack to find my notebook, and, disaster! it was gone. It was invaluable to me and, sick at heart, I told the guide that I must have left it at Pompolona. At almost the same time the telephone rang and another guide asked for me by name: "They've found some papers which belong to you at Pompolona. They'll send them back to the Te Anau Hotel and you can pick them up there."

What a relief!

Later the guide said that the party before us had flown in some grog the night before and had a big party that didn't break up until five o'clock in the morning.

I related this interesting bit of news to the international American executive and wondered if we shouldn't convey this to one of our Kiwi friends to see if perhaps something should be organized.

The guide suggested to all in the warm hut that they shouldn't stay too long because the legs tended to cramp up. Don't go singly, he said, because you are going to cross over some ice left by an avalanche and there are a few holes.

We took off down the face of the mountain. Out of the wind of the summit, it was open mountain country with a relatively easy path down the face. The evidence of the icy avalanche was by then only a token.

The Lady Navigator and I were by ourselves and we found that to be the best of walking.

At Arthur's Hut was a sign which said: "Arthur's Walk. Ten minutes longer. Ten times the views." We were tempted but tired. The twelve-pound shoulder packs, true to prediction and despite our strap-padding, were now beginning to weigh in the area of a hundred pounds. We took the shorter route.

Those who took the Arthur's Walk came in hilarious. They had encountered a foot bridge which had many of the planks missing and many of the planks broken. Getting across had been frightening and, of course, when completed, highly comical. They also reported glorious waterfalls and generally rubbed it into those who didn't take the "ten minute" path which, they conceded, must have taken another hour on the trail. Oh, the New Zealand *ten minutes!*

The last three miles to Quintin Hut from Arthur's Hut was again in forests, but of more of a rain-forest nature, thickly wooded, steep and wet. The going underfoot was trickier and we were again thankful for dry weather.

Hot tea and a shower were the first two things we had at Quintin and, without any trouble, a nap.

The regrouping of the walkers that night began to show feelings of a new-found camaraderie. Barriers were breaking down. First names became more frequent and new groups began to form and dissolve and new groups would form again. The Sixth Party was starting to take form. The family feeling was shaping.

The American executive ignored any Kiwi short-cut and was already in communication with Milford and going around taking preferences for beverages.

A blond farmer from Canterbury broke out a bottle of Scotch he had packed on his back from Te Anau and shared it with his bunk-mates. Generosity and brotherly love in their highest form!

Packets of Epsom salts which the Lady Navigator had purchased in Wellington proved a life saver to our Australian major, who had bruised his foot.

There was a woman, probably in her fifties, accompanied by a mature daughter who suffered severely from asthma but who had a tremendous desire to make the Milford Walk and had gone into careful, long training to achieve her ambition. No one commented on it but everyone took quiet pride in her arrival at Quintin Hut at the end of the hardest day.

Everybody agreed that the Quintin Hut cuisine was superb. It has always had that reputation.

That night there was a slide show, games and early bed. Happy sleeping.

The next day was a day of "rest". Options included hiking up to Sutherland Falls, in the morning, scenic flights if weather permitted, "pot-holing" and assorted other side hikes in the afternoon and glow-worm caves at night.

Everybody turned out for the Sutherland Falls hike at nine in the morning, almost the full body electing to take the arduous "view" route and only half a dozen taking the "easy" route – which, in fact, wasn't that easy.

The party hadn't lost its enthusiasm, despite losing the sun, which had gone for the day behind a high cloud cover, and pushed off immediately which may not have been caused by exuberance as much as the sandflies. The sandflies settle on you like a small cloud when you aren't moving but tend to leave you alone when you are moving.

The hike up the mountain took less than an hour but was a stiffer climb than any we had been called on to make before. The pauses for breath were frequent. The group, contrary to pattern, stayed together hoisting one another up the gigantic boulders. Finally we were at "May's View" and could see Sutherland Falls in full fig.

The falls have a magnificent descent of 1,904 feet . . . dwarfing the Empire State Building in New York City . . . coming down in three stages through a six-foot-wide aperture at the top. When the mountains are hit by a solid rainstorm, which is frequent, the water shoots out like a giant fire hose and, clearing the lower terraces, crashes down in a spectacular straight fall to the pool below. At such times it can drench spectators 200 yards away.

The falls were first discovered in 1880 when Donald Sutherland, known as "the hermit of Milford Sound", together with John Mackay explored the upper reaches of the Arthur River. On a flip-of-the-coin agreement, the first falls were named after the winner, Mackay. However, in reality Mackay was the loser because the giant falls which were discovered last were appropriately called Sutherland Falls.

In 1888 the Government of Otago approved a surveying party to accurately measure the Falls. By coincidence, at the same time Quintin McKinnon and his companion, Ernest Mitchell, were successfully getting through what was to become the Mackinnon Pass which was to open up the Milford Track.

McKinnon even came across the warm ashes of the surveyors' campfire in a just-vacated camp site in the valley.

The Sixth Party then descended in easy stages to the foot of the Falls although there was one bridge crossing carrying a sign reading: "Christie's Crossing. Don't Walk on Slippery Rocks. Hidden River. Fall In. Don't Come Back."

At the bottom of the Falls everybody wore parkas to keep off the heavy mist.

Looking from the bottom to the top, up the sheer walls, it seemed like an impossible climb yet it was accomplished alone by a young surveyor, William Quill, in 1890. The danger of the climb can be appreciated in that it was not repeated until 1950.

The lake at the top of the Falls is named after Quill who was killed a year after his daring climb when he disappeared over a precipice, never to be found.

Our guide that day had made the ascent the year before. "Never do it again," he said. "Even coming down was a bit of a grunt." Then, clapping his hands for attention: "All right, who wants to go behind the Falls?"

About nineteen hikers raised their hands including, it was quickly pointed out to me, the Lady Navigator, which brought the party to twenty adding one non-volunteer.

The behind-the-Falls party retreated far enough from the mist to strip themselves of cameras and, surreptitiously, beneath the parkas, anything else that would come off and then re-assembled at the bottom of the falls.

"Hold hands and don't let go," yelled the guide.

School-children fashion we skirted the Falls and then edged along the cliff. The noise became louder and louder. The mist became heavier and heavier.

Soon we were completely enveloped in the swirling mist directly behind the Falls. We might as well have been in the middle of the Falls. Water was over the top of the boots. Water came up underneath the parkas, crept through every crevice of clothing. It was thunderously loud. It was icy cold. In other words it was marvelous!

The party came out the other side gasping and grinning.

Somehow we all thought we'd circle around behind the Falls and then go to dry ground. But once through the Falls it was obvious that we were trapped by the river running out of the bottom of the pool. How did we get over the river?

"WHERE DO WE GO FROM HERE?" was shouted at the guide.

"YOU GO STRAIGHT BACK THROUGH!"

There was a loud rebel yell, half in protest and half in glee, and then holding hands again, back through we went.

On the other side those who had stripped were grateful to have dry clothes to slip back into. Those who didn't had a wet walk home to

Quintin Hut which was the "easy" route less than two miles away.

The hot shower at Quintin was long and satisfying.

The weather was worsening, which compounded a problem. Not only would it mean non-delivery of our "merchandise" but it also certainly meant that the arrangement that our packs were going to be flown out the next day if we were willing to pay a $1 fee . . . and almost everybody was willing to pay a $5 fee if asked for such a delightful reprieve of burden . . . would be scrubbed.

The gathering of the clan at afternoon tea was not altogether cheery. By the end of tea when card games and scrabble and back-gammon had started in all corners of the room, there was a loud noise passing overhead.

Great Bacchus, it was a helicopter!

Everybody rushed outside as the pretty, pretty bird, one of the best nature sights we were to see, completed a pass and then landed and was soon disgorging all sorts of packages.

It didn't mean saving our packs but it certainly saved the evening festivities.

The gathering that night of course was a huge success. The family feeling of the Sixth Party was now complete. What had started out as a rather motley group of strangers had welded into a tight bunch of buddies.

The American executive who had engineered the beverages said in good executive fashion: "My job is done. Your job is to collect the money."

The collection proved painless as people kept dropping money into my lap all evening. We collected 80 per cent more than we needed to cover our bill and the American executive was accused of missing his profit forecast by 20 per cent. The balance of the funds was donated to the kitchen staff with loud cheers.

Certificates for accomplishing the Milford Walk were awarded with much clapping. I proposed a toast: "To the Sixth Party! Always swift! Always dry!"

Quintin Hut to Milford Sound . . . Fourteen Miles

At five o'clock in the morning it started to pour.

Despite the rain everyone was cheerful. This was to be the longest day – fourteen miles – and obviously we were going to get our taste of "Milford weather". So be it.

People were exchanging addresses ... there was much names calling ... high spirits everywhere ... pick up your waxed paper bundle of sandwiches and a juicy fresh orange.

For the second time a miracle happened. Overhead there was a close sound of an airplane doing a pass-by.

Airplane? Packs! Packs will fly out.

From an instant-freeze position the room changed into a blur of instant action. Bodies were moving everywhere, singular in purpose. Get your dollar and get your pack.

The airplane landed despite the close ceiling in this little rocky strip cut into the valley and taxied to Quintin Hut. Packs went on to the plane.

At one time Quintin Hut was supplied by ferry from Milford Sound to Sandfly Point. Tractored to Doughboy Hut. Ferried on Lake Ada to Boatshed. Horse from Boatshed to Quintin. Now it is entirely supplied by airplane.

For the first time all the rain garments were on display.

The Salisbury ladies and their Auckland friend were in blue "issue" THC parkas and they moved out on the first stage of the last day looking like the Sisters of the Holy Order of Arthur River.

The first stage was six miles to Boatshed. It was raining and the path underfoot was rocky, as we were told in the previous night's briefing that it would be, but the cascading waterfalls in all directions were worth the rain. Glorious.

The Boatshed's tiny cabin was full of steaming bodies. Everybody was having an early lunch. Spaghetti sandwiches. The Quintin cuisine reputation took a beating but the succulent orange made up for it.

After lunch a long swinging bridge took us across one branch of the Arthur River and then another. We turned back up the river until we reached Mackay Falls (pronounced, not "ma-*kay*" but "*mak*ee").

Mackay Falls has the power of runaway horses. It booms and crashes and surges at you from the platform built for its viewing.

Nearby is Bell Rock which evidently had been holed out by water of centuries of time and then, lighter of weight, moved over the Falls by the rushing water where it ended up at the side of the river with the hollow side down. You can crawl underneath and there is room inside its cavernous interior for several people.

The walk now continued down the left side of Arthur River. Soon we were skirting Lake Ada, which is loaded, the guide said, with brown trout.

The rain picked up a notch and so did the waterfalls. The largest was the Giant's Gate Falls with a swinging bridge where you could get your umpteenth thousand waterfall picture.

At the end of Lake Ada was the open Doughboy Hut with awaiting sandflies. We decided the relaxing was not worth the biting and we pushed on.

With the heavy rain the Arthur River was in full flood. So were the tributaries feeding it. We were ankle-deep and knee-deep crossing and fording the rising streams but we didn't care.

The mile signs alongside the track indicated that the last stretch was in front of us. Without packs, we were now swinging in the rain. We hated to see the last mile go.

In a way we didn't see it go . . . at least by foot. When we reached Sandfly Point, there was a sign indicating that we were thirty-two miles from Glade House. But the sign had said "33 Miles To Go . . . and Good Luck" when we left Glade House.

Then we realized the last mile was the launch trip to Milford Sound Hotel. The last mile was "free".

In the cabin at Sandfly Point everybody was congratulating everybody else and everybody was soaked to a squishy.

The launch to Milford Sound arrived early and we were squeezed on board having a welcome paper-cup of hot tea and we were out on the Sound. It was not a day for sight-seeing but most of us stood out in the rain to get a better look at Bowen Falls, a landmark on the Milford Sound cruise. The rain-swollen Bowen Falls were incredible, a huge spout of water thundering out into the Sound.

In only a few minutes we were at the dock.

Those for the hotel were shunted in a mini-bus and those for the hostel were crammed into a truck like prisoners of war. The Sixth Party was beginning to break up . . . and we resented it.

At the hotel we dripped across the carpets . . . and we dripped up to our room where we found our rucksacks and our suitcases forwarded from Te Anau.

Our own bathroom. Our own bathtub!

There is a lot to say for civilization.

We filled the bathtub with hot water and had a most platonic, long-lasting soak in sudsy waters up to our submerged chins.

After taking our sopping clothes to the drying room and after a nap, a knock on the door said the clan was gathering for cocktails and dinner. We missed the cocktails, which obviously had been several, and joined the remnants of the Sixth Party for dinner.

After much wine and laughter a survey was made.

What was your favorite part of the walk?

The variety that Mr Turnbull had spoken about quickly manifested itself, everybody finding his or her favorite part.

The Salisbury ladies found the garden party of the Glade Walk to their liking. The Australian major, the fish in the Clinton River. To many the power and the glory of standing on top of Mackinnon Pass, next to nature, next to God, with king-of-the-mountain vistas and with a grand sense of personal achievement, was the crowning moment.

To the broad-shouldered cricketer from Brisbane it was the hilarity of the hand-holding exercise behind Sutherland Falls. Many voted for the last day itself with the fun of the rain and the spectacle of the mountains covered with fresh waterfalls.

It was the tough American executive who put his finger on the missing variation which Mr Turnbull, probably purposely, didn't mention. "For me the most enjoyable part of the walk was watching the melding together of people."

Oh, yes, chorused the remainder, the people, the people.

A strong contingent of the Sixth Party came over from the Johnston Hostel for after-dinner drinks.

All was hilarious.

I lost a Brioni necktie and gained a Canterbury scarf. The camaradarie was warm and hearty.

And then the Johnston contingent had to take the last transportation back to their quarters and the curtain came down on the Sixth Party.

It was over. The Milford Walk had ended.

Milford Sound . . . The travel poster comes to life
What a joy to photograph!

Unless the rain is pouring in your camera lens . . . and that is possible . . . the most amateur, box-brownie novice can get a snap of Milford Sound worthy of blowing up and hanging on the wall.

The deep royal blue of the glacier-carved waters contrasted against the sheer granite cliffs streaked with white streams of waterfalls are the contrasting ingredients to please the eye and the camera.

The mighty Mitre Peak, looming a mile high, commands the surrounding country in lofty splendour and becomes the signature mark of the photography.

You can get splendid pictures from the lawn in front of the Milford Sound Hotel. You get even better pictures when you take one of the launch trips out on the Sound.

The trips vary in length but all are worth while. Seen from the water and from various angles, Stirling Falls and Bowen Falls and Mitre Peak are worth the trip alone.

Getting to the Milford Sound by way of the Milford Track is glorious . . . but go by any means available. There are buses, limousines, rental cars and airplanes. Just remember that reservations for transportation, launch trips and hotel accommodations in the December-January high season are essential.

The drive to Milford Sound is on good road but should be taken early in the morning so that the sun is behind you which lights the scenery to advantage and also is better for photography.

You are advised to take insect repellent to ward off the sandflies ". . .exceedingly numerous and are so troublesome that they exceed everything I ever met with. . ." wrote Captain Cook in 1773. They still are.

And a raincoat. The rainfall in the Milford Sound area is around 240 inches a year.

The drive or bus trip to the Sound starts off by skirting the shores of Lake Te Anau. After reaching Te Anau Downs the road then follows up the Eglinton River (good fly-casting) to Cascade Creek.

This portion of the road is the Avenue of the Disappearing Mountain which you will see on your return trip . . . a distant mountain seems to melt into the earth. Also when you pass the boundaries into Fiordland National Park the Eglinton Valley will probably be alive with lupin. Lupin is not a native plant and the rule of the Park is that only native plants are allowed to grow in it. However, the story goes, a disgruntled park worker in a retaliatory gesture went to town and bought lupin seeds and threw them into the headwaters of the Eglinton and today's lupin fields are a result. They may not be native but they are beautiful.

At Cascade Creek there is a stop for tea, postcards, rest rooms.

From here the road skirts Lake Gunn and Lake Fergus and climbs to Homer Tunnel.

Homer Tunnel was started as a make-work project for unemployed labor in 1935 and the tunnel, delayed by war and avalanches, was not opened until 1952. It is a one-way tunnel with traffic flowing for twenty-five minutes in one direction ... and then twenty-five minutes in the other. There are fine scenic views from each entrance to the tunnel.

The road to Milford passes "The Chasm" which will be marked on your left. In a few minutes' walk, very pleasant, through the woods, you are at a platform where you can look at the remarkable stone sculpture carved by the rushing waters of the Cleddau River.

The distance between Te Anau and Milford is seventy-four miles. Taking the launch trip and having lunch makes it an all-day affair. *(Warning:* it makes a *long* day.)

A time-saver is to fly to Milford on Mount Cook Airlines from Te Anau or from Queenstown. Actually Queenstown is closer by airline miles than Te Anau. If the weather is good and a visitor is limited on time, the air trip has a great advantage.

Early in the morning, slightly track-tired and party weary, we took a last picture of Mitre Peak – such a *loud* camera – and boarded the 7:45 bus for Te Anau. By eleven o'clock we had retrieved "The Yellow Rose", the remainder of our baggage and the precious, lost notebook.

We were shortly on our way to Queenstown.

It is an uneventful, two-and-a-half-hour drive taking the Five Rivers cut-off. You pass through the fishing headquarters of Garston – the bartender said a visitor had pulled a nine-pound trout out of the river just behind the hotel the day before – and then Kingston Junction where the *Kingston Flyer,* a 1915 vintage railroad engine, operates during the summer.

You pass along Lake Wakatipu, cross the bridge of the Kawarau River and you are at Frankton Junction. Airfield golf course to the right.

Frankton Junction to Queenstown is four miles with motels dotting the way.

17. Queenstown: The Vacation Town

**Sheep and Deer and Gold and Tourists ...
Vintage Cars ... Vintage Steamship ... A
Sky-high Lunch**

Queenstown is a vacation town.

There are hotels of questionably modern architecture and a plethora of motels.

Take your choice of action: restaurants, golf courses, tours and cruises, boutiques, nightlife, *(nightlife!)*, horseback rides, jet-boat trips, chair lifts to mountain tops.

Even rainbow trout are taught to come to the dock-side and entertain the visitor.

Coming immediately after the nature-quiet solitude of the Milford Track, Queenstown seemed over-crowded and touristy. No matter. It is a favorite playground for many New Zealanders and a popular tour stop for overseas visitors.

It was not always so. In 1860 two men who had pioneered the region for sheep grazing owned stations on each side of the lake. One of them, William Rees, had his camp on what is now the site of Queenstown.

Two years later the tranquility exploded. The rumor of gold was confirmed with rich findings on the Arrow and Shotover rivers.

Thousands of miners swarmed to the shores of Lake Wakatipu and Rees, who was now forced to abandon his farming, turned to ferrying the miners from Kingston to his campsite and supplying them with provisions. Subsequently he tore down his woolshed and erected the Queen's Arms Hotel on the site now occupied by Eichardt's Hotel.

Thus Queenstown was born.

Eichardt's Hotel is at the foot of an arty-crafty shopping mall which also contains the local Public Relations office. Here we plotted a day's activity to include the Deer Park, lunch at the top of Bob's Peak, a visit to the vintage motor museum, a steamship cruise and a sheep station stop.

Deer parks are an increasing standard tourist attraction throughout New Zealand, certainly in the South Island. The Queenstown park is first rate not only for the animals ... elk (wapiti), deer, Himalayan thar, chamois, and mountain goats roaming freely in their special hillside sections ... but also for the hilltop, sweeping views. On one side you look over the Kawarau River, Frankton and the airport to Lake Hayes, a little jewel in the distance and the remarkable Remarkable Mountains.

On the other side you look over Queenstown, the lake, and in the distance Coronet Peak where you can ski in the winter or, for more views, take the chairlift to the top in the summer.

You also look over the peninsula facing Queenstown with an attractive golf course on its tip. We visited this fine par-71 course set mostly in woods, but never played it. The Queenstown Golf Club, as it is designated on the scorecard is ten miles from Queenstown by car ... or 380 yards by water. There is a water taxi service to the golf course.

On the return to Queenstown we passed the zoological gardens and also the Golden Terrace Mining Village, both of which are recommended by guidebooks.

We were anxious to get to lunch at another recommended facility, the *Skyline Restaurant* on Bob's Peak reached by overhead cable cars. The four-seat gondolas take off seemingly straight up 2,400 feet where there is a restaurant, lounge (bar), upstairs café and souvenir shop.

Lunch with a bottle of white wine looking out over the lake was extremely peaceful. What was lacking in the kitchen was made up for in the scenery.

At the bottom of the lift is another tourist attraction: Queenstown Motor Museum which must be the most comprehensive in New Zealand. That such a collection should be gathered and shown here in Queenstown with a population of about 3,000 is indicative of the Queenstown tourist drawing power. There are classics and oddities in the collection including several excellent Rolls Royces and Bentleys. Many of the cars are privately owned and are on loan to the museum, the owners occasionally taking them out for antique-car rallies. All the cars are operational.

Another vintage attraction in Queenstown is the *Earnslaw,* one of two steamships in the southern hemisphere to be powered by handshovelled coal. You can take a luncheon cruise on the *Earnslaw* or a

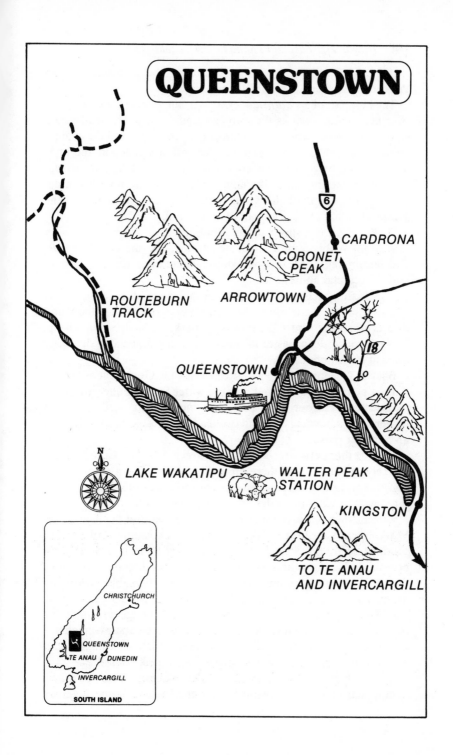

longer afternoon cruise to a high-country sheep station, Walter Peak, named after a son of William Rees.

The best part of an *Earnslaw* cruise is to stand on the walkway grill over the engine room as the ship gets underway while two firemen stoke the boilers – which take a ton of coal an hour – and the engines begin to turn over with a great sputter and hiss of steam and mysterious brass wheel-handles are turned in every direction, the fire shadows flickering about the engine room and the sound of ding-dinging ship's signal bells. Good stuff. The other attraction of the *Earnslaw* is that there is a quaint bar forward.

Walter Peak is a sheep station doubling as a commercial visitor attraction. Wool spinning is demonstrated. Handicraft is for sale. Old farming equipment is on exhibit. There are attractive gardens and the original homestead.

The highlight is a demonstration of sheep dogs at work. A "header" or an "eye" dog who never barks but who gathers and directs the sheep. And a "huntaway", a barker, who drives the sheep. It gives you a deep desire to witness the championship sheepdog trials in the autumn.

Back in Queenstown we had time to visit the Government Tourist Park, a peninsula jutting out into the water forming one side of the Queenstown Harbor. The park has meandering walks through flower beds, a bowling club and two tennis courts costing 15c per half an hour per person.

Despite the tourist crowds in Queenstown, Lake Wakatipu itself is scarcely populated and there are enjoyable country picnic, exploring, tramping and fishing expeditions to be had. Jet-boats can be hired with or without guides and with or without tackle.

Queenstown is also the starting or ending point for the Routeburn Walk. In contrast to the Milford Track which is only walked from south to north, the Routeburn can be traversed in both directions, northbound and southbound. The trip in either direction takes four days with three nights spent in the two lodges available exclusively for the guided tours of the Routeburn. Two nights are spent in either the Mackenzie Lodge or the Routeburn Falls Lodge and the third night is spent in whichever lodge was not used the first two nights.

Guided parties are limited to twelve and as the track is higher than the Milford Track, it is comparatively free of pesky sandflies.

The track goes from the head of Lake Wakatipu over the Harris Saddle and ends ... or begins ... on the Milford Sound highway halfway between Cascade Creek and Homer Tunnel.

The cost of the four-day, three-night privately-operated Route-burn is $74 in contrast to the $111 seven-day, six-night Milford package put out by the Government-controlled THC. The Route-burn is also open to "freedom walkers".

Our reservations for the Routeburn had to be cancelled in order for us to make the all-important Picton Ferry back to the North Island. After the introductory experience of the Milford Track, we were deeply disappointed.

The Longer Way to Wanaka

We took Highway 6 to Wanaka with a by-pass to Arrowtown.

We stopped twice. Once at Frankton to inspect the Wakatipu Golf Club adjacent to the airport which is a very flat, treeless, 9-hole course.

From the scorecard: "Rule 5: *BALLS OUT OF BOUNDS near or on runways of Aerodrome MUST NOT be retreived* (sic) *while plane is landing or taking off. Non-adherence of Rule No. 5 will result in disqualification of playing on this course for all time.*"

We no sooner cleared the Frankton Junction and the golf course than we had to stop again. Strawberry stand. Huge strawberries. Honor system 60c a basket (chip). The gallon tin in which we drop-ped our coins produced such a noise that we were sure the trans-action was noted in the farmhouse up the hill.

Detouring off of Highway 6 took us by Lake Hayes, which has a reputation for brown trout, but they can only be reached by boat in the middle of the lake and we didn't see any place to rent a boat.

It is a short distance from the end of Lake Hayes to Arrowtown.

You can also reach Arrowtown by taking a road out of Queens-town through Arthur's Point which was the location of a rich claim staked out by Rees's shearers, and further on is Packers' Arms, a restored inn *circa* 1860 with much of the original walls and a repu-tation today for a good kitchen.

Arrowtown today is an ice-cream stop for tour buses.

The most interesting thing in Arrowtown is the Lakes District Centennial Museum, an excellent small museum with many quaint relics from the goldrush days.

Two Americans were prominent on the scene. One was William Fox, a veteran of the California gold fields, who was responsible for the first important digging in the Arrow River. For some time he and his colleagues were able to keep their important gold discovery a secret although it was rumored that he had been seen cashing in large amounts of gold dust. Trying to follow him became the sport of Hunting the Fox. Eventually the secret was discovered and the rush was on.

It brought forth another American, the terrible "Bully" Hayes who was a blackbirder in the Pacific and who gathered about him a notorious reputation wherever he went. In Arrowtown he ran a pub and finally left town when it was discovered, as rumored, that his ear had been snipped, a branding given him in California for card sharking.

If you see a four-colored calendar of New Zealand, you will probably find one photograph of Buckingham Street in Arrowtown with the sunshine coming through the autumn-colored sycamore trees in front of the row of remaining miners' cabins.

Across the street from the museum is an antique-store. It is almost as good as the museum but more expensive.

From Arrowtown there is a short cut to Wanaka across the Crown Range. The road is tortuous at all times. Dusty when dry, dangerous when wet.

We had taken this road during our first trip to Wanaka on a particularly hot, dry day. We were promised a cold beer by our twinkly New Zealand driver at the famous Cardrona Hotel. Of course the *famous* Cardrona Hotel proved to be the miserable remains of an old goldrush bar, long closed.

This time we took the more comfortable route via Cromwell, twenty-six miles longer but much easier driving. The highway leading to Cromwell follows the gorges of the Kawarau River and there is a waterfall at the Roaring Meg marking the 45-degree parallel.

At Cromwell the Kawarau joins the mighty Clutha and continues to Lake Roxburgh and the Roxburgh hydro-electric station.

More dams are to be built on the Clutha which will flood the lower portion of Cromwell plus much of the surrounding orchard country. It is a sensitive local matter which a stranger would do well to avoid.

Going up the Clutha, the country is tussocked and flat. Soon to be flooded, much of it remains unworked. In the distance the snow-covered mountains of Mt Aspiring National Park can be seen.

Running alongside the west side of the highway is the Pisa Range dominated by Mt Pisa. Finally the low-profiled, somber Mt Iron is in front of you and just beyond it is Wanaka.

18. Wanaka: The Golden Country

A Vacation from a Vacation . . . How to Fish and how to Cook . . . A High Country Station . . . Birds, Beauty and God

If you wake up in Albert Town to the singing of larks and look across the Clutha River where it is joined by the Cardrona River and the sun is sliding down the St Bathans Range with the Hawkdun Range as a stage setting behind it and to the south the Dunstan mountains are getting their first touch of morning gold and the valleys are still in purple evening shadows and the tall larch trees and poplars are waving green leaves back at God – it is so painfully beautiful you want to cry out.

Wanaka is everything Queenstown is not. It is not developed although there is the fine Government-owned Wanaka Inn. There is a golf course and horseback riding and fishing in Lake Wanaka and its sister Lake Hawea and in the Clutha River. But there is no large development. No hawking of cruises, safaris and helicopter rides. It is very quiet.

A sign on a lakeshore cabin reads:

Marine Rentals
Power Boats
Mini Golf
Trampolines
Gold Mining Equipment

The cabin is unattended. That's Wanaka.

Wanaka has always been quiet country. Even the Maoris had no permanent settlement here of any size, only coming to net eels and snare birds.

Those Maoris who had lived here were chased out by a northern war party, never to return. Two plump young maidens didn't serve dinner, they were served *as* dinner to the protein-starved warriors, it was reported.

Sheep stations became the established way of life in the Wanaka country; the Morven Hills station, first established by Jock "Big

247

Mac" McLean, ran to half a million acres in 1858.

The pastoral face of the country was disturbed for a period of time with the goldrush to the surrounding areas. Even the Cardrona had a flurry of successful diggings, first by the Pakeha miners and then by the Chinese, and Albert Town became a ferry crossing and supply point. Not one but two hotels stood on the riverbank. The grey-wooded, tottering-plank remains of one can still be seen.

But even with the aftermath activity of quartz mining and dredging, Wanaka soon returned to its sleepy traditions.

We were ready for Wanaka.

After almost five weeks of packing and unpacking, driving, hiking, exploring, researching, we had need of a vacation from a vacation and accepted an invitation to stay at the Albert Town holiday home of friends from Dunedin.

Our host was half leprechaun and half pixie. His wife was half Billie Burke and half Julia Childs. For three days he taught us how to fish and she taught us new dishes to cook.

People in New Zealand have a talent for good living.

We remembered again the previous trip we had made to the same country. We had been fishing since dawn at nearby Lake Hawea. Came away empty handed. We tried fishing at the head of the Clutha River. Empty handed.

We adjourned for lunch.

Lunch was a barbecue on the ten-acre, lakeside estate of a retired couple from Dunedin. Five couples made up the company and everybody brought "something to nibble on".

The host had gone to the local hotel in the morning and had several gallon jugs filled with cold draft beer. The "jug beer" was sampled liberally and frequently.

Three fires were started.

One was for smoking fresh rainbow trout and freshwater salmon. Heavenly. Everyone has a sizeable portion of each.

The second fire was for barbecuing "sausages" which were what we would call frankfurters. A half a dozen each.

The third fire was for barbecuing steaks . . . one each . . . and lamb chops . . . two each.

As an accompaniment there were barbecued onions, pineapple rings and bananas and fresh rolls.

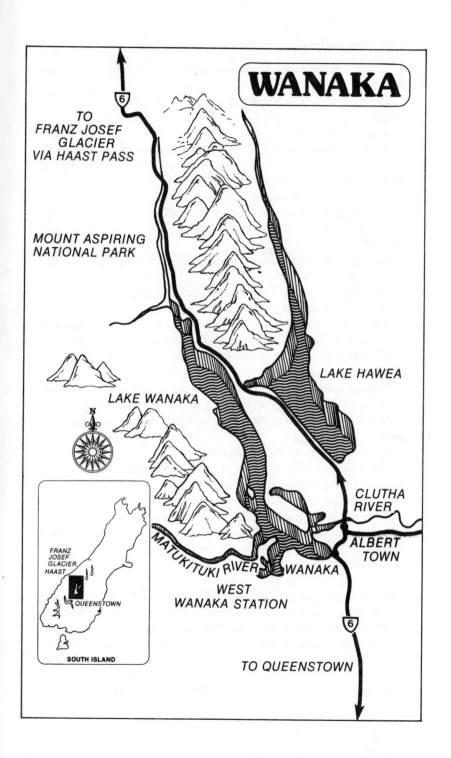

For dessert there were garden-picked fresh strawberries piled high with whipped cream.

The beer flowed freely along with gin for some and scotch for others.

A gargantuan meal.

After the barbecue my Dunedin fishing authority whispered to me on the side and we sneaked off like two errant school boys to try our luck at sunset fly-casting in the Clutha.

Share a moment of magic.

You are standing on a sand bar in the middle of a river fifty yards across. The music of water running through the shallow rapids is all around you.

The sun has already disappeared behind an alp-like range of mountains, and shadows deepen in the valley. You can see your fly fall gently on the surface and rush quickly downstream but soon the fly begins to disappear in the twilight.

You retreat to the river bank and change from fly-casting to thread-lining. There is only your companion and another fisherman far downstream and both are soon blotted out in the deepening dusk.

The last touch of yellow melts out of the sky. The river banks are dark. But the river stays a glistening pewter tone, catching the last reflected light from overhead. It seems to be lit from underneath. It glows.

Finally you are casting without any light.

You can hear the lure hit the water with a gentle *plop* but that is all. You cast again and again until it is totally black.

"One last cast," a voice comes across the dark.

"One last cast," you reply.

You leave because you have to. No fish. No strikes. But a fulfilment that comes from sitting in the lap of nature and being mothered.

After being pampered by fishing guides who do everything but jump in the water and hook a fish on the line for you, finally we had a coach who sat us down and taught us the rudiments.

How to tie a leader to a line. How to tie a fly to a leader. How to tie a knot.

We were made to do our lessons over and over and over again. Until we could do them in the dark. Which was exactly the purpose.

He taught us how to fish downstream with a wet fly and how to fish upstream with a dry fly.

We fished in the early morning and we fished at night until there was only a moon out and a sky full of stars.

Oh, yes, the coach had a pocketful of keys to private paddocks and we'd go bouncing off a sheep-pasture road to reach pools untouched but by a blessed few. There was always a quart of beer in back of the car in case of an emergency celebration.

The wind was strong from the northwest and the fish were few, but those which did get on the line lived up to the Clutha reputation for being fighting fish. I caught my first brown trout.

(The coach said they were fed on raw whiskey and raw meat but people from Dunedin often talk in such a manner.)

Our hostess cooked trout in a tempera light batter that would make the best Japanese chef jealous. She shared the recipe with us.

Hilda Turner's Golden Trout

Make a hole in the middle of 1/3 cup flour.

Separate two eggs.

Drop yolks into flour and swish slowly.

Add: 1/3 cup milk and mix until creamy and thick. Let mixture stand a minimum of 10 minutes.

Beat egg whites stiff-stiff.

Mix and add to flour mixture:

    1 teaspoon lemon juice
    1 teaspoon salt
    2 teaspoons melted butter

Fold in egg whites gently.

Heat one-half inch oil of your choice (Hilda prefers sunflower oil) in frypan. She warns that less than one-half inch of oil in pan will result in the oil penetrating the fish.

Dry fish fillets and dip into batter and fry to golden brown, turning as necessary.

Trout . . . or any white fish . . . prepared this way is excellent served cold on picnics.

Visiting a high-country sheep station is an education.

Through friends we were invited to West Wanaka station, an established station of 48,000 acres, operated by the Scaife brothers who had grown up on the property and who had been raised into the sheep business.

We skirted Wanaka looking up the Matukituki River to Mt Aspiring, which rises 10,000 feet in the Southern Alps. Its singular pyramidal peak bears a resemblance to the Matterhorn.

The West Wanaka station lies just across the mouth of the Matukituki River mostly snow-fed and comparatively placid, but in a rainstorm it can turn into a wild torrent of water. At one time a substantial concrete bridge had been built across the mouth by the Government, contrary to local advice, and in an ensuing storm the concrete bridge was swept away, part of it never to be found.

Gerald Scaife, an affable New Zealander in his mid-forties and the younger of the two brothers, met us at the swing bridge which now connects the station to the outside world.

A pickup truck and a battered Wolseley car took us through a tree-lined lane up to the station houses.

The two homes which house the two families are pleasant and unpretentious. There were gardens and trees and views over Lake Wanaka.

Margaret Scaife, Gerald's wife, a slim, handsome lady, met us in a sundress and showed us her garden. Although recent frosts had taken their damage, it was obvious she took a pride in her flowers and vegetables.

After meeting their pretty daughter, home for the holidays, we piled into Gerald's pickup truck for a small turn around the paddocks.

The station runs 7,000 sheep and 1,500 head of cattle. As is most of the sheep country in New Zealand, the Scaife station is Government-owned "Crown land" and is leased for thirty-three years. The lower land, fertilized annually by airplane, is green and lush.

The upper land no longer carries sheep because the loss of sheep in the high country winters made it unprofitable.

We later visited the woolshed where they had recently completed shearing the 7,000-head flock. There are ten power-operated shearing stands in the shed. Everything is geared for speed with the least amount of waste motion.

The sheep are held in pens next to the shearing stands. A shearer grabs a sheep out of the next-door pen, shears the animal in two minutes and then thrusts it down a chute to a lower level. An automatic counter at the exit slide keeps tally of the number having been shorn.

The shearing is done under contract at about $50 per hundred.

The contractor provides food for his shearers.

The West Wanaka station, described in *"Historic Sheep Stations of the South Island"* (Reed), is operated by only the two brothers and one hired hand. Extra help that is needed seasonally such as for mustering and shearing is contracted for on the side.

It is demanding work, with the strains inherent in stock-raising created by the uncontrolled weather and the uncontrolled market. In a bad year a sheep shearer can make more money than a station owner.

Gerald was philosophic about station life. Each of the brothers has a son. The older brother's son works at another station. Gerald's son was currently mountain climbing in Europe.

In the ambience of the living room Gerald poured drinks for the guests. "In the past generation," he said, "it was a custom for the son to follow the father. It's not that way today and I don't disagree with it. I wouldn't force my son into farming. Farming is hard work with a marginal future."

The kitchen in the home could feed a small army and Margaret, who confessed she couldn't boil water when first married, quickly learned to feed as many as twenty-two at mealtime. With "contract" farming that chore has been eliminated.

Today she plays golf in Wanaka with the ladies on Tuesdays and with her husband on Saturdays. She gardens. She loves to muster with the men and, we were told, unconsciously uses the musterers' language but that remained unproven.

The wife of the owner of the nearest station, thirty miles away, recently had won her helicopter licence, the second woman in New Zealand to do so, and that week she was going to fly over and pick Margaret up to fly away for a "do".

"Isn't it hard to live with 7,000 sheep all of the time and be faced with preparing mutton or lamb for a meal?" Margaret was asked.

Gerald patted his stomach with satisfaction, "She does all right."

We asked for her mutton recipes:

Margaret Scaife's Mutton Casserole

Cut up into cubes one leg of mutton. Put in casserole. Mix in bowl:

2 cups water	2 tablespoons vinegar
1 teaspoon sugar	1 tablespoon soya sauce
1 tablespoon Worcestershire sauce	salt and pepper to taste
½ teaspoon mustard	2 tablespoons flour

Pour over meat. Add one large chopped onion, carrots, parsnip and peas. Cover casserole and cook in moderate oven at 300°F for two to three hours.

For variety add: 1 can pineapple, 2 teaspoons curry.

Roast Stuffed Leg of Mutton

Bone leg and rub outside and inside with salt and pepper. Make stuffing of:

2 cups soft bread chunks
½ teaspoon celery seed or celery salt
½ teaspoon mixed herbs
1 small chopped onion
1 egg
¾ cup crushed pineapple (optional)

Stuff pocket with mixture and close. Brush with melted butter and sprinkle with ½ teaspoon of ginger and 1 tablespoon of lemon juice. (Optional: make slits in top of meat and insert slivers of garlic.)

Bake in open roasting dish at 325°F for three hours. Top with red currant jelly for glaze and roast another 15 minutes. Remove roast from pan and make gravy in the pan from the remaining juices.

Makes delicious cold cuts combined with almost any kind of salad.

We asked the gracious lady what a typical day's menu might contain at a high-country station. She wrote the following:

Breakfast – Fruit, cereal or porridge. Fried chops, bacon or sausages with eggs, tomatoes or omelettes. Toast with marmalade, syrup. Tea, coffee.

Morning Tea – Scones, toasted sandwiches, *pikelets* (a little sweet pancake served cold and buttered), tea cakes, sausage rolls, *mouse traps* (grilled cheese toast), bacon and egg pie.

Lunch – In winter, soup. Cold meats, fried potatoes, beet salads, pickles. Hot ground-meat (mince) dishes or stews. Macaroni-cheese dishes and the like. Scones, bread, jam, Marmite.

Afternoon Tea – If the men are about, tea or coffee with sandwiches or biscuits and cheese plus fruitcake and one iced biscuit or "just what I happen to have in my tins. Nowdays we don't bother very much with afternoon tea."

Dinner – Roast mutton, boiled mutton, grilled chops, casserole, chicken dishes, roasted pork or beef dishes with potatoes and two or three other vegetables and trimming e.g. mint sauce, horseradish sauce, gravies or red currant jelly. Dessert of all varieties, some days cold, others hot, e.g. fruit and ice cream, apple pie, plum pudding, *sago* (custard), caramel shortcake. Tea or coffee.

All this from a woman who didn't know how to boil water when she was first married. "I do love feeding working men and visitors," she concludes.

The hospitable visit to the West Wanaka station had given us a new insight into station life. The graciousness and the unaffected manners of our hosts was not surprising . . . it is a New Zealand way. But any idea of a gentleman-farmer who doesn't get his jodhpurs dirty and whose wife lives a lady-of-the-manor existence were erased.

It's a gum-boots-and-kitchen-drill way of life which must have great satisfactions but is never removed from tough reality.

In the autumn the poplars lining the lakes of Wanaka country turn into gold. They stand like royal guards on the shore fronts. The air is soft as nature starts to tuck everything neatly away for the winter. It is a favorite time and place for New Zealand landscape artists.

19. The Haast Pass And The Glaciers: The Wonder Of Our World

The Miracle Fish . . . "The Worst Roads Since Yugoslavia" . . . The Wonder of Our World

You should have three things on leaving Wanaka:
1. An early start
2. A ready raincoat/parka
3. A reservation where you are going to stay that night.

Although the distance from Wanaka to Haast Bridge on the West Coast is only ninety-one miles you should schedule at least a half day to make the trip if the sun is out.

An early start also puts the light behind you which gives you easier driving, better views . . . which are super . . . and better photography, of course.

If the sun is not out, and this area has one of the highest rainfalls in the country, then you need your raincoat because there will be times when you want to get out of the car regardless of weather.

Your destination will probably be either the Fox Glacier or the Franz Josef Glacier where accommodations are comparatively limited in relation to the attraction of the popular glaciers, particularly in the summer season.

We left Wanaka at seven o'clock in the morning because our host wanted to give us one last fishing experience . . . landlocked salmon.

The sun was with us and we were to keep it until we reached Haast Junction.

Getting away smartly was one miracle.

Getting the sun all the way through the pass was another.

Would there be a third? There would be.

We passed Lake Hawea hydro dam which has lifted the lake to feed the downriver Roxburgh power station. Here on the nearby rocks, lazily fishing almost two and a half years before, our host had described how he had moved into that time-frame of life when you start burying your friends who thought that their businesses couldn't survive without them. There had to be more to life than dropping dead at a desk of a heart attack, he said.

We both agreed, profoundly, that this was true and we both agreed that we would do something about it . . . and we had. We were both now semi-retired and on our way fishing again. Free men.

There is a little bay halfway up Lake Hawea where the waters of the lake and those of Lake Wanaka are less than a mile apart. This is known as The Neck.

You can swing off Highway 6 to the bay and deep water is before you, filled with landlocked salmon. We saw them but we didn't catch them.

The time came for our departure . . . but we cast again and again and again . . . a quarter of an hour beyond departure time . . . a half an hour.

"Let's roll."

"One last cast," pleaded the Lady Navigator.

("One last cast" – oh, that litany of the defeated fisherman! She had five more casts, we said our tearful farewells and we were away.)

Golden Wanaka country.

From the top of The Neck you can see both Lake Wanaka and Hawea and you follow the shores of Wanaka until you reach the head of the lake at Makarora.

The AA strip map says in this area: "Pass a sliding hill face which may suddenly block road at any time." We flew past it.

Descending down to the lake level, there is a perfectly framed picture of Mt Aspiring with the lake in the foreground.

And then it happened. It is painful to repeat. Let me just reprint a letter I sent back to our Wanaka host, Gordon Turner.

Dear Coach –

It was like this:

We left you with our fishing gear pretty much still at-the-ready in the back of the wagon. Went through the first pass and arrived at the head of Lake Wanaka where Mt Aspiring, snow-capped, is reflected in the lake. A picture.

We stop the car. Take a snap. "Isn't it beautiful?" we say to each other before scampering down the road . . . halt . . . what is that bubble on the lake? . . . and that one? . . . and that one? Fish! (They weren't fish, we learned later, they were bubbles from underground springs.) And then . . . heart pounding . . . louder on the organ, Joe . . . alongside the shore is a fat brown trout . . . over there! There's another!

Riot squad goes into action. "Here, Lady Navigator, here's your pole. Go over to that head of rocks and start casting." She disappears.

My pole is partially disassembled and I hook in (1) the chilly-bin (2) her Dallas-suede coat (3) my left thumb. I'm trembling but progressing and confident.

Off-stage shriek from lakeside: "JAWWWWAN! HELP!"

I look around in time to see a giant brown jump thirty yards out at the end of her line. I'll be gawdamned.

First cast, Coach, and I swear with that heavy salmon lure you put on her line at Lake Hawea, she didn't catch that monster in the mouth. She speared him through the head.

She hauled him in like a live sack of coal, beached him . . . no net, of course . . . together, with eyes averted, we hit the fish behind the head with stones, hunting knife and finally a huge hunk of wood. It finally died just to put us out of our misery.

She cleaned it. Be-headed it. De-tailed it.

And that night, at Franz Josef Glacier, she cooked it in butter. I must say it was delicious . . . but living with her ever since . . . ?

Coach, you don't have an old sleeping-bag, do you?

Your loving pupil . . .

That was the third miracle.

From that time on we always carried rods ready for action in the back of the car, a simple precaution we should have taken from the time we first hit the road in New Zealand.

The Haast Pass is the newest road to cross the Southern Alps although it is the lowest of all the passes and one of the oldest. (In early Maori days it was a known trail to the greenstone country.)

The Maori war party which later had maidens for dinner came through this pass. (It was a remarkable military manoeuvre. The party had started from the most northern part of the South Island and, in a flanking movement, fought its way down the entire west coast, came through the pass and was only defeated less than fifty

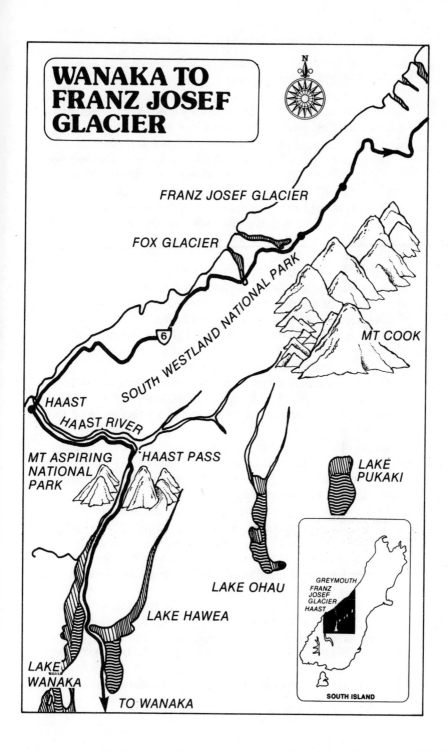

WANAKA TO FRANZ JOSEF GLACIER

N

FRANZ JOSEF GLACIER

FOX GLACIER

SOUTH WESTLAND NATIONAL PARK

6

MT COOK

HAAST

HAAST RIVER

MT ASPIRING NATIONAL PARK

HAAST PASS

LAKE PUKAKI

LAKE OHAU

LAKE HAWEA

LAKE WANAKA

TO WANAKA

GREYMOUTH
FRANZ JOSEF GLACIER
HAAST

SOUTH ISLAND

miles from the south coast when it was surprised in camp and slaughtered. The march took over a year.)

In 1863 the pass was first traversed by white men. The explorer was Charles Cameron, a gold prospector whose accomplishment was doubted until his powder flask was found at the summit of what is now Mt Cameron in 1881. Second was Julius von Haast.

The pass was named after von Haast, an Austrian who had been brought to Christchurch as the Canterbury Provincial Geologist.

Work started on the pass in 1929 as a project for the unemployed but it was not until 1965 that the entire road was completed, linking the west coast with Wanaka. Originally it was estimated that the road could be completed for very little money. Its eventual cost was $11 million.

Makarora was once a timber town where surrounding forests were felled, milled and tied into rafts and floated down Lake Wanaka and then down the Clutha River to the budding gold towns on the Clutha. There must have been some wild rides.

There is a Mt Aspiring National Park information office at Makarora, after which are a series of alpine meadows until you pass over the Makarora River and start climbing.

There's a beautiful gorge on the right from which the Makarora flows and further on is Fish Bridge, a dizzying height above the river below it. (We stopped to get a look and nearly got rammed from behind.)

Shortly after passing over Fish River Bridge you reach the summit of Haast Pass, which is at an elevation of only 1,847 feet. A stone monument marks the spot. Directional signs point to the original pack trail used by drovers in earlier days.

Two miles after leaving the summit you will see Fantail Creek Falls from the road on the right. Have your camera ready.

The Haast River is on your right and drops down a gorge called the Gates of Haast and then on to Pleasant Flat Bridge and Clarke Bluff, which is a good place to have late morning tea in the sun. And have a what-the-hell cast in the milky river.

The country continues to open out and the Haast River continues to widen and you are at Haast Bridge. The Haast Pass is behind you.

Later that night at our motel an Englishman with a sign pasted on the back of his car reading "COVENTRY, ENGLAND" (which would indicate something about his personality, wouldn't it?) sputtered on and on about the Haast Pass. "It's the worst road I've encountered in my entire life! I've driven all over the world. I've even driven in Yugoslavia. That road is worse than a road in Yugoslavia."

We could hear him crying but he never touched us. We hoped that he would experience the Kauri Forest road in the rain when it was under repair. Yugoslavia, hah!

Our friends in Wanaka and Dunedin had told us to take the time to take the walks. There are walks designated along the Haast Pass at Davis Flat, Gates of Haast, Thunder Creek Falls, but suffering the time penalties of fishing, we didn't and felt guilty.

Our friends also said to fill up the gas tank at Haast Junction and we did. At Haast Junction you cross one of the longest bridges in New Zealand. It is almost a quarter of a mile across and was completed in 1962 at a cost of a half a million dollars.

Heading north again on Highway 6 you go along the coast and through much winding forest country.

At Lake Moeraki we stopped overlooking the lake and had a picnic lunch. A little waterfall across the road supplied clear, cold water for drinking and for wiping off the picnic plates and rinsing out the cups. Perfect.

There is a scenic wild-ocean lookout at Knights Point just before reaching Lake Moeraki. Mark it for a stop.

The road continues inland, past Lake Paringa and on to the coast again at Bruce Bay, once a settlement for prospectors who came to pan gold from the beach. As the expression goes, it didn't pan out and they moved further north.

You are now coming to Westland National Park and it is time to look at your map more closely. The country in front of you comprises one of the most interesting topographical areas in New Zealand. As you look at the map, you can appreciate how close the top of the Southern Alps is to the coastline. In a relatively short distance the ground goes from sea level to 11,000 feet as if nature had taken the earth and suddenly tilted it up to this severe angle – which is exactly what happened.

A giant fault-line lies under the earth here and runs up the spine of the South Island. Parts of the fault line can be seen from the air.

The results of the tilting topography are many. Naturally such a shield, facing the winds of the Tasman sea, blocks the moisture-laden air, creating much rain on the lower level and much snow on the upper level.

The amount of snow has been of such huge proportions in the past that it has been unable to melt and succeeding packs have weighted the snow down with such force as to create solid ice, thus forming glaciers which at one time ran clear down to the sea.

Even today the faces of the Fox and Franz Josef Glaciers are only short distances away from fern groves and subtropical plants. Nowhere else in the world does this phenomenon of nature exist.

Looking in the map at the giant escarpment which runs from Milford Sound to beyond Arthur's Pass making up the Southern Alps makes you appreciate Tasman's description as a "land uplifted high".

The AA map will also indicate the tremendous amount of land in this area that New Zealand has protected for future generations: Fiordland National Park, Mt Aspiring National Park, Westland National Park on the west side of the Southern Alps. Mt Cook on the eastern side of the Alps.

You drive past the scenic drive entrance to Fox Glacier and go first to the Westland National Park Visitor Center where you will find displays and free brochures. A complete set of informative mimeographed papers for 20c details more than you can absorb about glaciers.

.To the west of the little community center of Fox Glacier there is a hotel, souvenir shop, tearoom, post office and an air strip. A road leads to Lake Matheson which is perhaps one of the most photographed lakes in New Zealand because of its magnificent views of reflected mountains. Not when it's raining. A rowboat can be hired at the hotel to take you to the far side of the lake where the setting is superior.

Doubling back a short distance on Highway 6, you enter the scenic drive to the face of the Fox Glacier. From the road the moraine or mass of rocks and sands left by the retreating glacier is not pretty in itself nor has the face of the glacier the ice-cream-parlor, snow-white purity you'd imagine.

The impressiveness of a glacier is either to walk on it or fly over it, both of which can be arranged. Again you have to pray for a break in the weather.

There are many interesting walks and drives in the area. Slide shows and talks are given at the Visitor Center. A glow-worm cave is almost within the community center.

From the Fox Glacier to the Franz Josef Glacier is one of the more tortuous roads in New Zealand. The twists are measured in the hundreds. However one of the mimeographed sheets at Fox details each part of the interesting drive and if you have a good Lady Navigator, you may not be able to see it all because your eyes are fixed on the road, but at least you can hear about it.

At Franz Josef, which was named by von Haast after his Austrian emperor, there is the National Park headquarters. More displays and broadside informational sheets.

Within walking distance of park headquarters is the St James Church, a stopping place because of its Tudor architecture and the view from the sanctuary rail towards the glacier. At one time the ice of the glacier could be seen through the window but it has now retreated out of sight.

If the church is closed, you can walk around to the window and get the same view from the walk.

There is also an air strip at Franz Josef.

The Franz Josef Hotel is north of town which is not to be confused with the Franz Josef Glacier View Motel, further north, or the Motel Franz Josef, still further north.

Visiting the glacier is most enjoyable. There are signposted side jaunts which take only minutes. Peter's Pool, for example is a "kettle" lake on top of a knoll. The pool – a kettle – is the result of melted ice. Clear and placid, it is a mirror for reflection photographs.

Sentinel Rock is a commanding viewpoint from which to see the glacier's path. At the time of the glacier's discovery it fronted the face of the glacier.

The car park ends at a fascinating mountain of smooth rock which humpity-humps over a large area leading almost to the glacier face. Wear your tennis shoes.

We played children-in-the-park over the rocks and had a delightful time working out our driving kinks.

Guided walks on the glacier can be arranged through the Franz Josef Hotel and include the proper equipment. Park headquarters has information about the various drives and walks that take from two minutes to all day. There is also fishing and hunting in the park.

The advancement and the retreat of the glaciers is one of the more fascinating aspects of the Park. Their present retreat cannot be predicted to continue. There have been past instances where seasons of heavy snow have created the incredible pressure on the body of the glacier that squeezes it forward with a terrible relentlessness crushing mountains into sandpiles.

Two theories are put forth saying that man is responsible, beyond the normal cycle of an interglacial period.

The "greenhouse" theory says that man, having dumped millions of tons of débris into the atmosphere in only the last 100 years, mind you, has created a greenhouse where light and heat energy from the sun are trapped and instead of their being reflected away by the atmosphere, the atmosphere is warmed leading to reduced snowfalls and therefore glacial recession.

The second theory is in reverse of the first. Man is creating a belt of stratospheric pollution with high-flying aircraft and atomic explosions, aided by volcanic explosions. This high belt of particles is reflecting heat energy away and cooling the atmosphere. The theory continues that if the same rate of cooling from 1945 to 1970 is maintained, we won't be 25,000 years away from another ice age, but only 500 years.

Take your pick of theories.

We asked the manager of the motel if she would like some trout. She said no, her son had caught a salmon the day before in the lake just up the road.

That's all we needed.

20. Westland And Home

A Little Light Fishing ... Gemstones and Gin Mills ... Panning for Gold at Shantytown ... "Hoke" and "Grey" ... A Little Heavy Rain ... The Frightening Earthquake ... The Beautiful Buller ... Watching the Shearing ... The Happy Stretch Home

You could make a dream world of travel in New Zealand by just stopping at every pretty lake and river and throwing a fishing line in and, in between, stopping at every pretty rest area and having picnics and teas.

In the early morning light, with visions of a repeat of the Miracle of Wanaka before us we cast into Lake Mapourika and again at Lake Wahapo without any action and pushed on towards Hokitika, known locally as "Hoki".

It is not a road for fast travelling, which makes you take the time to appreciate the scenery of forests and mountains and rivers. Something seems out of character for New Zealand travel and you realize what it is: there are no sheep ... a few head of cattle but no sheep.

Heading towards Hoki, you cross multiple rivers and streams, many of which show signs of having been worked by gold dredges.

After leaving Harihari you skirt the wooded shores of Lake Ianthe and then pass the historic goldmining town of Ross. You pass over the Totara River, once known for its gold and now known for its whitebait. An optional road to Hoki comes up on your left which will take you by Lake Mahinapua, a favorite boating lake in the area.

Hoki doesn't appear very attractive to the casual visitor, although a visit to the museum and a gemstone factory are recommended by travel authorities. The town enjoys a colorful reputation in New Zealand. It is known for its independent spirit, the number of its bars ... which in the past ignored any formal laws of opening or closing ... and for its unique band.

At one time the town consisted of a calico store on one side of the Hokitika River and a few tents and a couple of stores on the other side of the river. Then in 1864 gold was found.

Hokitika, according to some sources, jumped to 16,000 people overnight and had a population of 50,000 less than two years later.

265

(These figures are in dispute, however.) Among the miners were a large number of Irish who remained to give the west coast a sizeable Irish population today.

At the height of the immigration over sixty ships were moored at one time inside the terribly treacherous harbor entrance. A local pastime was to watch the boats negotiating the harbor mouth and to bet on the potential success or failure. Boat after boat was wrecked.

In the following twelve years over $27 million of gold was taken out of the west coast, of which Hoki was the center.

The Kokotahi Band of Hokitika reflects the spirit of the goldrush days. Made up of volunteers in a miner's dress of red shirt and black bandana, they play a variety of instruments, mostly of their own invention, producing a noise which has the virtues of being both loud and happy. The thirst of the band is as well known as its music.

The West Coast Historical Museum is a neat but small museum reflecting the history of the country's gold-digging past. It includes a large collection of photographs and clippings from old newspaper stories. Among the oddities is the story of Guy Menzies, a twenty-one-year-old Australian who flew solo in 1931 from Sydney and, diverted by bad weather to Westland, landed in a swamp near Harihari where his plane turned over on its back. Having no other recourse the adventurous pilot undid his seat belt and fell out on his head! A cut lip was the extent of his damage. Like "One-Way" Corrigan, Menzies had filed a flight plan from Sydney to Perth, Australia, but secretly took out over the Tasman Sea to make the first solo flight in history between the two countries.

Although gold provided the west coast with temporary riches and a permanent population, the historic Maori treasure of the coast was greenstone. Today it supplies the local jewelry industry.

Greenstone is a jade (nephrite) which the Maoris prized for cutting tools, chisels and adzes because of its hard substance. They also used it for making war axes and the flat hand-held *patu* club used in battle as a slashing weapon to break bones, necks and heads. Also, ornaments of greenstone were valuable and the tribal neck pendant, the *hei-tiki,* duplicated in every souvenir shop in New Zealand today, was made of the precious stone.

The rich fields of greenstone were found in the country of Westland, particularly around the Arahura region, just north of Hokitika, where Kupe supposedly made a landing.

There are two greenstone factories in Hokitika where the visitor is

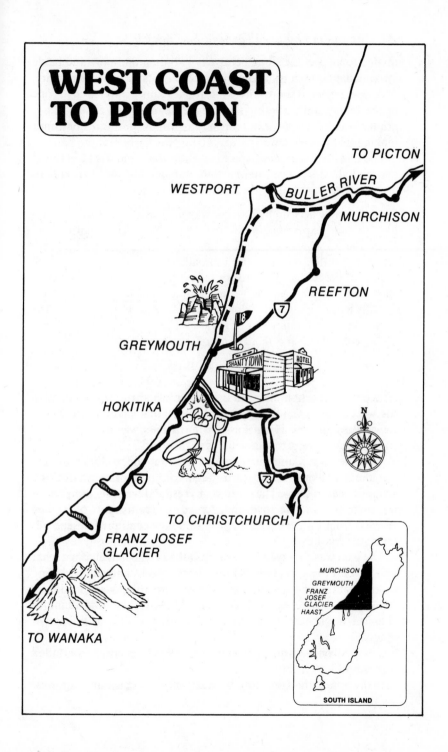

invited to inspect the stone being cut with diamond saws and made into pendants, earrings and other decorative ornaments. There are, of course, adjacent shops where the articles can be purchased . . . one of the better, authentic buys in New Zealand. (It is rather incongruous watching New Zealand men of rugby size and demeanor making the delicate jewelry.)

The Lady Navigator also found an antique shop and for $7 bought two leaded glass panels out of a china cabinet. She loved Hokitika.

If you are now accustomed to one-way bridges in New Zealand you have a new experience waiting for you between Hokitika and Greymouth, where you twice not only share the bridge with oncoming traffic but also the railroad whose tracks go down the middle of the bridge. The broken railing from previous accidents on each side commands your respect immediately. You learn, especially in the rain, to drive slowly and to keep your wheels out of the railroad tracks. Getting out of the tracks can cause the car to lurch out of control . . . and there is all of that broken railing to remind you.

At Kumara Junction the road is joined by Highway 73 which links the west coast to Canterbury over the Arthur's Pass road. Like the Lewis Pass and the Haast Pass, Arthur's Pass was used by Maori tribes to reach the greenstone fields in the west.

The citizens of Canterbury wanted a road to the goldfields hoping that the gold would flow back through Canterbury instead of being sent overseas in ships. The citizens of Westland however didn't need the road or want the road and, forced to pay for part of it, they seceded from Canterbury Province. And they continued to send out their gold by ship.

The pass was surveyed by George Dobson who, when asked what was the best route, replied, "Oh, Arthur's pass is the best," referring to his brother who had found the pass across the Main Divide in 1864 when he was twenty-three years old. Arthur became a famous engineer in New Zealand and was knighted in 1931 at the age of ninety.

George Dobson who completed the road to Canterbury was killed by road robbers in 1866.

If the communication link between the east coast and the west

coast was at first a failure, the creation of a road for both coasts to
Arthur's Pass National Park was a success.

The Park covers over 200,000 acres. There are winter sports. Outdoor ice skating, skiing, tobogganing. There is hunting: Red deer,
chamois, thar. Hunting permits can be obtained from Park headquarters located in Arthur's Pass township which is on the east side
of the Divide.

There are many varied walks of all durations in the Park and
several pleasant places to camp or just have a picnic. The Arthur's
Pass National Park Handbook is recommended.

At the south side of Paroa, close to Greymouth, are signs pointing
towards Shantytown. Your friends have recommended you visit the
re-created gold town and you do.

Shantytown is only a few minutes off of the Highway 6. The idea
of the tourist attraction was launched in 1968 after a meeting called
by the Public Relations Office in Greymouth brought together
people who were interested in vintage steam engines and cars and
the history of goldmining. A visit by one of them to Knotsberry
Farm in Los Angeles sparked a vision of having a similar attraction
in Westland. In 1971 Shantytown opened its gates and has been
increasing in popularity annually.

One of the first unique attractions at Shantytown was a gold claim
where the visitor could pan for gold and was promised "color" for
the effort.

Today there are authentic buildings and re-created buildings including a bank, general store, Golden Nugget Hotel – precious –
printing works with a "Columbian" printing press made in 1837,
cobbler's shop, barber shop, a 106-year-old church which originally
was built in No Town, twelve miles from Greymouth, a jail (gaol),
authentic gallows and stocks – a favorite photographic spot ...
though in fact hanging in public was never practised in early New
Zealand and the stocks were never even heard of ... livery stable,
fire station, blacksmith shop, engine sheds and tearooms.

There is a 1900 railway station which serves as ticket dispenser for
the Infants' Creek Bush Tramway, a short-line run through the
native bush. The passengers ride in a specially built carriage pulled
by the *Kaitangata,* a genuine steam engine which employs a cer-
tificated engine driver.

Shantytown must be considered Greymouth's tourist attraction. "Grey", as the city is called locally, has 8,000 people but offers little to the visitor although it serves as the farming and timber center of Westland.

Nearby rivers carry good trout.

With nothing better to do we travelled outside the city, three miles up the Grey River and played golf on the Kaitata Links of the Greymouth Golf Club: par 72, flat, tree-lined.

Almost immediately it started to rain, which steadily increased until we quit at the end of nine holes under a danger of drowning.

Looking down the river you could see the notch in the limestone cliffs which forms a funnel compressing a river wind into a fierce, cutting gale that blows through the city. It is known as *The Barber*.

"Grey" indeed.

We stopped at a fruit stand on the way back to the motel. It was December 15. We asked the Irish-faced proprietor, "Have you had much of this weather?" He answered quickly without looking up: "Since last Christmas."

We laughed and then he looked up. "You don't believe me? They've had seven *yards* down the road!"

We always carried a plastic ice tray with us.

Motels frequently did not have a full tray in the refrigerator and just as often these would be a pathetic little line of cubes and the trays would often be broken. Having our own tray meant that we had a full tray in the morning to dump into the chilly-bin, keeping the contents cold and allowing for enough ice in the evening on arrival to have at least one drink.

At Greymouth there was no ice tray at all. I went to the manager's office and asked if I could have some ice and also an ice tray. Mrs O'Donnell asked in a gentle way: "You're an American?"

"Yes. How do you know?"

"Americans never ask first: 'How are the beds?' They say, 'Where's the ice?' "

There are no antique stores in Greymouth.

Greymouth To Picton ... To Taupo

The traveller has a choice of routes to make the all-important rendezvous with the Picton Ferry to Wellington.

One route continues up the west coast on Highway 6 to Westport and then follows the Buller River to the Inangahua Junction. The other is the inland route to the Inangahua Junction through Reefton on Highway 7. The Highway 7 route looked easier and was our choice. It was another mistake. Fellow-trampers from the Milford Track made the crossing the next day with us on the Picton Ferry and they raved about the Pancake Rocks and the blowholes on the Westport road and said the Buller Gorge was not to be missed. Another advantage of the coast road was to visit historic towns once famous for gold and now sustaining their existence by mining the country's main supply of bituminous coal.

Happy in our ignorance, we tootled along on our chosen route, first driving along the Grey River to Ikamatua and then following the Inangahua River to Reefton.

Reefton once had the super glorious name of Quartzopolis. In 1870 rich goldbearing quartz veins were found here and it became the scene of feverish activity. Speculative companies were formed and, aided by the telegraph, the town was the center of a gold boom on paper. The predictable crash that followed broke many companies and investors. However the quartz veins were real and millions of dollars were pulled out of the mines before the end of the century.

One of the curiosities of Reefton is that it had electric lights only six years after New York City was getting its first electric lighted streets. Thanks to an English engineer who installed a demonstration 1-kilowatt lamp in Dawson's Hotel, now the Masonic, Reefton had an early taste for electricity which developed into a public utility. By 1888 the little town out in the middle of nowhere was enjoying the benefits of hydro-electric power.

The Buller River is a happy river to look at. The sun had returned and we followed the road's winding course up-river with the Lady Navigator behaving like a sheep dog wanting to go to work. The waters looked like they would be so full of trout. And they are. However we never found a place where we could descend to the riverbank and try our luck. You really need local knowledge.

At Lyell there is a frightening reminder that you are riding along the main earthquake fault line of the South Island. On the opposite side of the river from the highway an entire mountainside collapsed during the 1968 earthquake, totally blocking the river for several days. It looks like it happened yesterday and tends to hasten your passage. Another twelve miles further on a tablet by the side of the highway describes the "fault-line" upthrust created by the 1929 Murchison earthquake and you can see on the other bank of the river how the earth has been moved both horizontally and vertically.

We reached Murchison in time to scurry to Mrs Collins' tearoom only to find that we were too early for the scones. Crushed.

From Murchison we continued to Kawatiri Junction and then turned east on Highway 63 again, following the Buller River to its headwaters at Lake Rotoiti in Nelson Lakes National Park.

Lake Rotoiti is a little jewel of blue water set in surrounding hills of tall trees.

At the entrance end of the lake there are tame trout and a sign asks you not to fish there. According to our fishing guide in Canterbury, there is excellent trout fishing at the other end of the lake, but it can only be reached by boat.

A larger, sister-lake, Rotoroa lies seven miles off of Highway 6 turning east at Gowanbridge.

From Rotoiti to Blenheim is a mostly straight road following the gradually widening Wairau River.

During our travels in the South Island we had seen sheep recently sheared and we had seen sheep about to be sheared. Three times we had passed pens at high noon time when shearers were off to lunch.

Just outside of Blenheim there was a woolshed by the highway. Newly shorn sheep and cars parked around the shed indicated there might be action inside. It was almost one o'clock. Still at lunch?

"Do you think we should?"

"Of course we should."

"They might throw us out."

"All they can do is throw us out."

"I don't think we should."

"Drive in."

Sometimes it pays to have a strong navigator.

We drove up to the shed among the dogs. A man appeared in a shed window.

"Good afternoon," we said.

"Hello."

"Do you think we could watch the shearing?"

"Don't know why not."

He disappeared from the window and then reappeared at the shed door. He came down the steps and over to the car. He had the twisted Celtic face of a character actor in a John Ford movie. His hair was a burnt red and curly. His tattered, knitted sweater fell over him like an old tea-cozy.

"We don't start for another ten minutes and we only have a few rams to do, but if you want to watch it's all right."

We chatted. People are kind to strangers in New Zealand.

Our new-found friend was Alex Boyce. He was a free-lance shearer – that is, he didn't work for a contractor – and he was paid $28 per hundred sheep sheared. He probably would shear between 200 and 300 sheep in a day. Shearing took up about eight months of his time during the year and the rest of the time he repaired fencing and worked at farms.

He didn't do competitive shearing but often acted as a judge in A & P shows where shearing competitions were a standard event.

Inside the shed there were three shearing stands. Three thousand ewes had already been sheared and there were only four rams each for the three shearers to finish.

Each shearer provides his own shearing instrument, which costs $125 plus the blades. The blades are wide, made in Australia but illegal for use in Australia where a narrower blade is mandated.

The record number of sheep shorn by one man in a day in New Zealand, he said, was 600!

The huge bales of wool were marked "AIRFIELDS", the name of the station.

When the time came to go to work, each shearer went into an adjacent pen, took a headlock on a ram . . . some of them weighing 300 pounds . . . and hauled the animal backwards, butt-down, to the shearing stand.

The ram was constantly under a variety of wrestling holds that prevented him from moving in any direction and in four minutes . . . being larger he took twice as much time as a ewe . . . he was nude and pushed down a chute into the cold, cold world.

We were shown how the shorn wool is separated, trimmed and folded and put into a wooden bin, then compressed into a bale.

The master of the operation was a handsome, serious young man who didn't want us to have any illusions about the sheep business:

"It's not sheep in a pasture and into the shearing sheds and walked off to the meat works. We have 3,000 sheep. Last year we had some foot-rot and three times during the year we treated and dipped the sheep. That makes 9,000 sheep treatments plus the shearing and the crutching."

(Crutching sounds like what you think it is. Messy sheep.)

"In addition we grow and bale 10,000 bales of hay. That's just on the side. If you consider that a half million dollar investment in a station, plus a few tons of sweat, is going to net you three per cent, you have to think there is an easier way to make a living."

Shades of West Wanaka station.

Blenheim toasts itself as the *Sunshine City*. It was raining when we arrived and raining when we left. It is the capital of the Marlborough province and has a colorful, sometimes burlesque history.

The Wairau Affray, a confrontation between Maori and Pakeha, cost the first band of Nelson settlers their lives and cast long shadows on the development of the country.

Blenheim shares with Picton a happier occasion in early January when an army of volunteer hikers make a traditional march from Picton to Blenheim. Those who complete the seventeen-mile journey are awarded medals.

Outside of Picton is a nine-hole golf course. Inside Picton there is everything a holiday town can offer.

The 3,500 residents play hosts to many thousands of vacationing New Zealanders who come to fish and enjoy the waters of the Marlborough Sounds.

Picton is a pretty place. You look up the throat of the Queen Charlotte Sound and on each side are forest-covered mountains. Guest-houses are spotted in many of the little bays in addition to all of the accommodations within Picton itself.

In addition to tennis courts, walks, drives and boat charters there is the Smith Memorial Museum, heavy on the relics of the whaling industry, a flourishing industry of the district for nearly 140 years.

Today the name of Picton is synonymous with the ferry, the umbilical cord linking the "Mainland" of the South Island, as it is sometimes called, to the North Island.

In Picton we were just happy to put together the loose ends of our five week journey and rest in the motel for the final day home.

The next morning we were promptly in line for our Picton Ferry appointment. We were shuttled to the upper deck in precisely the same parking spot we had coming over.

The crossing was in the rain but we didn't care. Comfortably ensconced in the game room we played backgammon and ate our picnic lunch.

On our way out of Wellington we were slowed down by the police directing traffic around an accident. It started us thinking back. In our entire South Island tour we hadn't seen even a scraped-fender accident.

At "Paraparam" the Lady Navigator bought antique bone-handled knives, in Otaki a pile of fruit, in Bulls a steak for dinner.

The sun came out as we drove through the exquisite river hills of Taihape.

Passing through the Tongariro desert the sunshine was lost again but was replaced by a rainbow that seemed to follow the car down the desert road.

By the time we reached Lake Taupo the light was beginning to fade but we were like we were on the last stretch of the Milford Track: grateful to reach the end of the road. Sorry it was all over.

It was dusk when we pulled into the lakeside cottage at Taupo. "The Yellow Rose" was relieved of her eighteen articles of equipment . . . luggage, food, sports equipment, curious odds and ends . . . and we soon had a fat fire going in the fireplace.

Christmas trees and Christmas shopping were around the corner. I poured a fat drink to go with the fat fire and proposed a toast. "Here's to a great trip. Here's to 'The Yellow Rose'. Here's to the Lady Navigator. Name it. What would you like for Christmas?"

The Lady Navigator lifted her glass.

"In an antique, satin-lined box –."

"Yes."

"Wrapped in expensive, colored paper –."

"Of course."

"Tied with multi-colored, fancy ribbons –."

"Yes. Yes."

The glass moved higher.

"Just give me New Zealand!"

And then we both got misty-eyed and had a quiet cry.

21. The Nineteenth Hole

Six months in New Zealand, going from corner to corner, drinking-in the scenery, taking advantage of the many sporting facilities, leaves you with a singular conclusion: pound for pound New Zealand is the richest country in the world.

The visitor will frequently hear the phrase directed to him: "We don't have any rich in New Zealand . . . but we don't have any poor either."

Don't you believe it.

Everybody is rich.

True, it may not be cash in the bank . . . but what can cash in a bank buy?

There is clean air and clean water in New Zealand. How much is that worth?

There are millions of acres in national parks. Additional millions of acres in scenic reserves, forests, Government domains, city parks. How much are all these acres worth?

The food is abundant, of superlative quality and relatively inexpensive. Put a price tag on it.

The medical facilities, the educational, welfare, police, transportation systems are of enviable standards. The New Zealand people pay for these benefits through high taxes but in the end isn't that what money is for?

Above all New Zealand is a tranquil country. No amount of money in the bank can pay for peace.

Oh, to be sure there are some problems. There are bike gangs, robberies, isolated cases of violence and union frictions and minor racial confrontations. But compared to world standards today, New Zealand lives in a domestic paradise.

And nobody works too hard. The frantic push-and-pull, the pressure of modern society, self-inflicted slavery is missing in New Zealand.

These riches are for everyone to enjoy.

Generally the New Zealander knows he is well off. But he'll hide it under that damned inferiority cloak.

We were playing golf in Taupo after having been in New Zealand for over four months and we were joined at the first tee by a vacationing Wellington man looking for a game. On the eleventh fairway, after chatting about this and that, he complained, "Oh, but we're not at all sophisticated."

"That's not true."

"Oh, it's true all right. Not sophisticated at all."

I didn't know whether to hit him with a 9-iron or a sand wedge. "Where are you not sophisticated?" I kept my voice just under a shout. "In the things that count?"

"Well, I —"

"Are you without sophistication in your medical knowledge?" The sand wedge had all that nice weight to it but the 9-iron on the other hand had a better cutting edge.

"Oh, no, dear sir, we have one of the highest degrees of medical–."

"Do you lack knowledge in agriculture? In feeding your people?"

"Good heavens, no, our record for sheep and cattle farming is unmatched. The price of our food is so low–."

"Is it welfare, then, that lacks sophistication?" My voice was getting louder. I'd settled on the 9-iron.

"Please! Everyone knows we established a level of welfare when most of the world didn't know how to spell it."

"Then it must be the lack of spiritual sophistication that you are talking about."

"No, no! We had bishops before we had bathtubs–."

"Then tell me where you aren't sophisticated. In making a dry martini? In ordering in French in a Continental restaurant?"

The Wellingtonian had retreated behind his trundler and golf bag but the confrontation was interrupted by the Lady Navigator.

"Your shot, Luv."

If I'd shanked, I would have killed him.

You look at the people in the Members' Stand at Ellerslie, you look at the number of yachts in the marinas, you see the countless vacation homes around the lakes and ocean beaches.

You won't see any mansions. You'll never see a chauffeur-driven limousine except by the diplomatic corps in the capital. There are no ostentatious displays of superwealth.

But as you look around in your travels it would appear that in addition to everyone being rich, there are some people who are richer than others.

Six months of travel in New Zealand make you feel the richest asset of the country is *space.*

"You can go for miles and never see anyone."

A friend of mine wrote the following in a speech to a tourist conference:

"Crowding is the single, most significant factor which is precipitating unsettling changes in our world today. Crowding changes life-styles. Crowding affects mental health. Crowding results in pollution of a hundred kinds. Crowding lowers the quality of everyone's life."

New Zealand is so uncrowded. With half the population living in four main metropolitan centers there is a lot of space left unoccupied.

The critical point is that it is such beautiful space.

Previous trips to New Zealand didn't prepare us for the magnitude of the variety of scenery which would greet us. In six months we could cover California to every last hideout. In New Zealand we couldn't get it all tucked in.

The paradox about uncrowded New Zealand is that the crowded world hasn't found it.

Literally millions of Americans go tramping off to Europe and suffer a sardine holiday, overcharged, overbooked and overhustled. Yet a little more than 300,000 overseas visitors come to New Zealand every year, most of them from Australia. Less than 55,000 Americans. Incredible.

The tourist industry, the second largest industry in the world, has left a potentially rich industry in New Zealand comparatively untouched.

Perhaps it is just as well. If the average New Zealander thought that doubling the tourist arrivals might cost him five seconds more at his boat ramp, he'd turn down the new tourists in a flash.

He wants his beautiful uncrowded New Zealand just the way it is. And who is to blame him?

KAITAIA

BAY OF ISLANDS

KERIKERI

WHANGAREI

GREAT BARRIER I.

AUCKLAND

NORTH
ISLAND

TAURANGA

HAMILTON

ROTORUA

TAUPO

NEW PLYMOUTH

GISBORN

NATIONAL PARK

NAPIER

HASTINGS

WANGANUI

PALMERSTON NORTH

MASTERTON

COOK STRAIT

WELLINGTON

NELSON

BLENHEIM

Scale
150 miles

200 kilometres

CHRISTCHURCH